NORTHERN CONNECTION

NORTHERN CONNECTION

INSIDE CANADA'S DEADLIEST
MAFIA FAMILY

Peter Edwards

Optimum Publishing International
Montreal, Ottawa, Toronto

Northern Connection: Inside Canada's Deadliest Mafia Family
By Peter Edwards

Foreword by Michel Auger

Copyright © Ottawa 2006 by Peter Edwards and Optimum Publishing
International

Published by:
Optimum Publishing International Inc
Michael S. Baxendale, Publisher
PO Box 524, Maxville, ON
K0C 1T0
www.optimumbooks.com

Library and Archives Canada Cataloguing in Publication

Edwards, Peter, 1956-

Northern connection: inside Canada's deadliest mafia family / Peter Edwards :

foreword by Michel Auger.

Includes bibliographical references and index.

ISBN 0-88890-245-X

1. Cotroni family. 2. Mafia—Québec (Province)—Montréal—History
3. Mafia—Canada—History. 4. Organized Crime—Canada—History. I. Title.

HV6453.C3E383 2006   364.1092'271428
C2006-902341-7

Book and Cover Design: Optimum Publishing International
Editor: Craig MacLaine
Cover Photo: Michel Auger collection
Author Photo, Back Flap: Barbara Hanson

Portions of this book were published by Key Porter Books in 1990 under the title of Blood Brothers.

Printed and bound in Canada on acid free, recycled paper.

Contents

Part One
The Rise of the Cotronis

Part Two
Holding Power

Part Three
Upheaval

Part Four
Convergence

The Connection's *Who's Who*

Joseph (Joe Bananas) Bonanno. Head of the New York crime family with which Vic Cotroni was aligned.

Salvatore (Bill) Bonanno. Sophisticated son of Joe Bonanno.

Maurice (Mom) Boucher. Leader of Quebec Hell Angels.

Tommaso Buscetta. Biggest turncoat in Mafia history; lived briefly in Toronto and Montreal.

George Cherry. Montreal boxing figure who credits the Cotronis with giving him a break from the poverty of his youth.

Vito Ciancimino. Former mayor of Palermo, Sicily, and an associate of Cotroni money-launderer Michel Pozza.

Francesco (Santos, Frank, The Big Guy) Cotroni. Brother of Vic and Pep Cotroni and last hope of the Cotroni brothers. He wanted to move to Toronto.

Giuseppe (Pep) Cotroni. Older brother of Frank and younger brother of Vic Cotroni. Lots of ambition but less success. He was interested in drugs, securities and pizza flour.

Nicodemo and Maria Micellota Cotroni. Parents of infamous Cotroni brothers. Their Christian names live on in numerous Cotroni offspring.

Vincenzo (Vic, The Egg) Cotroni. Former head of the Montreal Mafia and Canadian branch-plant manager for New York mobsters. He was a conciliator and problem-solver, in the classically Canadian sense.

Claude Faber. Frank Cotroni's lieutenant who married into the family. He doesn't look like much but is deadly.

Tony Frank. Early Montreal mobster from same downtown neighbourhood that produced Vic Cotroni and his brothers. He comes from the days when you could be a big Montreal mobster and not be under an American thumb.

Carmine (Mr. Lilo) Galante. Former big gun in the Bonanno crime family of New York and Vic Cotroni's ticket to the big time. He yanked Montreal mobsters into the American orbit.

Louis Greco. High-powered Sicilian associate of Vic Cotroni who helped him rise in the 1950s.

Giacomo Luppino. Old don of the Hamilton mob and father-in-law to Paolo Violi.

Stefano (The Undertaker) Magaddino. Old don of Buffalo and jealous cousin of Joe Bonanno. He had a strong influence over southern Ontario.

Eddie (Hurricane) Melo. Frank Cotroni's Toronto bodyguard, a former boxer and former organizer for Local 75 of the Hotel and Restaurant Employees Union. Had a $15,000 bounty on his head, and was murdered in 2001.

Ciro Niegri Nieri. Former associate of early mobster Tony Frank, and turncoat.

William (Willie Obie) Obront. Cotroni money-launderer whose front was as a meat wholesaler. He gave Cotronis links to Jewish mobsters.

Johnny (Johnny Pops, The Enforcer) Papalia. Hamilton mobster connected to the Cotronis who was murdered in 1997.

Pacifique (Pax) Plante. Flamboyant Montreal crime-buster of the 1940s and 1950s.

Michel Pozza. Cotroni money-launderer who had ties to both the Sicilian and the Calabrian wings, as well as to Sicily.

Palmina Puliafito. Vic Cotroni's sister and a wealthy businesswoman.

Phil (Rusty) Rastelli. Head of the Bonanno family after its heyday. A former Montrealer, he was popular with the Cotroni gang.

Nick Rizzuto. Bitter Sicilian enemy of Paolo Violi who passed time in Montreal and Venezuela.

Vito Rizzuto. Son of Nick and an avid golfer.

Réal Simard. Montreal driver and killer for Frank Cotroni.

Domenico Violi. Father of Paolo Violi and old-time Calabrian mobster who moved to Parma, near Cleveland, Ohio.

Paolo Violi. Heir apparent to Vic Cotroni. Calabrian-born, but a Canadian nationalist of sorts.

Who, Where and Why

WHEN MY BOOK about Canada's most powerful crime family first appeared in 1990, the Cotronis ruled an empire. *Blood Brothers* told the story of how the Cotronis had used brains, muscle and a vicious ruthlessness to reach the top of the Canadian crime world. Since then, so much has changed. Most of the key figures in the story have died — many violently. The biker gangs showed they could be more than just deadly errand boys for the Italian mobsters. And they have taken over much of the lucrative crime businesses that nourished the Canadian mafia during their glory days.

With the death of godfather Frank Cotroni, the end of an era became official. I felt I had to finish the story. The first part of this book comes directly from *Blood Brothers*. The last part tells how the empire collapsed in a wave of bloodshed and violence.

This book draws from interviews with police, criminals, journalists, academics and assorted others, and the research for it took me to Montreal, New York, Marseilles, Rome and Palermo. Whenever possible, I visited the locations I describe, including mobster homes, crime sites and favoured restaurants. Conversations quoted are from wiretaps, courtroom or hearing transcripts or the memories of credible sources. None has been reconstructed for dramatic effect.

On a couple of occasions, counsel for Frank Cotroni said I could not interview Cotroni. Hamilton mobster John (Johnny Pops, The Enforcer) Papalia made the same point in blunter terms, saying, "Take a walk…parasite." Fortunately, I was helped far more than refused, reminding me of Blanche Dubois in *A Streetcar Named Desire* who says, "Whoever you are — I have always depended on the kindness of strangers."

Some former strangers are now friends, thanks to the book. Michel Auger never turned down a chance to help. All Canadians owe him a debt for his courage in exposing organized crime even after he became one of its victims. He has made us all safer and richer for his efforts. James Dubro of Toronto, a pioneer in this field of journalism in Canada, and Pierre Tremblay, of McGill University and the Université de Montréal, read early drafts of the book and offered intelligent comments and considerable help. Thanks as well to Pino Arlacchi, Margaret Beare, Daniele Billitiere, Ralph Blumenthal, George Capra, André Cédilot, Miro Cernetig, Yves Chartrand, Paul Cherry, Andrew Chung,Sandro Contenta, Lee Davis Creal, Don Dutton, Pamela Erlichman, Jennifer Glossop, Rocky Graziano, Corp. Reg King, Jonathan Kwitny, Mario Latraverse, Lizette LeGal, Paul Legall, Carol Lindsay, Patrick Mahoney, Bob Menard, Cal Millar, Bob Mitchell, Barry Moody, André Noël, Nicholas Pileggi, Claude Poirier, Stephen Rodger, Ron Sandelli, retired RCMP Chief Superintendent Ben Soave, Richard Starck, Bernard Tétrault, Sergeant Joe Tomeo, Staff-Sergeant Larry Tronstad and Gwynn (Jocko) Thomas. Whatever errors might remain, as well as all opinions, however, are those of the author.

The book must not be interpreted as anti-Italian. The Cotronis and other Mafia families are Italian in heritage, but so are many police officers, including some I quote. So, indeed, were most of the Cotronis' victims. As I worked on the book, I thought of one Canadian police officer active in fighting organized crime. Although born in Italy, he is cited in print as a "Canadian" police officer. Frank Cotroni, who was born in Montreal, is labelled "Italian."

In recent years, I have had the privilege and pleasure of working with Antonio Nicaso, who has done much to educate people that the modern Mafia is a global phenomenon, with roots around the world and no respect for the laws or borders of any country. Some of my best sources were police officers who spoke on a not-for-attribution basis. I respect their work enormously.

My thanks to the late Wayne Braun of the *Toronto Star* for letting me bend my labour beat there at times when I felt there was a good mob story at hand. And of course, as always, my agent, Daphne Hart of the Helen Heller Agency.

There is a reason this is dedicated to my mother, the late Winona Edwards. She was the best editor and supporter a child could have, and I might never have had the nerve to go into journalism, let alone report on the Mafia, if not for her. Her memory and that of my father, the late Kenneth Edwards, continue to guide and inspire me. Finally, I would like to thank Barbara, James and Sarah, for constantly reminding me what's really important.

Peter Edwards, April 2006

Foreword

FOR THE PAST four generations, the Cotroni family name has been part of the history of Quebec and Canada. By the time I was leaving the woes of adolescence, the name of this crime family was already known by the public, even if, officially, neither the police nor other authorities were saying much about them. In the newspapers, Vincent (Vic) Cotroni was portrayed at this time only as a very well-known businessman.

That was true, but it wasn't all of the story. It wasn't until the 1960s that we started to read more accurate, rounded descriptions of Vincent Cotroni's lifestyle and the precise nature of his business. The Cotronis had a chosen place in the local underworld from the time that the American Mafia installed itself in Montreal at the beginning of the 1950s. Vincent Cotroni wasted no time forging alliances with Carmine Galante, the rough American envoy for Joe Bonanno, who was putting the underworld house in order, so to speak.

Back then, the Cotronis were politically connected. This wasn't in the realm of grand theoretical debates, but in the way in which politics were actually practised in Quebec. The Cotroni people were election workers. It was through helping political parties that the people of the underworld would later receive government favours. Their organized-crime businesses of gambling, prostitution and cabarets benefited greatly from the favours of elected officials. Help was given, and help was returned.

As a cabaret proprietor, Vic Cotroni was also one of the pioneers who popularized Québécois songs; at that time the shows in Montreal were almost solely American and staged in the English language.

Much was written about the Cotronis, and they were also prominently featured on major radio and television reports. However, it required the attention of Peter Edwards to pull together the complete history of this Montreal family. Since the publication of his original English-language version of *Blood Brothers* in 1990, several authors have attempted to chronicle new developments in the life of this turbulent family, but the work of this journalist from the *Toronto Star* is the most accomplished.

Peter Edwards knows his craft as a journalist. He is a strong storyteller who portrays the grand moments in the careers of the four Cotroni brothers — little-known brother Michel, as well as his more notorious brothers, Vincent, Giuseppe and Frank. Their careers are well described by my colleague from Toronto.

This new book *Northern Connection* adds the recent activities of Frank Cotroni and his entourage to the history, helping us to better understand why the Cotronis were leading players in the criminal world. Peter Edwards shows us the diverse corruption — the illicit trafficking and the laundering of dirty money. He also ranks the importance of the Cotronis in the North American and world Mafia hierarchies. Finally, he describes the decline of the Cotroni empire and the rise of outlaw motorcycle gangs in the Canadian criminal world. He explains how the Hells Angels and the Mafia worked together to fix the price of illegal drugs to maximize their profits.

This is a unique book about crime history written by a journalist who understands the underworld and who writes about it in a lively and direct style — Peter Edwards is an investigative journalist who presents his material well. This work is extremely useful to everyone who wants to understand what happens behind the scenes in the underworld.

— *Michel Auger*

Note: Michel Auger is French Canada's leading crime reporter. He writes for Le Journal de Montréal. On September 13, 2000, a biker gunman pumped six bullets into Auger. But Auger survived. And he continues to report on organized crime.

For Winona Edwards,
And fresh harbours

PART ONE

The Rise of the Cotronis

"Here, it's more important to have a friend than to have a right."
- Old Sicilian saying

Chapter One

Death of the Godfather·

"What is the mafia?"
— Vic Cotroni

It rained heavily on the day of Vincenzo (Vic) Cotroni's funeral, but that didn't stop the curious, the reverent or the authorities from attending his north Montreal send-off. In life, Vic Cotroni had been quiet and outwardly modest. In contrast, his death was accompanied by a seventeen-piece brass band. Spectacular floral arrangements filling twenty-three cars escorted him to the afterlife.

Everyone on the streets of north Montreal who heard the funeral dirge that September afternoon in 1984 knew Vic Cotroni didn't need grand gestures or flashy clothes, quick movements and loud words to announce his importance. The 5'5" great-grandfather with a bad heart and arthritis had been powerful enough to kill or enrich a man with a nod, a gesture or a few softly-spoken words. But Cotroni preferred mediation to violence, and his finesse and ability to generate respect had earned him that rare Mafia luxury: a death in bed of natural causes. Some former associates who shared Notre Dames des Neiges Cemetery hadn't been so wise or lucky or well-connected, and had been lowered into the ground with their bodies disfigured by buckshot and bullets.

But Vic Cotroni's considerable achievement of holding all enemies, except time, at bay and dying a peaceful death in his seventy-fourth year was no consolation for his daughter Rosina, now a mother approaching middle age. She clutched a large crucifix and wept uncontrollably in the rain by the grave while staring at the coffin, as if unable to believe that her father, once arguably the top Canadian in the Mafia, was finally dead.

Vic Cotroni was eulogized as a family man who served as "a father to many" and who "had a special mission in life." Mourners were offered consolation that Cotroni, who had lived surrounded by professional killers, believed in an afterlife. At the instant of his death from cancer, they were told, Vic Cotroni was watching the papal visit on television. Denied the comfort of those words were Cotroni's sister, wealthy businesswoman Palmina Puliafito, who was rushed to hospital hours after her brother's death, apparently with inflamed stomach ulcers, and his brother Francesco (Frank, The Big Guy), who was behind bars at the Parthenais Jail in Montreal on charges of smuggling $3 million in cocaine.

Frank Cotroni asked for a day pass to attend the funeral. He was turned down. But when authorities said he could visit the north-end funeral home that held his elder brother's body, it was Frank Cotroni who declined. An associate explained that it was all a matter of family honour: "Frank's children and a lot of his friends will be attending the funeral, and Frank's a proud man. Nobody wants his picture in the paper sharing a pair of matching chrome bracelets with some burly screw [guard]."

Vic Cotroni had been considered by police as the top Canadian in the New York Mafia crime family of Joseph (Joe Bananas) Bonanno. Cotroni's organization was every Canadian nationalist's worst nightmare — it showed that even our crime world was hope-lessly wedded to the economy of the United States, with Canadian crime profits siphoned off to head offices south of the border. Vic Cotroni appeared on police charts as head of a "*decina*," or arm, of the Bonannos, making Vic Cotroni, in effect, the manager of an American branch plant.

There was something very Canadian about all this, and the rise of the Cotroni organization was a dark, nasty mirror image of the growth of Canadian business in general. But while other branch-plant managers might grumble about murderous office politics, such complaints would not have been hyperbole for Vic Cotroni. Like other Canadian branch-plant managers, Vic Cotroni wielded great power at home but was ultimately deferential to his head office, which in his case was located on the streets of New York City. He had warm feelings towards his native Italy, but also realized that the *realpolitik* of the mob made New York the centre of real power. His attitude wasn't just smart politics, it was also a prescription for survival. Like other branch-plant managers, he intuitively knew how far he could safely push his interests, which helps explain how he managed to live to a ripe old age. He held his position with the Bonannos for more than a quarter-century, and authorities said he amassed a fortune through loan-sharking, prostitution, gambling, extortion, and drug-running, and by smuggling into the United States some of the most fearsome killers in the underworld.

While Cotroni's operation was a branch plant, it was big league by Canadian standards, and any young man serving under him could expect to serve a five-year apprenticeship before being considered a full family member. They then became part of something huge. When police peeked into the bank account of one of Cotroni's four main money-launderers, they found it had been a conduit for no less than $83 million. And during the heyday of Cotroni's illegal gambling rackets, police estimated his American bosses siphoned off some $50 million yearly as their cut.

Vic Cotroni's northern empire touched politicians, heroin addicts and killers, as well as average Canadians. His name meant the threat of scandal for Canadian police officers, politicians and ostensibly respectable business leaders. And when the separatists of the FLQ tried to wrench Quebec away from the rest of Canada, they considered Vic Cotroni's family name important enough to include on their manifesto. Vic Cotroni's influence wasn't confined to the management side of business; he also had a hand in construction, hotel and restaurant unions. It was possible to bite into a pizza of which every ingredient had been supplied by businesses run by Cotroni or his associates. And if you had a little spumoni ice cream for dessert, you were again enriching the Cotronis. This food monopoly reached its peak in Canada's centennial year, when Cotroni enterprises managed to monopolize fast-food contracts at Expo 67, allowing Cotroni to fill thousands, perhaps millions, of stomachs from across the world with diseased hotdogs.

Branch-plant managers are not by definition flashy people, and Vic Cotroni was no exception. His face had a certain dignity, but was not handsome or ugly, not scary or even memorable; it was the serious face of a quiet man who knew much and said little. His eyes, world-weary and encased in pouches of sagging flesh, had an intensity that belied his age and might have been considered a sign of great intelligence or of reptilian awareness.

No one is quite sure how Vic Cotroni got his nickname "The Egg." It may have referred to his power to grant continued life in his murky milieu, or perhaps it was just a description of the clean oval shape of his head. Another riddle he chose not to clarify was the spelling of his name, which appeared in court and police records alternately as Cotroni, Coutroni, Controne, Catrino, Citroni and Catroni. But his headstone revealed that he had preferred "Cotrone." By this point, though, both his family and the authorities had agreed on the "Cotroni" spelling, the lie having become the truth. Whatever the spelling, the name generated power in the underworld. While Vic Cotroni spoke softly, his words travelled a great distance, and secret police flowcharts linked him with major criminals in Italy, Mexico, Brazil, Venezuela, the United States and across Canada, from Edmundston, N.B., to Vancouver. People listened when Vic Cotroni spoke to them. When, in a wiretapped conversation, Cotroni told leading Ontario mobster Johnny (The Enforcer) Papalia he could easily have Papalia killed if his debt wasn't settled, The Enforcer whimpered, "I know."

Vic Cotroni wasn't a man for great shows of emotion, but it was an open secret that he was passionate enough to feel the need for a mistress as well as a wife, and that he was the father of an illegitimate son with a considerable crime career of his own. Much of Vic Cotroni's time was spent in a luxurious penthouse on the edges of the monied, WASP-ish Westmount district of Montreal. He also owned an estate about an hour's drive away, near Lavaltrie, complete with vineyards, greenhouses, a full-time gardener, a boathouse and high-intensity lighting. Like its owner, the country home was solid, respectable and unspectacular from the outside, but its inner walls were swathed in oak and marble and held six bathrooms — five done in marble and one with double urinals — and a conference room that could accommodate thirty people and was lit by twelve crystal chandeliers. In the basement was a specially constructed pool table that looked solid and big enough to support a small truck. The house was clearly built to shelter and entertain respected guests, and if its thick walls could talk, they could tell volumes about Canada's crime history. But if they could talk, odds are they would have been levelled years ago.

But Vic Cotroni looked too small, too benign, too dignified, too simple and — to some people who didn't look closely enough — too dumb to be the repository of great evil and great secrets. This apparent dumbness was a matter of skill, not ineptitude, and he once instructed an underling to study and copy his performance on the witness stand, summing up his tactics with the words: "I act stupid." For his part, Cotroni told those bold enough to ask that he was just an illiterate pepperoni salesman who had met with good fortune. "What is the Mafia?" he asked a reporter shortly before his death. "I made my money in clubs and in gambling. All the rest is nothing but talk."

Despite his insouciant act, in his declining years Cotroni couldn't escape his responsibilities as *Le Parrain* (The Godfather) of Montreal. And that power followed him to his grave, as if understanding he was perhaps the only one with the diplomacy and strength necessary to bind together the disparate Calabrians, Sicilians, francophones and anglos who made up his crime confederacy. When he was finally buried, a member of the Montreal Urban Community Police's anti-gang squad told a reporter, "We'll have to watch closely who comes into Montreal. It's still New York that has the final decision over what happens in Montreal."

Such talk had amused Vic Cotroni in life. "If I'm such a bad criminal," he once asked, "why am I still walking around free?"

Vic Cotroni was the product of a complex crime subculture properly known as the *'ndrangheta,* which had its genesis in Old World neglect and later flourished in the fertile climate of North America. Vic Cotroni was born in 1910, the son of a poor carpenter in Mammola in the southern Italian region of Calabria, where opportunities were few and criminal societies were a fact of life.

The term "Mafia," in its truest form, refers only to organized crime in western Sicily. Today it's popularly understood to also include the *'ndrangheta* or "honoured society" of Calabria; the Camorra, the Naples underworld, which had its genesis in that city's prisons; and the North American hybrid of these groups, La Cosa Nostra, which translates to "Our Thing." Lines between the groups have been blurred somewhat, as on the streets of Montreal, where Vic Cotroni managed to pull together Calabrians, Sicilians, New York La Cosa Nostra members, and anyone else interested in making money outside the laws of the state.

The *'ndrangheta* began more than a century ago as peasants in Italy's poorest regions struggled to cope with changes that threatened their already meagre lifestyles. The early *'ndrangheta* was a loosely-organized rural phenomenon, engaged in cattle-rustling, control of water supplies, smuggling and protection rackets. But, more importantly, it offered the hope of real or vicarious honour for the least honoured members of society, the peasantry. In those early years, theft wasn't a particularly lucrative business since the peasants of the Aspromonte mountains of Calabria had little worth stealing.

The new Italian state, founded in 1870, offered myriad complex laws but little real help. Its bumbling ways taught residents of the Calabrian deep south, or Mezzogiorna, and neighbouring Sicily to view crusaders and reformers with a wary eye. But since the peasants had little political clout with which to restrain outsiders, they responded instead with diffidence, by retreating into their families and by mass emigration. Villagers who could not change the world were determined at least to not appear foolish while struggling through life. Those most prone to the codes of the *'ndrangheta* were therefore those least honoured by society, the peasant classes.

At the core of the *'ndranghetista* system was *omertà,* a double code of conduct that set different moral codes for dealings with those inside and outside one's family circle. This code made it acceptable for families such as the Cotronis to control prostitution and pornography rackets while righteously guarding the women of their own families. The root of *omertà* was "uomo," or "the ability to be a man." Mafiosi or *'ndranghetista* behaviour involved a heightened sense of one's own being and a total inability to live under the rules of others.

The machismo ethic of the *'ndrangheta* was deeply ingrained in Vic Cotroni. Once when he was approached by a CBC television crew from the *Connections* series, he mistook these strangers for hitmen preparing to kill him. Cotroni instinctively covered his genitals, hoping to preserve the symbols of his manhood, if not his life. In the world of Vic Cotroni, murder was the assertion of one's manliness over that of another man. It was also a prerequisite for a mafioso hoping to inspire fear and ultimately respect. As a member of one crime family said, "Law is force, and can never be separated from force."

Chapter Two

Beginnings

"I know who the real public enemies are. But they are men who have the respect of the public...men who wear silk hats, who are apparently of standing inthe community."
— 1930s Montreal mob-buster J.J. Penverne

Vic Cotroni was fourteen in 1924 when his parents, Nicodemo and Maria Micellota Cotroni, brought him to Montreal. The family was part of a tidal wave of immigration from Calabria that followed the war. The Cotronis made a brief stopover in New York before heading north and settling in an apartment near the corner of Ontario and St. Timothée streets. The three-storey rowhouses there ran together for block after block, each unit pressed tightly against the road, leaving no room for lawns or children's play. Adults found escape in nearby gaming houses and brothels, one of the most infamous of which was just around the corner from the Cotronis' new home.

This district was Montreal's original Italian section, where urban decay translated into cheap housing and frequent violent crime. Already, it was being replaced by the Mile-End region to the north as the destination of choice for Italians. The new settlement boasted an Italian parish church, Madonna della Difesa, and fresh greens and grapes around what is now Jean-Talon Street, instead of the innercity stink of the crowded St. Timothée slums.

Montreal served as the first stopping point for most European immigrants hoping to start new lives in Canada. Industry badly needed cheap, docile labour for the new nation's railways, mines and smelters. The government's immigration policies were directed towards Swedes, Finns, English and Germans of northwest Europe, but steamship agents soon found there was money to be made by stoking the fires of industry with immigrants from eastern and southern Europe, including Calabria. Steamship companies were paid senseria, or bounties, by North American employers to provide cheap, seasonal European workers, and little time was lost abiding by immigration laws or honouring promises made to migrants. By the 1921 census, Montreal's northeast Italian district had 13,922 residents, mostly from Calabria. While their numbers were rapidly growing, Italian immigrants were still a minority among minorities, far behind the 34,484 Irish immigrants and 42,817 Montrealers classified as "Hebrew."

While on the job, recent immigrants could expect crude extortion attempts from the Blackhand, a primitive forerunner of the Mafia. Even the most powerful immigrants weren't immune to such threats. In 1904, Antonio (King) Cordasco, a banker, steamship agent and labour recruiter, received a letter in his Montreal office displaying a menacing drawing of a black hand, pointing to the letters "M" and "A," accompanied by a crude sketch of a coffin, two skulls-and-crossbones and what appeared to be a snake under the hot sun.

Cordasco himself was not averse to making a profit from the tensions between his newly arrived Mediterranean brothers and the Anglo-Celtic captains of industry. There was a fierce competition for *senseria* for immigrants recruited for steamship voyages to Canada. Young Calabrian men came to Canada, expecting a hostile reception from its people and its climate. They had left a culture based on face-to-face encounters and a system of honour with a strong emphasis on kinship and mutual respect. To them, employment was something to be temporarily cherished, not expected. With no plans of staying in Canada long enough to learn the language or customs of their new workplace, they were susceptible to the overtures of middlemen such as Cordasco who could function in the cultures of both the Old and the New World. As historian Robert Harney writes, "If one could see boss or banker as a patron, one could know the limits of exploitation."

Like Vic Cotroni decades later, Cordasco offered security and strength in a foreign world. And, also like Cotroni, Cordasco turned enormous profits, selling such provisions as sardines, anchovies and bread to worksites at hefty profits, while also tapping into the newcomers' savings by running boardinghouses and saloons. He sold workers a shield from the New World while at the same time preventing them from assimilating. As an Italian-language newspaper advertisement said, "If you want to be respected and protected either on the work or in the case of accident or other annoyances which can be easily met, apply personally or address letter or telegrams to Antonio Cordasco."

The Mafia had flourished in Italy because the law was out of touch with average citizens and had lost respect. Those conditions were rife in Montreal well before the Cotronis' arrival in 1924. A 1909 royal commission into municipal wrongdoing in Montreal uncovered a wide variety of ugly situations, including an apparent attempt by police to bribe a young boy and his little sister to inform on their mother who was to be a witness against the police in an upcoming sex trial. The head of the Montreal Light, Heat and Power Company testified that one alderman tried to squeeze $10,000 in campaign contributions from the utility. The alderman's defence was that the power utility had attempted to bribe him with stocks and cash. Either way, the smell of corruption at top levels of the city's power structure was enough to make one's nose burn.

The Cotronis arrived in Canada midway through the American experiment with prohibition under the Volstead Act. At first, Canadian authorities had winked at the illegal sale of liquor into the United States; entrepreneurial Canadians were, after all, just taking advantage of what was widely considered to be a foolish, unworkable law. Unfortunately, the smugglers could not be trusted to break the law on just one side of the border. Liquor was being run into "dry" Ontario, and smugglers heading into the United States reasoned that they might as well return home with contraband silks, jewellery, tobacco, narcotics, cars and cotton clothing. For some American manufacturers, this offered the chance to dump excess goods into Canada while keeping their American prices high. For others, it meant being the victims of wholesale hijackings. Average Canadians who were able to buy goods at a cut price didn't mind that the smuggling was hurting Canadian firms. The rackets bringing goods into Canada cost the country an estimated $10 million to $15 million yearly in lost duties, $30 million to $40 million yearly to Canadian manufacturers in lost orders and $15 million to $25 million yearly in lost wages for workmen. Fines for smugglers were so low and so infrequent as to be considered a national scandal. Those goods that were confiscated often went mysteriously missing, leading one Crown attorney to accuse the Montreal Customs House of being "one of the greatest clearing houses for stolen goods in Canada."

When the Cotronis arrived in 1924, Montreal was in the midst of a sensational trial that triggered a judicial inquiry into police wrongdoing. Both the trial and the inquiry hinted they would bring to light a cocky, powerful and fast-growing underworld that held the police, politicians and courts tightly in its grip.

The central player in the drama was Tony Frank, a Montreal mobster so powerful that other career criminals paid him a tithe for the right to commit crimes in his city. That tax was also supposed to grant them access to the wide-ranging legal connections of which Frank boasted. The Sardinian-born mobster haunted the courtroom corridors of his new city, always well-dressed and frequently at the side of lawyers and judges. Frank was also a constant and prominent fixture along downtown Cadieux Street where prostitues, dope pedlars and bootleggers worked their trades. Often with him was his less-affable associate, Frank Gambino (aka Mike Capuano), whose criminal charges ranged from window-smashing to attempted kidnapping, attempted murder and murder.

Other key members of Frank's gang were Mike Valentino (aka Jack Foster) and bodyguard Salvatore Arena, who could often be seen holding court at *L'Ancien Club des Musiciens* at 141 Cadieux Street and at an Italian social club at 315a St. Laurent Street. The leaders of the gang weren't physically present when a half-dozen hooded robbers gathered on Ontario Street near Moreau Street, about a mile east of the new Cotroni home, on April 1, 1924. But the influence of the Frank gang's leadership was unmistakeable and everywhere as the criminals prepared to rob an armoured car loaded with payroll funds.

The thieves had paid Frank $200 for the use of his Winchester deer rifle and a sawed-off shotgun, which had its pellets replaced by leaden lozenges so it could easily blast a gaping hole through soft human tissue. They augmented their firepower with an 1881 model .38 special U.S. service revolver, a Smith and Wesson .38 and a pair of Colt .45 automatic pistols. They felt further armed with Frank's purported abilities to keep them out of jail, as Frank had bragged, "Don't worry; if you get pinched, you will get right out." Robber Ciro Niegri Nieri (aka Mr. Linden, Edward Harris) also recalled Frank saying, "He would get us away in an automobile, over through Ottawa and Toronto, that way into Windsor, and if we got arrested for robbery or something, he had enough pull up there to get us all out." The heist had been carefully planned, but sparing innocent lives wasn't one of the considerations. Nieri later said one of the early plans was simply to "go by the bank door and shoot everybody."

With Nieri that afternoon was an assortment of criminals from Quebec, Ontario and the eastern United States. Their diversity was, in a sense, a tribute to improvements in automobile technology and road-building, as well as Canada's tightening bond with the United States. If railways built Canada as a nation, one could also argue that highways helped create an outward-looking Montreal under-world with strong links to New York City, just 385 miles down the road. That quick access to the richest North American market would be a constant factor in Vic Cotroni's strength, years later. Easy bail, fast cars and smooth highways meant a robber acquitted in Montreal on a Monday could be behind a pistol, robbing a store in New York or Toronto on Tuesday, and back on Cadieux Street, enriching Frank, on Wednesday. But, despite the American influence, there was no sign of American control over the Canadian gang. The presence of driver Leo Davis (aka Waimon), a Paris-born Jew, was a comment on the growing strength of Montreal mobs. Davis had had no known criminal record when he brought his wife and toddler north from poverty in the New York City area after hearing reports of how much money Canadian bootleggers were making.

Nieri was known to traffic in cocaine, morphine, opium, stolen goods and female flesh, and split his time between New York State, Montreal and the thriving underworld of Hamilton, Ontario. His companions included Mike Serafini (aka Mike Knight, Anderson), who was known to police in Sudbury, Ottawa and Toronto, having been expelled from Toronto on a weapons offence earlier in 1924; Adam Parillo (aka Adam Howard), who had been arrested in Bridge-port, Connecticut, and throughout New York State; and Harry Stone (aka Peter Ward, Warren, Powell), who was believed to be from Chicago and who had a record of opium-trafficking and smuggling and bail-jumping. The only Canadian-born male in the gang was Louis Morel, a former policeman and sports star, whose criminal life included drug-smuggling, robbery and helping rig Montreal civic elections.

The gang also included a Québécois woman, Emma Lebeau (aka Emma Leboeuf, Ciro), a prostitute who considered herself Nieri's

27

girlfriend. She had met Nieri at the Italian social club at 315a St. Laurent, and she said Nieri promised to marry her and free her from having to sell her body to strangers. But first he sent Lebeau off to earn a dowry in a brothel in North Bay, Ontario. After that, it was back to Montreal and another fleshpot at 321 Cadieux Street.

There was a wild exchange of gunfire as the robbers fled with $142,288 from the armoured car, and a young security guard lay dying on the pavement. Also cut down was Stone, whose body was left in the back seat of a Hudson touring car in the city's north end. A tip from neighbours pointed police to a west-end boardinghouse where Nieri and Lebeau were holed up.

The couple panicked at the thought of facing murder charges alone, and, in return for implicating the rest of the gang, they were spared the gallows. Nieri told authorities how Gambino took Stone's loss like a pro, saying, "What do we care if Stone got killed? We've got the money."

Nieri caused a sensation when he explained how decisions made on Cadieux Street reached far beyond the Montreal downtown.

> *Q:* Did you not go to Toronto to hold up a jewellery store?
> *A:* Yes, sir, with Serafini with the understanding I would be protected upon giving a share of 10 per cent…
> *Q:* To whom were you to give that 10 per cent for protection?
> *A:* Tony Frank, Mr. Gambino and Mr. Valentino.
> *Q:* And, as a matter of fact, they brought you back?
> *A:* Yes.
> *Q:* They paid for it?
> *A:* Yes.
> *Q:* Did you have anything to do with the holdup in a store of St. Lawrence Blvd.? I think it was a store kept by a Hebrew…
> *A:* Yes, that is, Mr. Gambino gave us that and he got 10 per cent for protection and 10 per cent for the tip.
> *Q:* Were you also in any way connected with the theft or highway robbery of Lowney's chocolate people?
> *A:* Yes, and the protector received $100 for that too.
> *Q:* Who was the protector?
> *A:* Tony Frank, Gambino and Valentino.
> *Q:* Did you give the money to Tony Frank or whom did you

give it to?
A: I gave it to Tony Frank himself.

No one claimed Frank, Gambino and Valentino were among the half-dozen gunmen who ambushed the bank car, but prosecutor R.L. Calder argued they were still guilty of murder because of the organized nature of the crime: "Let me ask you to notice as we go along how business-like robbery has become, and how people who intend to indulge in preying on society got to work as coolly and calmly as a man who has put through an agreement, or is contemplating a deal in futures or wheat."

All Montreal watched to see if Frank's connections were enough to free him from a date with the hangman. They weren't. The lives of Frank, Gambino, Morel and Serafini ended on the gallows of Montreal's Bordeaux Jail on October 24, 1924. Valentino and Davis had their executions commuted at the last minute. Valentino spent the waning years of his sentence in a Bordeaux Jail mental ward, and after being freed in 1939, he retreated to Little Current, Ontario, where he ran a modest diner. Davis was freed the same year after prolonged protests from American Jewish groups who argued he was no more than a bit player in the tragedy. He was returned to New Jersey where his family had lived on charity. By this time, the youngest of his children was fifteen, having been born the year Davis narrowly escaped a walk to the gallows.

Meanwhile, Supreme Court of Canada Justice Louis Codèrre had just finished his study of the Montreal police department. His findings appalled him. Testimony at the Frank robbery trial showed that police routinely sipped coffee with hoods and that Montreal's finest had been tipped off to the armoured car hold-up well in advance but did nothing. Codèrre concluded that the police department suffered from incompetent leadership, aldermanic meddling, petty jealousies and lax discipline. Despite the crushing of the Frank gang, Codèrre wrote that, "Vice has spread itself across the city with an ugliness that seemed assured of impunity."

Some cosmetic changes in the make-up of the underworld followed the Codèrre probe, but nothing happened that seriously threatened the criminals' take. The name of Cadieux Street was changed to de Bullion Street after a New York play made the old name notorious. But along the same pavement the same crimes continued. Passers-by were cajoled from brothels, and hookers advertised their trade within a hundred yards of police patrol wagons, and those men who succumbed to the sirens' call often found their drinks drugged and their pockets picked. The customers weren't the only ones suffering. Judge J.A. Robillard, head of the Montreal juvenile-delinquents court, concluded sadly: "Young girls of fourteen and fifteen are being found in increasing numbers in establishments which are permitted to hold pagan orgies nightly, to the detriment of future Canadian womanhood." By the mid-1930s, Montreal had returned to its old ways, with French police ranking it third on a list of the world's "most depraved" cities behind only Port Said and Marseilles. (One can't help but wonder if the tolerant attitude towards the "inevitable crimes" of vice would have been the same if women in Quebec had had the vote, as did their Ontario counterparts.)

Why the Cotronis chose to settle in Montreal in 1924 remains a mystery. But it's not out of the question that, like the unfortunate Leo Davis of the Frank gang, they wanted to be part of the flourishing bootlegging trade. Clearly the Cotronis found the liquor laws of their new country strange. They were constantly paraded through courts for bootlegging offences in the 1920s and 1930s. Nicodemo Cotroni ran afoul of the law for an altercation with a female liquor inspector, illegal possession of alcohol, theft and possession of stolen goods. Vincenzo, the eldest, didn't attend school; instead he accumulated a lengthy record of minor offences before he reached the age of twenty. Father and son are listed in court records as carpenters, with Nicodemo 's 1937 income listed as $35 a week and his total possessions valued at $1,500. The family had by then grown to eight. Vic's younger brothers were Giuseppe (Pep), Michel and Frank, and his sisters were Palmina and Marguerite.

As an adult Vic Cotroni carried just 135 pounds on his compact frame, but he had a deep chest which fanned up to broad, sloping shoulders that call to mind those of hockey star Gordie Howe. Cotroni used his strength to his advantage as a professional wrestler, grappling under the name of Vic Vincent. It was on the pro wrestling circuit that he met Armand Courville who would become both a friend and partner in crime and whose nephew would one day become a willing killer for the Cotronis.

As Vic Vincent, Cotroni moved beyond his neighbourhood and deeply into the downtown Montreal underworld of gambling houses and after-hours drinking spots. Those establishments were part of a vice industry estimated in 1936 by the city's mayor, Adhemar Raynault, to be earning $200 million yearly. During Prohibition,

Montreal was the only city on the continent where customers could legally consume alcohol.

As jazz historian John Gilmore writes, "Alcohol oils the gears of the nightclub industry and pays the salaries of its workers, and in Montreal alcohol flowed more liberally than anywhere else in North America." Mobsters tightened their hold on the city's nightclub industry while jazz musicians learned how to keep their eyes on their instruments and increase the volume, whenever violence erupted in gang-controlled nightclubs.

For Vic Cotroni, the Depression years were a time of financial and professional growth. A mug-shot shows a taciturn, neatly groomed young man, smartly dressed in a crisp white shirt, with what appears to be a silk tie, and a well-fitting double-breasted suit, sporting fashionably wide lapels and the wide pinstripes equally popular with mobsters and bankers.

By the end of the 1930s, Vic Cotroni's criminal record expanded to include possession of counterfeit coins and membership in the goon squads that were hired to terrorize voters on election days. During the city's "baseball bat" elections, thugs cleared committee rooms of rivals and stuffed ballot boxes in favour of their candidates.

Vic Cotroni's most serious charge at the time was for the rape of a young girl from Italy named Maria Bresciano who had turned down his proposal of marriage. Charges were dropped while he was out on bail when she agreed to become his wife. Italian sociologist Pino Arlacchi notes that the machismo of the 'ndranghentista system exists in continual tension with the idealizing of virginity and sexual shame for women. "Except among relatives, the two sexes represented qualities in constant antagonism: the *uomo di rispetto* ('man worthy of respect') had the task of demonstrating his virility at every opportunity, even if this meant committing violence against women or seizing them by force."

As Canada entered the Second World War, Ottawa feared an unholy alliance between Italian-heritage mobsters and Fascists. The Royal Canadian Mounted Police submitted secret lists to the federal government on hundreds of Canadians with suspect loyalties, and mass internments followed quickly. Anti-Italian prejudice was rampant. In one case, a Toronto man was confined for two years for no greater offence than playing the Italian lawn-bowling game of bocce with Fascist sympathizers. But the intelligence files also included an inventory of the Ontario Italian underworld and testify that, despite later denials by politicians, Ottawa clearly considered Mafia behaviour a serious security threat. Giovanni Durso of 200 Hess Street North in Hamilton is described in a secret RCMP report as a "criminalminded Italian and a member of the Mafia"; Charles Calogero Bordonaro of Hamilton is listed as "the leader of the Maffia [sic] at Hamilton"; and Dominic Belcastro, Thomas Rasso and Dominic Longo of Guelph are listed as "members of an international gang." But, while about a dozen Ontario residents are bluntly listed as Mafia members by Mountie intelligence, none of the hundreds of Montrealers interned during the war are listed as having Mafia ties. The closest the intelligence material comes to mentioning Montreal underworld figures is in June 1942 letters to the government suggesting Luigi, Michele, Vincenzo and Giuseppe Soccio be granted freedom only if they do "not belong to, or have any relationship with any secret society, band or gang, or any illegal organization."

The discrepancy between the numbers for Ontario and those for Quebec is initially puzzling, particularly since long-standing links between the Ontario and Quebec underworlds were highlighted by the Frank trial. But the omission starts to make sense once one notes that almost everyone on the Mountie lists for Montreal was a pro-Fascist, Sicilian-heritage immigrant connected with the Sons of Italy. This was relatively easy information to get, even for English-speaking policemen in Montreal. The omission of Calabrian-heritage criminals such as Vic Cotroni was more an indication of Mountie ignorance than underworld passivity. For Vic Cotroni, this was a good thing. He didn't need the notoriety for he understood that crime grows best away from the harsh glare of a public spotlight. Opportunities would soon arrive in Montreal to take crime far beyond anything Tony Frank could have imagined.

Vic Cotroni felt no need to enlist in the war effort for either side, instead investing in nightclubs frequented by both politicians and career criminals. But he managed to stay out of jail, which was a sign he was getting better at crime — not that he was retiring from it.

Chapter Three

Mr. Lilo

*"A new vision! A new hope!
A new soul for Canada."*
— John Deifenbaker,
Federal election campaign 1957

O pportunity for Vic Cotroni came in the short, scowling form of Carmine Galante. The Brooklyn mobster was, at the most, 5'5" tall but he cast a large and chilling shadow. He could overpower larger men with the sheer force of his personality, and was diagnosed by a prison psychiatrist as a psychopath. He was a man of sharp contrasts and paradoxes: he spoke in the "dese, dem, dose" patois of B-grade movies, but he also showed a fondness for St. Augustine, Plato and Descartes. Bespectacled and balding, he loved his children and his pipe and Don Diego cigars which brought him the nickname "Mr. Lilo" for "Mr. Cigar." He believed in simplifying life's contradictions and chaos with bullets, and he exercised this belief with gusto. The fact that he was also connected to creating countless drug addictions through international heroin-trafficking didn't stop Galante from considering himself a good Roman Catholic and an American patriot. In his worldview, the Mafia was a force against evil, setting up standards of loyalty and fair play.

Galante (real name Camillo Galante, though it was also spelled "Galente" on court records until roughly 1960) was born on February 21, 1910, in the slums of East Harlem. His father, a fisherman, moved as a child to Brooklyn from Castellammare del Golfo, Sicily. This was a good place for an aspiring mobster's family to be from, as it was also the former hometown of Joe Bonanno and fellow U.S. crime heavyweights Stefano Magaddino of Buffalo, Joe

Profaci of Brooklyn and Joe Aiello of Chicago. Young Galante was sent to juvenile hall at the age of ten as an incorrigible delinquent; he had graduated to Sing Sing prison on an assault conviction by seventeen, and by age twenty, he had been acquitted of murdering a police officer but found guilty of assault and robbery. The latter conviction, which brought Galante a twelve-year prison sentence, came after a six-year-old girl and a detective were wounded in a botched hold-up.

When finally paroled in 1939, Galante found the Italian-heritage mobs had changed considerably. They had come under the loose control of what was grandly known as The Commission, which regulated crime the way a chamber of commerce oversees merchants. As a general rule, there was to be no interference in the day-to-day operations of families, but Commission member Joseph (Joe Bananas) Bonanno explained, "The Commission, as an agent of harmony, could arbitrate disputes before it… It had respect only insofar as its individual members had respect. More than anything else, The Commission was a forum." The order formed a distinct pyramid within crime groups, with all monies going to enrich the top echelon. In return, leaders were expected to provide protection against police harassment or arrest. For those behind bars, the process was supposed to provide care for their families. Low-level soldiers weren't paid salaries but were expected to pay their bills by running criminal rackets of their own. Bonanno would explain that members of his "family" included shoemakers, tailors, barbers, bakers, factory workers, priests and politicians, and that only a few members engaged in illicit, full-time crime.

Upon his release from prison, Galante freelanced his services to the mobs of Bonanno, Profaci, Vito (Don Vito) Genovese and Lucky Luciano. It was Genovese who gave Galante the job that elevated him from minor-hoodlum status. Genovese was in Italy, dodging murder charges and attempting to curry favour with Benito Mussolini. The Italian leader was angered by frequent, caustic attacks from the pen of Genovese's countryman, Carlo Tresca, the outspoken editor of the New York Italian-language newspaper, *The Hammer.*

Galante's solution to the problem came at 9:40 on the evening of January 11, 1943, when the corner of Fifth Avenue and Fifteenth Street was darker than usual, the result of a wartime power-saving dim-out. Tresca was walking alone when a squatty man in a snap-brim hat approached him. The stranger, who had been loitering at the corner, reached into his pocket, extracted a .38-calibre revolver, and pumped bullets into the journalist's cheek and lung, and then fled in a dark sedan. All clues pointed directly at Galante, and a suspicious detective asked him where he was the night of the murder.

"I saw *Casablanca,* the movie, and I saw a girl," Galante replied.

"John Wayne was very good in *Casablanca, "* the detective deadpanned.

"Not so good," Galante replied.

"What's the girl's name?" the officer continued.

"I don't know," Galante answered. "She was not so good either."

From someone else, this might have been considered a joke. But Galante was not known for his wit. Although Galante couldn't even remember the movie's famous song phrase *You must remember this*, frustrated police had to release him for lack of evidence.

Galante's reputation shot up in the underworld. No longer a no-name thug specializing in grocery-store hold-ups, he was soon Joe Bonanno's driver and a "made man" in the Bonanno family. By the late 1940s, Galante began to look north to Montreal. What he saw was an enormous opportunity for profits if someone could force relative order on the city's underworld.

The north-south pull between Canada and the United States had been magnified since the 1920s. By the 1950s, clearly no market was more important than the United States for Canadian captains of commerce and crime. Branch plants in auto, radio and appliance manufacturing were appearing in Canada, and Carmine Galante planned to do the same thing for the varied criminal enterprises of Joe Bonanno.

Carmine Galante arrived in Montreal in 1953 with a suitcase full of cash and Napoleonic plans of expansion. The move north offered escape from the relentless publicity that had been generated by the televised proceedings of the U.S. Senate Crime Investigating Committee headed by Tennessee senator Estes Kefauver. This attention had chased American bookies into Canada, and Galante followed them to ensure the Bonanno group secured a cut of their earnings. More important, he also wanted to make the port city a focal point in the world's drug trade. There was now increasingly tough enforcement in the United States, which made it difficult to ship drugs directly into New York. For centuries, Montreal had been a trading and distribution centre for mainstream commerce, and was recently also a popular spot for French Corsican drug-traffickers who enjoyed its European ambiance and its familiar language.

Galante wanted to intensify things, a decision that brought both the promise of riches and the threat of violent death. For a few fortunate Montreal criminals, Galante's presence meant their careers would skyrocket as they gained supremacy over long-time rivals and access to the American marketplace. The lives of others would plummet, some all the way into the grave. Whose fates would be enriched and whose would be ruined were anybody's guess in 1953.

Galante set up shop in an electronics firm. When he ventured out, seldom without bodyguards, he was sighted with the likes of Frankie Carbo, the American underworld don of boxing. Galante was soon extracting protection money from gambling houses, after-hours drinking spots, houses of prostitution, night clubs, carnivals and abortionists, and pressing to extend his influence to truck drivers and butchers. Within a year of his arrival, he was the most potent force in Montreal's underworld, ending forever what one Montreal police officer wistfully called the "era of the gentlemen gamblers."

At the time, Vic Cotroni was a significant but not a dominant force in the Montreal underworld and an *éminence grise* of the arts scene who was credited with launching the careers of several Québécois folk singers. His *Faison Doré* nightclub in the city's tenderloin district attracted judges, lawyers and politicians to hear such international singing stars as Charles Aznavour and Tino Ross. It was also listed as a mailing address for French-born heroin-smuggler Antonio D'Agostino who was known on the streets of Montreal as "Michel Sisco."

Most likely, Vic Cotroni's relationship with Galante grew out of Cotroni's friendship with Louis Greco, a stocky pizzeria owner with thirteen years' served prison time for armed robbery. Greco soon became known as Galante's Montreal underboss, and he ruled the west underside of Montreal through his eatery where he still performed such common chores as mopping floors. Like Galante, Greco was a Sicilian traditionalist, with a middle-class home and modest lifestyle that belied his wealth and power. Vic Cotroni's status rose with that of Greco to the point that he had the honour of standing as godfather to one of Galante 's children, while Galante became godfather for one of his. To Mafia watchers, this was a clear sign that the Calabrian Vic Cotroni was a somebody.

The old criminal cartel was used to having its way in Montreal, with the aid, or at least the non-interference, of pliant members of respectable Montreal society, including politicians, police and the press. But the 1954 civic election was turned into a morality play by a pair of crusading young lawyers and a judge with a deft sense of timing. Mr. Justice François Caron tabled a long-awaited report on crime in Montreal less than a month before the civic election, ensuring that corruption would be an election issue. His 100,000-word study made for spicy reading. Newspaper readers enjoyed a glow of righteous indignation as they read that gambling houses thrived under the noses of bought-off or non-caring police officers and city fathers, and that madames were accorded the courtesy of twenty-four hours' notice before whorehouse raids.

Caron's report was a godsend for one of his researchers, Jean Drapeau, who was running for mayor as the reform candidate for a new group calling itself the Public Morality Committee. The crime establishment fought Drapeau with bribes, baseball bats and bullets. Police raided mobster Frank Pretula's well-appointed home in Beaconsfield and discovered in a bathroom wall safe a notebook that detailed how the criminals spent more than $100,000 fighting Drapeau's reformers. The notebook also listed at least a half-dozen journalists who were on the mob payroll for laundering the image of the mob and sullying that of the reformers.

Vic Cotroni's north-end gang did what they considered their democratic duty — they stuffed ballot boxes when they were not threatening the opposition. But zealous newcomer Drapeau easily won the election, and appointed as police chief his old associate Pacifique Roy (Pax) Plante who had worked with Justice Caron in researching the report. A thin man with thick, horn-rimmed glasses, Plante, in the words of journalist Stuart Keate, looked like "a third violinist or a prosperous beauty salon proprietor." But once Plante was in the morality squad, neither church bingos nor Vic Cotroni were safe from his passion for order.

The Drapeau years didn't wipe out the mob, but they had annoyed it. In 1955, Galante was called upon by the RCMP and the Immigration and Revenue departments to explain what he did for a living. Unable to do so to the satisfaction of the authorities, he was deported. He dispatched his brother-in-law, Antonio Marullo, north to handle business. But he, too, was deported.

When the 1957 civic election came around, American Salvatore (Little Sal) Giglio was in charge and mob patience was exhausted. During the election campaign, Civic Action League president Dr. Reuben Lévesque was savagely beaten. Then, when Drapeau went on television vowing not to be intimidated, goons trashed his campaign headquarters. One night while returning home, Drapeau spotted two strangers in a sedan by the side of the road The sedan's lights were suddenly turned on, and the car raced after Drapeau. The mayor was able to duck into the safety of his garage only because he had an electric garage-door opener, a curiosity in 1957.

Drapeau wasn't under attack just from criminals. Quebec premier Maurice Duplessis had fought Communists, unionists and even Jehovah's Witnesses, but he drew the line at the mob. And, in the election of 1957, Duplessis threw his considerable might behind the anti-Drapeauites, participating in what even his sympathetic biographer Conrad Black described as "the most disgraceful election campaign the Union Nationale ever ran, before or since. The combination of violence, salacious advertising and good, old-fashioned corruption was an offense to all honest citizens."

The onslaught was too much for the reform slate. Drapeau lost to former Liberal MP Sarto Fortier, who campaigned for a "wide-open but honest" Montreal. Stunned and hurt, Drapeau protested he had been robbed by a "pack of wolves" who cast 20,000 phony ballots and financed their campaign with hot money. Plante was shuffled into the city's legal department and then fired. He fled to a small village in Mexico where he was said to be living in fear for his life and spending much time with his Doberman pinschers.

Predictably, the rackets rebounded. Sal Giglio charged bookmaking houses $200 a week, plus a quarter of the profits, as a business tax. After-hours drinking holes, known as blind pigs, channelled $300 a week plus a quarter of the net profits to the mob, while prostitutes were billed $35 weekly for the privilege of renting their bodies to strangers. In an effort at public relations, streetwalking was discouraged, and bartenders at blind pigs were told to serve honest drinks. Giglio expanded Galante's old heroin-trafficking network, tightening ties with his associates Lucien Rivard and Vic Cotroni. But it was cigars and cigarettes, not heroin, that drove the dark-eyed little mob chief back to the United States. Police found 240 illegal Cuban cigars and 880 American cigarettes in Giglio's possession that hadn't been declared at Customs. Ottawa seized the opportunity, declared Giglio an undesirable, and gave him two days to leave the country. Giglio was the last American sent north to handle the Bonanno interests. After he was deported, the job would be handled by a Canadian — a small step for Canadian nationalism and a giant leap for Vic Cotroni's career.

Events overseas also helped make 1957 a watershed year for Vic Cotroni. In October, across the Atlantic in Palermo, Galante, Joe Bonanno and legendary mobster Lucky Luciano met with Sicilian boss Salvatore (Ciaschitteddu "Little Bird") Greco and rising young Sicilian mafioso Gaetano Badalamenti. Also in attendance was Tommaso Buscetta, who would later work with Vic's younger brother, Frank, and who later still would become the most famous turncoat in the history of the Mafia. The meeting took place in the most opulent setting the island of Sicily had to offer, a sharp contrast to their grubby topic of conversation. They chatted in the courtly Hotel des Palmes, with its red carpets and marble statues, and at the tables of the luxurious Spano restaurant. They discussed how to expand the world's heroin traffic and resolve disputes the trade would undoubtedly bring.

The drug ring they set up would become known as the "French Connection." Turkish opium was sent to Marseilles, where it was converted to heroin, then shipped through Montreal and into the United States. Support from French Corsican gangsters was secured by offering them an unlimited American market, while Cuba was brought into play as a warehouse for American-bound heroin. The set-up had enormous significance, and not just for the countless North American ghetto residents whose lives would be ruined by heroin. It also changed the Mafia itself as criminals began to look beyond their communities to their roles as international entrepreneurs. The set-up also tightened Montreal's ties to New York. And it offered the mob the potential for riches and for disaster, as Vic Cotroni and Galante would soon know only too well.

Chapter Four

Big Money, Big Risks

"I like you. You are quiet.
You don't make anybody
know your business."

— Guiseppe (Pep) Cotroni praises a man
who says he wants to be a drug dealer

The potential profits in the heroin trade were breathtaking. A kilogram of raw opium could be bought in Turkey for $35, and by the time it was refined, diluted and sold on the streets of Harlem, its value had been pumped up as high as $225,000. But that promise of riches brought equally magnified risks. Convictions meant heavy prison sentences, since destroying neighbourhoods with the narcotic wasn't winked away as were morals crimes such as gambling and prostitution. The thought of decades behind bars made even stoic criminals queasy — and sometimes talkative with police. The lure of huge profits also made normally obedient mob soldiers greedy enough to think of striking out on their own, bypassing the mob's pyramid-shaped power structure.

Vic Cotroni's younger brother, Giuseppe (Pep), knew this all too well. A jowly, balding, outwardly pleasant man, Pep Cotroni made a great deal of money doing nasty things, including wholesaling heroin into New York. Police trailing him once noted him buying twenty ties at $15 each and paying with cash. He was overheard musing that he could easily spend his afternoons counting thousand-dollar bills, should he have the whim. He was co-owner, with Carmine Galante and his brother Vic, of the plush Bonfire restaurant. The Bonfire's previous owner, Frank Pretula, was missing and presumed dead at the hands of his business's new management. Not all Pep Cotroni's rivals were so firmly subdued. In 1958, strychnine was found in a bottle of anisette in his posh Ste. Adèle cottage, but the list of suspects was too long for police to make an arrest. Possible culprits included Pretula loyalists angry over the treatment of their former boss, and more pragmatic underworld figures concerned that Pep Cotroni's crime interests were spread too widely and too thinly and that his conviction could collapse any number of criminal enterprises.

Whatever his problems, Pep Cotroni wasn't one to snub a chance to make money, and there was a great deal of it to be made in the new French Connection heroin ring. Pep Cotroni paid careful attention therefore when a stranger in his thirties came calling, to say he wanted to help expand the business. The stranger, who wore sunglasses night and day, was accompanied by a bit player in the city's underworld named Eddie Smith.

"Why did you come to see me?" Pep Cotroni asked.

"We know you are involved in a lot of rackets," Smith replied. "Maybe you can help us."

"What is your full name?" Cotroni asked the man behind the sunglasses.

"Dave Costa."

"What is your nationality?"

"Italian."

"Where do you come from?"

"East Holland."

"Do you know anything about junk?"

"Yes, I sold junk."

Pep Cotroni gave the newcomers a crash course in narcotics trafficking. He explained the Marseilles system of rating heroin by applying heat, since different purity levels meant different melting points, and he told them how to use codes to relay pay-phone numbers at which he could be reached. If Cotroni mentioned a number, Costa and Smith were to subtract two from each digit, except zero and one, which remained the same. And there was a written code, in which any vertical line represented zero and various angles represented different numbers. Pep suggested Costa should go to New

York to get a "trap," underworld slang for a hidden compartment built into furniture. Chevrolets were the car of choice for drug runners, especially the two-door and convertible models, since their back-seat arm-rests were easily converted into secret storage compartments. The best time to drive across the border was around two in the morning when Customs security was at its most lax.

Cotroni wasn't impressed when Costa put in an order for just two kilos of heroin. And he made it clear he wasn't a man to be trifled with by telling Costa that a man had been "knocked off" for owing him $30,000. Over coffee and cake in a restaurant, Cotroni added he preferred to deal in cash, not credit, "...although there will be times that I will not be able to go along with this. Because you will have some good customers and that these customers you can't let down, either they will not have the money or they will need the narcotics, and you will have to learn how to feel them out, and when you get to know them, you will know which ones to trust and which ones not to trust."

But then plans for a deal were suddenly called off by Cotroni, who said he didn't want to anger top New York mobsters. Cotroni told of drug dealers with Runyanesque names like Bootsie and Angie, and explained that in New York the heroin traffic was handled by just five men. "You have to take into consideration . . . [that] by you going into the picture," he told Costa, "you will take anywhere between a $150,000 and $200,000of business away from these people."

Costa protested that he had brought $14,000 with him in good faith and deserved a chance. Cotroni eyed the envelopes of cash and relented. He outlined a scheme that would allow them to do business together without tipping off Frank (Chow) Mancino, a Brooklyn drug dealer who didn't want any extra competition. "In order for us to do business, you will have to go back to New York, see Chow and tell him that I am no good and that I don't deal with narcotics and I am a phoney, et cetera. Then within forty-eight hours I will know if you did it or not, and if everything is okay, you can come up here secretly or without anybody knowing your business, and we will do business."

Cotroni said Chow Mancino knew people and had "been to college," underworld argot meaning he made powerful connections while in prison. The right cellblock in the right prison was to a young

criminal what the Harvard Business School was to an aspiring businessman. Cotroni warned Costa that Chow was a man to be watched
carefully. Once a drug-runner between Montreal and New York,
Mancino had tricked Cotroni out of $100,000 and now didn't dare
set foot in Montreal.

Costa and Smith went to New York and encountered Mancino
on Marcy Avenue in Joe Bonanno's old Williamsburg neighbourhood
of Brooklyn, in a brick working-class home a few blocks down the
street from Carmine Galante's equally ordinary house. Mancino was
on his roof, feeding his pigeons, and seemed to believe his visitors'
lies. When they returned to Montreal, Pep Cotroni was more than
eager to complete the deal, saying, "The next time you come up,
you know where to come. You come to the same place."

Privately, Cotroni told Costa that Smith was a nice person, but
useless as a drug-runner. Cotroni feared Smith wasn't being smart
enough to notice if police were trailing him or bugging his room.
Worse yet, he wasn't discreet, and a good trafficker is neither loud
nor obvious in his movements. "You, as well as myself, know that
in this business you can't do that. I like you. You are quiet. You
don't make anybody know your business. You know what the score
is as far as narcotics go."

Pep was right. Costa did know the score and wasn't obvious in
his movements. He was really Patrick Biase, an undercover FBI
agent working alongside the RCMP. In June 1959, he arrested Pep
Cotroni in the biggest narcotics bust in Canadian history.

So strong was Vic Cotroni's image that a myth grew to explain
away his brother's arrest. Some Montreal criminals believed Pep
Cotroni's arrest was not an attack on Vic Cotroni's organization,
but rather a dramatic manifestation of Vic Cotroni's will. One well-
placed mobster would argue years later that a Mountie tipped Vic
Cotroni off about the arrest hours before it happened. The mobster
asserted that Vic kept quiet, willing to let his brother pay the price
for violating the law—not the state's law but Vic Cotroni's law. Vic
Cotroni was said to be against drug-dealing because he was old
enough to feel paternal towards children and successful enough not
to need to deviate from more traditional sources of income such as
gambling and extortion. This theory is extremely unlikely, but it
does show the power of Vic Cotroni's reputation. A more probable
explanation comes from a police officer who sees Vic Cotroni's
hands on virtually everything in Montreal's Italian underworld, but

his fingerprints nowhere. The officer notes that Pep Cotroni was a decade younger than his powerful brother and stuck with high-risk jobs. "I'm sure [Vic] used Pep as protection against being out front. Vic was the boss so his brothers were expected to be the guys out front, protecting the eldest from any direct involvement in anything."

Pep Cotroni must have felt a knot in his stomach when he learned that all his dealings with Biase had been recorded. Strapped to his leg, the undercover officer wore a radio transmitter, roughly the size of a package of cigarettes, that relayed Cotroni's words to an RCMP listening-post. As if that wasn't enough, the prosecution was to be handled by a young zealot named Jean-Paul Ste. Marie. Ste. Marie wanted Pep Cotroni to suffer nothing less than fourteen years in prison, stiff financial penalties and the lash.

The jury was told that Pep Cotroni was a top international drug smuggler, with ties to Cuba before and after the revolution, as well as to Europe and New York. But there were doubts they'd hear from star witness Eddie Smith. Smith was terrified that a return to Montreal would mean his murder. Instead, he wanted to testify before a special travelling court session in a New York City hotel. The judge agreed, and the next day everyone in the Montreal courtroom but a haggard-looking Pep Cotroni and his lawyer registered surprise when Pep Cotroni whispered that he was guilty.

With Pep Cotroni's conviction and that of his friend and part-time spaghetti-house waiter René (Bob) Robert, police crowed that they had locked up two of the most important drug-traffickers on the continent. Ste. Marie likened Pep Cotroni's crime to wholesale murder and demanded the sentence reflect its seriousness: "The death penalty is prescribed for a killer, and a man who traffics in narcotics is just as certainly a killer as is a murderer. His nefarious trade takes the lives not only of hundreds of addicts but breaks their families' lives as well in many instances. Unfortunately, the maximum is only fourteen years and the lash." Jail wasn't enough, Ste. Marie argued. He called for "the largest possible fine" against Pep Cotroni: "We have tried repeatedly to get back from him the $28,800 he received from the agents, but without success. I would like to see this man broken financially by the court's sentence, for I know that no matter how stiff a penitentiary sentence he may get, the most effective punishment will be against his pocket."

Pep Cotroni seemed unaffected when Judge Wilfrid Lazure sentenced him to ten years in prison. But the mobster winced when

Lazure added that he was fining him $60,000 and ordering him to return the American agents' $28,800. "Your ramifications extend to the Orient, France, Italy and the United States," Lazure lectured. "You fooled the police by operating as a spy network. ...You rose rapidly in the underworld." Lazure noted the "enormous expense" of the joint RCMP, FBI and U.S. Treasury department operation, adding, "I could have ordered the lash for you in addition to the penitentiary sentence."

Lazure continued: "The traffic in narcotics is one of the worst plagues of society. It does incalculable harm and I hear that the Montreal-New York trade has reached figures not in the millions but in the hundreds of millions of dollars. It's almost unbelievable."

Winding down, Lazure remarked that he had been struck by the energy and reasoning of Ste. Marie: "It is not normally my practice to compliment the Crown prosecutor. But I must in this instance pay tribute to the fine manner in which the mass of telling evidence was presented by Mr. Ste. Marie, assisted by his counsel, special prosecutor Ezra Leithman, Q.C."

Innocuous as they seemed at the time, those final words would take on a strange, even frightening, ring.

Pep's worries weren't over. In April 1960, five months after he had been convicted in the biggest drug bust in Canadian history, he was on trial, facing charges of masterminding the nation's biggest bank robbery. And, to make matters worse, his prosecutor was once again Jean-Paul Ste. Marie. The huge robbery had an unlikely location, the quiet eastern Ontario community of Brockville. Employees at Brockville Trust & Savings arrived at work one May morning in 1958 to find that someone had chiselled and torched through the bank's ceiling and into the vault, leaving not a fingerprint where $9 million in cash and securities had been.

Police from Canada, the United States, Interpol and Switzerland rushed to sleepy Brockville. Pep Cotroni's undoing in the case came through the personal peccadillo of one of his men, René Martin, who, for reasons only he knew, liked to carry his personal bank book when robbing a bank. This time, the passbook fell from Martin's pocket into the rubble, where it was found by a bank employee. Martin wouldn't talk, but that wasn't necessary, since he was found with half a million dollars of the Brockville loot. Police knew he was an associate of Pep Cotroni and soon linked both Martin and

Cotroni to a Marseilles money-launderer named Gabriel Graziani, whose connections extended throughout Europe, North America and the Middle East, and who regularly banked stolen funds in Switzerland.

Pep Cotroni had used the stolen bonds to pay a Sicilian immigrant who was remodelling Cotroni's tavern. Pep's bar was in the Ontario-de Buillon Street neighbourhood where Tony Frank once thrived, just a few minutes walk from the old Cotroni family home. The immigrant was also employed as a waiter in a blind pig, an afterhours drinking spot, managed by Cotroni. Now he feared for his life. The witness was hidden in the homes of various Montreal police officers. He told the court he believed he had narrowly escaped a grim end at the hands of Pep Cotroni's enforcer, René Robert. Robert had suggested they take a car ride together, but instead the engineer fled to a barber's shop where he hid under a towel until police arrived. "I felt something was going to happen to me if I had gone on the ride with Mr. Robert." On another occasion, he was beaten by Pep Cotroni after being interrogated by police. After the beating, Pep Cotroni changed his tactics, offering him $10,000 and saying ominously, "You need a rest and you should go away."

The immigrant witness wasn't the only one in Montreal's Italian community who worried. Co-editors of the Italian-language weekly *Cittandino Canadese* were warned not to continue writing about Pep Cotroni's legal woes. Two thugs visited them, saying it was "not respectable" to publish such stories. Nothing was said about the respectability of smuggling heroin or robbing banks. Montreal's other Italian language weekly, *Le Courier Italien,* made no mention of the securities case. But Nick Chamara, owner of the defiant *Cittandino Canadese,* was undaunted, boldly saying, "Publicity is my best weapon."

Ste. Marie was again impressive on the attack, persuading the court that Cotroni was too dangerous a man to be allowed out on bail. This time, his efforts brought a seven-year sentence for Cotroni, who grimaced but said nothing when the jury delivered its verdict. Ste. Marie prematurely boasted that the conviction meant the end of the "hot bond" traffic, although just $3 million of a total of $15 million in loot was recovered. In an effort to make amends for the missing money, Ste. Marie launched legal proceedings to seize all Pep Cotroni's assets, so that the mobster's life would be less comfortable once his prison time was served.

Things were going no better in Brooklyn for Vic Cotroni's senior associate, Carmine Galante. He was one of the underworld notables summoned before a federal rackets grand jury after police stumbled on a top-level Mafia gathering at a farm at Apalachin, New York, on November 14, 1957. Fifty-eight mobsters were scooped up by police, while untold others, whose ranks were said to include Montrealers Louis Greco and Pep Cotroni, dashed through the bushes and brambles, and around a police roadblock, to freedom.

In 1958, Galante's fortunes worsened. He was among thirty-six mobsters indicted for international drug-dealing. An assistant U.S. attorney charged that Galante was "intimately acquainted with practically every important underworld figure in the United States." Galante tried to flee his prosecutors by going to Montreal, then sneaking back to New York, where he enjoyed a life of luxury on the run until he was picked up by police in June 1959 on the Garden City Parkway.

Some key witnesses in the trial were murdered. Others were officially listed as suicides. Jurors were attacked in the courtroom, both verbally and physically. The sixty-eight-year-old jury foreman was flung down a flight of stairs, and his spine was smashed. His crippling came after testimony had been heard from seventy-five witnesses and the prosecution and defence had rested their cases. The result was a mistrial. During Galante's second trial, one of his co-accused heaved a fifteen-pound chair at a prosecutor. Another had to be gagged and shackled during the proceedings, leaving his lawyer to argue his client was not sane enough to stand trial. When a verdict was finally reached in 1962, no one got less than a twelve-year term, and a total of 276 years of sentences were meted out. Galante was given twenty years, with a $20,000 fine tacked on for screaming verbal abuse in the courtroom. Federal judge Lloyd F. MacMahon ruled: "If criminal conspiracy trials can be frustrated or reversible error willfully created by the defendants' concerted efforts to prejudice their own rights, we might just as well close our courts and let organized criminals take over the country."

The lengthy terms were eloquent testimony that international drug trafficking was a far riskier business than old-style Mafia extortion and gambling rackets. It seemed Galante was finished at the top levels of the underworld. He would begin to serve his time at age fifty-two, and few people could have believed he'd once again be a major player on the world-crime stage. To Vic Cotroni, who had lost a benefactor and a brother, the world must have seemed a riskier, lonlier place.

Chapter Five

The Home Front

*"I'll show you who's boss
around here."*
— Frank Cotroni

Vic Cotroni made it clear he was around to stay despite the imprisonment of his brother Pep and his friend Galante and the headaches of the Drapeau-inspired crackdowns. Mobsters don't announce they have been promoted by taking out an ad in *Report on Business,* but they nonetheless let people who matter know. Vic Cotroni didn't declare his improved status by shouting or shooting or boasting; he built a house. His summer home, custom built in 1959, was a symbol of his status in the underworld. He was firmly anchored at the centre of what might be termed a crime board of directors. Its centre was in the Italian district of St. Leonard and its influence extended to the Jewish criminals of west-end Montreal and French Canadians in the north and east. Cotroni also controlled enterprises that were ostensibly legitimate, while letting front men, such as a scrap-metal dealer and a major contractor, perform day-to-day management chores.

As the 1960s began, Vic Cotroni was tied to everyone who mattered in the Montreal underworld. At the same time he kept a business-like distance from them, savouring respect and showing no great need for affection. It wouldn't be long, though, before he would reach out beyond his borders, since even branch-plant managers can have ambitious plans.

At a time when many Canadian nationalists were wringing their hands over growing American investment, Vic Cotroni was rejoicing in the wealth his southern ties had brought him. The sturdy little man with the voice that seemed both remote and forceful had a chauffeured limousine, a duplex in Rosemount and the new palatial summer home on the St. Lawrence River in Lavaltrie. An hour's drive from Montreal, the new home stood well back from the highway and any prying eyes. There was thick walnut and white-and-pink marble throughout. The marble also wound through porches and along a forty-foot walkway to a swimming pool, and around its deck. The home's centrepiece was its conference room with an enormous, hand-crafted walnut boardroom table. Cotroni may have learned how to make crime business-like from the Americans, but his grand table recognized his birthplace as well, with inlaid crests noting the regions of Italy and the word "Italia" carved onto the chairs at the table's head and foot. The boardroom overlooked the St. Lawrence, and a sundeck was held up with the twenty-four-inch steel beams sometimes used in bridge construction. The deck capped an auxiliary power supply, in case the house's 400-amp service failed. There was also an expensive back-up power system for Cotroni's stainless-steel fridge, a walk-in industrial model the size of a small office, with meat hooks along one side and shelves on the other. The stove was also top quality, a stainless-steel Galardo industrial model one would expect to find in a fine restaurant, not in a private home.

Despite the opulent kitchen, there was no doubt this was a man's home and that the man of the house was very particular about workmanship. Two urinals stood amid the white marble of one main-floor bathroom. A heavy slate, professional-sized Brunswick pool table dominated the recreation room, where there was also a built-in movie screen framed by two twelve-foot floor-to-ceiling speakers sunk into the walls. Cotroni was still married to the former Maria Bresciano and they now had a daughter, but his wife kept very much in the background, as was shown by the summer house's layout. (Even farther in the background was his French-Canadian mistress, who maintained a home in Montreal and was mother of his son.)

There had obviously been much thought given to entertaining respected people. The guest bedroom upstairs was a mirror image of the master bedroom, so important guests would not be upstaged. Each room had a view of the St. Lawrence, a walk-in closet so big it included a small desk, and a white marble bathroom with the weighscales and toilet-paper holders discreetly hidden into the walls. Between the bedrooms was a sitting-room overlooking the river, big and grand enough to pass for a living-room in an average home. But in the summer home of Vic Cotroni, the sitting-room appeared almost tiny. To reach the master bedrooms, one went up a winding staircase, through another sitting-room, and under tens of thousands of dollars' worth of crystal chandeliers.

Attempting to show that his good fortune was his people's wealth, Vic Cotroni gave generously to north-end Montreal churches and charity groups. For a mobster, such actions are more convenience than conscience — it's always nice to have friends when you're in a dangerous line of work. Vic Cotroni was able to detach himself from the grubbier day-to-day crime of his career both physically and practically. Enforcement duties were handled by his younger brother Frank, twenty years Vic's junior. Frank had been born in Quebec, and his French was better than his Italian. Vic Cotroni hoped this cultural difference would translate into tighter links with French-Canadian criminals.

It was Frank's hands-on role in the family business that brought him and a gang of associates to Montreal's Chez Paree nightclub on Stanley Street near Ste. Catherine early in the morning of November 4, 1960. Just a few years before, a trip to the Chez Paree meant the opportunity to view top cabaret reviews and such jazz legends as Charlie (Bird) Parker and Woody Herman. But, by November 1960, jazz had given way to rock and cabarets had fallen to television variety shows. Couples who had once spent pleasant evenings dancing to Nick Martin and his orchestra now stayed home and watched Ed Sullivan. The lovely Chez Parette dancers were replaced by strippers with names like Joy, Dasher, Sheba and Baby Doll who often doubled as hookers for the unaccompanied men who now outnumbered couples in the audiences. Musicians sleepwalked through "Night Train" and "Honky Tonk" instead of experimenting with bebop and jazz, and soon they'd be replaced by recorded music.

These were unsettled times for the underworld in the nightclub industry. Reform threatened to disrupt long-standing and profitable relationships. Mobsters fought to control a union that represented club workers and acts booked into nightclubs. Newfound co-operation between suburban and downtown police made it more difficult for gambling spots to leapfrog from downtown to suburbs and back to avoid arrests. Reform also threatened to cost some criminals their liquor licences, and a strong hand was needed to squeeze profits from protection rackets amid the rapid change.

Frank Cotroni and roughly thirty associates weren't at the Chez Paree early that morning to lament the downtown's cultural decline, but to do business. Frank Cotroni was known to police as more impulsive than his brother Vic, and not as sharp a judge of character. He could usually be found up front, at the cutting edge of the action, and at the time of his visit to the Chez Paree he was out on bail for carrying a gun capable of firing armour-piercing bullets.

Inside the Chez Paree early that morning, a piano was knocked over, a television was thrown into the bar, and liquor was splashed throughout. The Cotroni men methodically swung baseball bats at every piece of glass in sight, causing an estimated $30,000 in damage, while their twenty-nine-year-old leader, Frank Cotroni, shouted, "I'll show you who's boss around here... They will pay me, even if I have to wait until I die."

The downtown Montreal jail was full of the usual flotsam of the streets, including a violent young drunk whose offence was hurling a case of beer into the face of a policeman. Also in the cell was a gaggle of cowering McGill University students protesting their innocence. They had been jailed after late-night revelry had gotten overly boisterous. They complained that the wrong students had been arrested and that it was another band of liquor-addled academics that had committed the minor act of vandalism for which they were being held. One student was particularly uneasy, shivering amid the stench and dampness of his own vomit, when the Cotroni gang entered after being picked up in the Chez Paree bust. Years later, the student, now a successful newspaper editor, would recall with wonder that the Cotroni men didn't act like thugs. Frank Cotroni's voice was soft, his manner gentle, as he gestured towards the cold, nauseated student. Then Cotroni took off his fine camel-hair coat and handed it to the student, giving him both warmth and a strange feeling of security. The next morning, the students were freed to return to classes and their normal lives, but first they made a call for Cotroni to the mobster's lawyer. They may not have realized it at the time, but the undergraduates had been given a lesson in mafiosi behaviour that night: that if you do someone a small favour, you can often get a larger one in return.

The Chez Paree mêlée led to increased calls for a gangland clean-up. In 1962, Jean Drapeau, who had been re-elected mayor in 1960, called for federal aid to keep the civic election clean. The Cotroni group reportedly spent $1 million trying to unseat the austere reformer. Another $690,000 was offered to bring illegal pinball machines into the city. The gambits failed. But Vic Cotroni kept his cool, waiting for the right opportunities as his fortune and influence quietly grew.

He was clearly confident his American ties were more durable than any experiment with reform.

PART TWO

Holding Power

"Here the question arises: is it better to be loved than feared, or vice versa? I don't doubt that every prince would like to be both; but since it is hard to accomodate these qualities, if you have to make a choice, to be feared is much safer than to be loved."
— Niccolò Machiavelli, *The Prince*

Chapter Six

The Boss Comes North

"It's a wonderful city. That's all I can tell you."
— Top mafia boss Joseph (Joe Bananas)
Bonanno explains why he wants
to move to Montreal

A t the top of Vic Cotroni's world, even above the now imprisoned Carmine Galante, was Joseph (Joe Bananas)
Bonanno, a vain man who projected the haughty certitude
of a soap-opera leading man. Bonanno grew up in Castellammare
del Golfo, Sicily, puffed with the desire to lead men and proud that
his father chose a life in the Mafia over one in the priesthood. "He
could have been more self-centred, placing personal tranquillity over
sacrifice," Bonanno bragged. "Instead, he chose to help his family."
Bonanno was twenty-six when he helped form the Mafia Commission in 1931 with the likes of Lucky Luciano and Al Capone.

But by 1964 things were exploding in "The Volcano," Bonanno's
nickname for New York City, and Bonanno stood accused of plotting the murder of three fellow Commission leaders. It had long
been clear that Bonanno disdained his fellow Mafia commision
members, some of whom had been mere car thieves and moonshiners
when Bonanno had become a don. But now Joe Bonanno was on the
fringe of the Commission, which took much of its direction from his
"distant cousin" Stefano (The Undertaker) Magaddino of Buffalo
and New Yorkers Thomas (Three-Finger Brown) Lucchese and Carlo
Gambino. Things were particularly poisonous between Bonanno

and his septuagenarian cousin, Magaddino, a bull-necked man who looked like a combination of Benito Mussolini and Elmer Fudd. Bonanno considered Magaddino a paranoid who "saw darkness in the middle of the day." In Bonanno's view, Gambino was also a poor excuse for a mafioso: "He was not a warrior. Given a choice, he avoided violence. He was a squirrel of a man, a servile and cringing individual."

Were Bonanno's contempt for and desire to control the Commission enough to make him plot the murder of the threesome? Would he kill his own cousin for ambition? Bonanno would later dismiss the charge as "baloney, fantasy, all garbage. Take it from Joe Bonanno." But that was the accusation made by an ambitious young mobster named Joe Columbo, who said he had been asked to carry out the killings. The Commission summoned Bonanno and his associate Giuseppe Magliocco (aka Joe Malyak) to account for themselves. Magliocco, a 300-pounder with high blood pressure, blurted out a confession and was fined $50,000 by the Commission. For this, he was allowed to go on living. Joe Bonanno considered himself above the judgment of his peers and fled. He hid out on the west coast under the name of J. Santone, then looked north to the friendly Canadian turf of his subordinate, Vic Cotroni.

The possibilities for Vic Cotroni were frightening. He couldn't have wanted to defy the Commission. But he also couldn't afford to offend Bonanno, who represented his link to the riches of the American market and who was, in effect, his boss. Lives would be lost, as well as money, if Joe Bonanno's bitter personal rivalries were allowed to divert energies from money-making to in-fighting. At the very least, Joe Bonanno's arrival disrupted Vic Cotroni's seclusion.

When Joe Bonanno arrived in Montreal with his wife, Faye, he told the immigration authorities he was not a big cheese in the mob, but rather an aspiring cheese-maker who was considering buying into the cheese-making company of G. Saputo & Sons Ltd. As proof, he produced a signed letter dated May 20, 1964, from Giuseppe Saputo, on company letterhead: "Italian Specialties: Mozzarella, Ricotta, Caciocavalli, Butirri, Pizza Cheese, Imported Cheese."

> Dear Mr. Bonanno;
>   We are happy to confirm our discussions leading, we hope, to your continued interest in our companies that are extensively engaged in the manufacture and sale of cheeses of all kinds. You have been very helpful to us over the years ad-

vising us and we are happy to have you take an active interest in our operations. As you know the Saputo family is interested in three companies, G. Saputo & Sons, Cremerie Consenzainc, and Cremeries Stella Inc., and we are prepared to give you an overall twenty percent in these companies upon your investment of approximately $8,000.00. We are of course most interested in your active interest in our affairs and I am sure you can help us greatly to expand our business.

We are now employing about twenty-five people and we fell *[sic]* sure tath *[sic]* with your help we will be able to expand this into a much larger business and increase the people employed at least double.

We are prepared to enter into this agreement with you as soon as you are ready and hope tath *[sic]* it will be soon.

Yours truly,
Saputo & Sons Ltd.

Bonanno, who gave his permanent address as 1847 East Elm Street, Tuscon, Arizona, told the government he had been involved with the Saputo firm for "the last three or four years." As a sign of his seriousness and wealth, he was accompanied by one of his lawyers.

"Have you any experience in cheese production?" he was asked at an immigration hearing.

"Yes, of course."

"What experience?"

"I am not to the point of being a professional cheese-maker but I know the process."

"Did you have some experience before?"

"Yes, a little experience."

"Where?"

"In California."

"How long, how many years of experience would you say you have?"

"Eight to ten years."

"You like Canada, Mr. Bonanno?" Bonanno's lawyer, Norman N. Genser, asked the mobster.

"Otherwise, I would not be here and I brought my wife because I want to be sure that she would like Canada as well," replied

Bonanno.

"And she likes it and you like it?"

"Yes, and Montreal is like San Francisco. It has a European atmosphere. I like it very much. It is a wonderful city. That is all I can tell you."

The inquiry officer pressed on, "Mr. Bonanno, is there anything else you wish to add on your behalf?"

"No, very simply I have given intention to reside here. First I like it and then I was to take responsible business."

Bonanno's professed liking of Canada touched off a flurry of memoranda between Montreal and the Minister of Immigration's office in Ottawa on Bonanno's activities.

J.K. Abbott, director of inspection service for the Department of Citizenship and Immigration, wrote on May 27, 1964:

> His record ranges from a 1930 arrest in New York City for transporting machine guns for the Capone mob in Chicago to attendance at the Mafia organized crime conference which was held in Binghamton, New York in 1956. During the U.S. Senate hearings on organized crime and illicit traffic in narcotics which were held in September and October of 1963 in Washington, Bonnano [sic] was named as the leader of a major segment of the crime organization exposed by Joseph Valachi.
>
> The criminals who are reported to be members of Bonanno's crime group have been involved in crimes which include extortion, strong arm and murder, counterfeiting, gambling and narcotics.
>
> He has been associated with Carmine Galente [sic] who is at present serving twelve years for narcotics violations and one-time owner of the Bonfire restaurant in Montreal and a major figure in illegal gambling.
>
> He has also been connected with Toronto-based criminals John Papalia and Alberto and Vito Agueci who were arrested in New York City for narcotics violations. Vito Agueci is now serving a fifteen-year prison sentence for narcotics, and his brother, Alberto, was brutally murdered in a gangland slaying near Rochester, New York, at the time of his trial.
>
> During Bonnano's [sic] recent stay in Canada, and prior

to his application for permanent landing, there have been indications that he has been associated with criminals in the Montreal area.

Bonanno admitted that he had not been altogether frank in his application form, but he said his intentions were nonetheless generous and honourable: "I was helping Canada reduce its unemployment." Bonanno presumably wanted so badly to help remedy Canada's unemployment woes that he tried, unsuccessfully, to bribe the Crown counsel. The lawyer was approached by a gambler who said he was representing Vic Cotroni's associate Louis Greco and "the boys." The gambler said it was imperative that Bonanno remain in Canada for at least three months, and intimated the Crown counsel would be rewarded if this could be arranged.

The Immigration department wasn't impressed with Bonanno's stated concern for Canada's jobless, and Bonanno was sent to Montreal's Bordeaux jail where he was stripped of his pinky ring, watch, cigars and $2,000 in pocket money. He found his quarters dank, dusty, poorly lit and cockroach-infested. The food was even worse. "The meat tasted as if it had come off a sick caribou. I spit it out."

But as word of his identity spread, Bonanno was treated with all the respect and gentility that can be mustered in such rude surroundings. And, as C.M. Isbister, Immigration department deputy-minister, dryly noted in a memo dated June 4, 1964, jail in Montreal was more congenial for Bonanno than freedom in the United States: "We are continuing to hold Mr. Bonnano [sic] in jail in Montreal, which he seems to prefer to being at liberty in the United States. This is a great compliment to Montreal and from a most surprising source."

Bonanno would later immodestly compare his reception from fellow prisoners to what might be expected for a screen star. Hoods chanted "Le grand boss!" applauded, and called out their names in hopes that Bonanno would provide them with employment, not necessarily related to the cheese industry. His guards were less vocal but equally solicitous, providing him with kind words, Cordon Bleu cognac and a box of fine cigars.

As news spread of Bonanno's trip to Montreal, his cousin Stefano Magaddino was livid, fuming, "He's planting flags all over the world!" Mob spheres of influence ran north-south. But, while Montreal was considered Bonanno turf, Magaddino feared Bonanno was plotting a push from Montreal into Toronto and the Magaddino sphere of influence. Bonanno would later argue that his trip north was simply part of an effort to divest himself quietly and peacefully of his interests in "The Volcano." But Bonanno did nothing to settle matters before the ruling Mafia Commission during this tense time. He haughtily refused to recognize the Commission's authority or to answer the murder-plot charges, despite the persistent entreaties of Commission emissary Sam (The Plumber) DeCavalcante. A wire-tap in DeCavalcante's Kenilworth, New Jersey plumbing and heating business gives us a window into Commission relations between August 1964 and July 1965. DeCavalcante, head of a sixty-man New Jersey family, was overheard to say he feared the Bonanno tensions could explode into "World War III." For his part, Sam (Momo) Giancana of Chicago recommended that his fellow commissioners take the direct approach towards Bonanno — "Kill, kill! Why don't you just kill the guy?"

The bug also revealed that DeCavalcante was edgy on September 21, 1964 as he tried to explain Bonanno's predicament to Joe Bayonne, a Bonanno family member and one of DeCavalcante 's closest friends.

"Joe, this is strictly between you and I," DeCavalcante said as Bayonne entered the office.

"Yeah?"

"If I didn't do this," DeCavalcante continued, "I'd feel like a lousy bum... The Commission doesn't recognize Joe Bonanno as the boss anymore... I don't know what's the matter with the guy, Joe. I've done everything possible."

The bug didn't pick up Bayonne's response clearly. Perhaps he gasped. Certainly he was jolted.

"They [the Commission] can't understand why this guy's ducking them," DeCavalcante said.

"Now . . . the Commission has no intention of hurting anybody. But Joe better not get any intention of hurting anybody either — that's most important for me to tell you."

"He's got no intentions as far as I know."

"Well, he might hurt people in his own outfit to cover up some of the story — his story. Do you understand what I mean? ... The Commission is out to hurt no one — not even Joe Bonanno. But they don't want no one else hurt either."

"Who?"

"Right in your own outfit," DeCavalcante replied. "When Joe [Bonanno] defies the Commission, he's defying the whole world."

Within a month, Bonanno was back on the streets of New York City after being deported from Montreal. He apparently planned to testify before a federal grand jury, but something strange happened on the night of October 21, 1964, the eve of his scheduled court appearance. Gunmen leapt out of the shadows in front of his lawyer William Power Maloney's apartment at 35 Park Avenue, fired a shot in the direction of Maloney, and then rushed Bonanno through the rain into a waiting car. But Bonanno was so devious that many who knew him doubted he was really abducted. The "slippery bananas" theory of his disappearance was that Joe Bonanno had orchestrated his own kidnapping to avoid having to testify before the grand jury. The bogus-kidnapping hypothesis was buttressed by the fact that no one seemed bold enough to make a move on Bonanno's Brooklyn fiefdom. It was also supported by the comic-book nature of the Bonanno-napping and by the fact that Bonanno was not simply shot dead on the street. But others reasoned that the Giancana school of thought had prevailed and that Bonanno was anchored at the bottom of the Hudson River.

That winter, Magaddino headed to Montreal in an attempt to win Vic Cotroni's support. The DeCavalcante bug picked up a December 23, 1964 conversation in which Bonanno family member Joe Notaro said the Montreal *decina,* or branch plant, of Vic Cotroni wanted to be left out of the hostilities. This meant not being pushed into the sphere of Bonanno's old friend Gaspar (Little Gaspar or Gasparino) Di Gregorio who had turned on Bonanno. "They want to be left alone," Notaro reported to DeCavalcante. "I said, 'All right, convey the message to Vic that as of this night, as far as we are concerned, they are at liberty to do what they want.' When we get this ironed out, we can go talk to them."

"How many people remain that are not with Gasparino?" DeCavalcante asked Vito De Fillippo of the Bonanno family.

"About twenty-five," Notaro replied.

"How many *caporeginas* [lieutenants]?"Notaro said there were five, including "Vic from Montreal" and they talked about a recent conversation with Bonanno, in which the old don grandiloquently stated, "Remove me or kill me."

Two weeks later, Bonanno's lawyer, William Maloney, called a press conference. He said Bonanno's son Salvatore (Bill) had informed him that the don was safe and would be returning soon to The Volcano. Maloney announced that Bonanno senior would be appearing before the grand jury on rackets, but that he wouldn't be testifying. Reporters and photographers packed Maloney's Wall Street-area office suite, and police were, in the words of one scribe, "as thick as flowers at a gangster funeral." All that was missing was the main attraction, Joe Bonanno. Maloney wasn't amused when some of the idle newshounds began singing, "Yes, We Have No Bananas." And when they tried to thrust bananas into the flustered attorney's hands for a photo, he snapped, "This is no time for gag pictures."

Throughout the next fifteen months, the bushy-browed mob chieftain would be reported to be, sometimes simultaneously, in Montreal, western Canada, Rome, Palermo, Algiers, Tunis, Mexico City, Haiti and Queens. Canadian immigration officials said there was no substantive proof to claims that Bonanno had spent most of his absence in Montreal with his associates in the Cotroni family.

Then suddenly, on May 17, 1966, showing no ill effects from his adventure, Bonanno appeared at the federal court house in Manhattan's Foley Square, looking tanned and chipper in a blue-grey suit and fedora. As a nice, symmetrical touch, it was the same outfit he had worn when he was escorted at gunpoint off Park Avenue. He had given a news photographer a tip that he'd be appearing in court and, knowing his photograph would be seen by millions, Bonanno had removed his glasses which detracted from his strong profile and accented his crooked nose broken by a punch decades before. He turned to the curious press and announced, with the air of a great centurian amused by the foolishness of lesser men, "I've got nothing to say."

Years later, he would explain his absence by saying that he was rushed to the Catskills by his "dear cousin" Magaddino. Bonanno explained that Magaddino let him go after six weeks, because, "maybe he didn't want my blood on his conscience. Maybe the retaliation from my people..." This explanation left the remaining nineteen months of his absence a mystery.

There was speculation that Bonanno re-appeared because the Mystery of the Banana Split focused enormous police and media scrutiny on mob activities. There had also been dark talk that his return would mean an escalation of inter-mob hostilities, as he sought to win back lost ground. For Vic Cotroni, there was still strong pressure from both sides to leave his neutral ground and join the fray.

In 1966, police had been carefully monitoring Vic Cotroni's operations, fearful that the upcoming Expo 67 world's fair would be a

Vic Cotroni (right) with his underboss Paulo Violi at a banquet. Cotroni (The Godfather) was born in Calabria, Italy in 1910. He emigrated to Canada with his family in 1924. From the fifties until his death from natural causes in 1984, Cotroni headed Canada's deadliest Mafia Family.

Underboss Paolo Violi was a fellow Calabrian and Cotroni's most trusted lieutenant. He was the son-in-law of wiley old Hamilton mobster Giacomo Luppino. His power came to an end in 1978 when he was gunned down during a card game at the Reggio ice cream bar he once owned.

Violi's demise, in combination with the death of much-feared Vic Cotroni a few years later, gave way to the Sicilian rule of the Montreal mafia under Vito Rizzuto.

A young Vic Contoni wrestled under
the name of Vic Vincent in the 30s.

By the time he was twenty, Cotroni had accumulated
a lengthy record of minor offences.

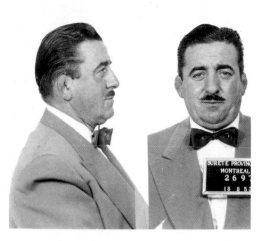

Long-time friend Armand Courville was Vic Cotroni's entré to the Montreal underworld of the '40s and uncle of hitman Réal Simard.

Murdered Cotroni adviser Pietro Sciara

Louis Greco was Vic Cotroni's confidant and connection to New York's Bonanno crime family.

Meat wholesaler William (Willie Obie) Obront was one of Cotroni's four main money-launderers.

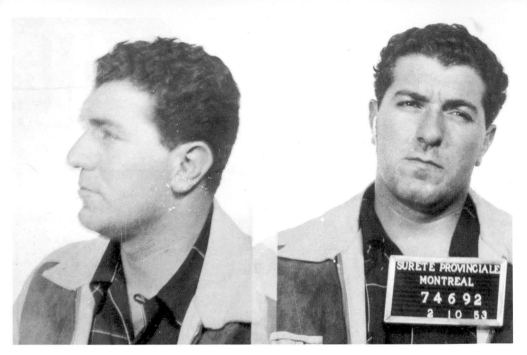

Santos (Frank) Cotroni followed the family tradition and was in trouble with the law early and often.

Frank Cotroni with Nancy Sinatra. He loved the glitz and glamour of the entertainment and sports world.

Frank Cotroni with trusted lieutenant Claude Faber at his shoulder.

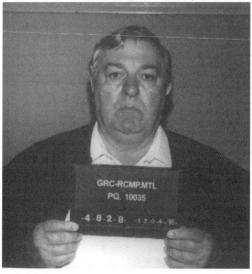

Brother Giuseppe (Pep) Cotroni. Heroin wholesaler served many long prison sentences.

In his later years, an overweight and ailing Frank Cotroni was in and out of prison.

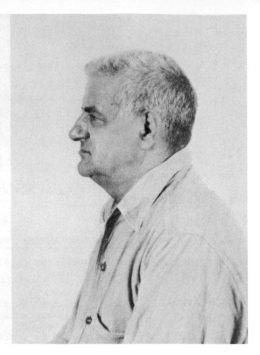

Joe Valachi, the Cosa Nostra's most celebrated snitch. The 1968 book *The Valachi Papers* by Peter Maas put to rest, once and for all, any question about the existence of organized crime in North America. Valachi died in a Texas prison of a heart attack in 1971.

Tommaso Buscetta. Mafia turncoat and associate of Frank Cotroni. Fourteen members of his family were killed by rival mafiosi. He died of natural causes in 2000 at age 71.

Michel Pozza. University-educated financial adviser to the Cotroni family and other major crime figures. Shot dead by Cotroni hitman Réal Simard in 1982.

Above: Vic Cotroni leaves Paulo Violi's Reggio ice cream bar.
Below: Frank D'Asti. The Cotroni soldier offered to help the Quebec government find Labour Minister Pierre Laporte who had been kidnapped by FLQ cell members. Laporte was later strangled by his captors.

Gerlando Sciascia, Vito Rizzuto, Giovanni Liggamari and Joseph (The Boss) Massino leave Capri Motor Lodge in the Bronx the day after three Bonnano family underbosses were slain in a Brooklyn social club.

Giuseppe Settecase—Mafia Mediator.

Réal Simard — Frank Cotroni chauffeur and hitman

boon to prostitution and gambling. They had noted with keen interest that Vic Cotroni had some important American visitors in late November 1966. The police noted a series of meetings between the Americans and Vic Cotroni; Louis Greco; Paolo Violi, Cotroni's energetic young associate; and Giacomo Luppino, Violi's father-in-law and the clever old don of the Hamilton underworld. The most significant of the Americans was Joe Bonanno's thirty-four-year-old son Salvatore (Bill), who presumably was in town to tighten the family's hold on Montreal. He was travelling with bodyguards Carl Simari and Peter Magaddino, a cousin of the family's bitter rival, Stefano Magaddino. Also with the Americans was Peter Notaro, cousin of the Bonanno lieutenant Joe Notaro, whose voice had been picked up on the DeCavalcante tapes, and Vito De Fillippo and his son Pat. Vito De Fillippo was thought by police to represent Canadian and American gambling interests in Haiti, with close ties to Paul Volpe in Toronto and Louis Greco in Montreal. When two cars carrying the American mobsters were pulled over on November 28, 1966, near the corner of Jean-Talon and Hutchinson Streets in Montreal, police found three loaded revolvers. But no major crime had been committed, and the best police could do was charge Bill Bonanno with driving without proper registration, a $25 offence. Ironically, when charged with minor weapons offences, each of his associates gave his occupation as "chauffeur." Fearing the worst, immigration officials rushed the Americans back to New York.

Bill Bonanno came to the mobs by a totally different route than Vic Cotroni. The Cotronis had been poor and Calabrian when top American mafiosi were almost exclusively Sicilian. While the Cotronis had to fight their way up, Bill Bonanno was to the manner born. He was named after his mafioso grandfather but was, in many ways, an unlikely gangster. He attended Arizona prep schools and the University of Arizona, where he was a leader of an ROTC cadet squad and presided over a club that passed out pamphlets on "how to have fun without drinking." But, like a warm Mediterranean breeze, his father, Joe, would arrive in Arizona each winter in expensive suits and gently, unintentionally push Bill towards the feudal struggles of the east coast. Bill Bonanno married a woman who had also grown up amidst the pomp and paranoia of the underworld. Rosalie Profaci was the niece of millionaire importer and Brooklyn mob boss Joe Profaci. Her cousins had married into powerful Detroit and West Coast families. As a child, she played with those cousins in Joe

Profaci's 328-acre New Jersey hunting lodge, once owned by Theodore Roosevelt, which included thirty rooms, one of which was a private chapel with statues of saints.

Bill Bonanno would later tell Martyn Burke of the CBC *Connections* series on organized crime that there was no question of what his duties were when his father's troubles began in the early 1960s: "Among the Sicilian people, the family unit is paramount. The family unit is a very, very closely-knit structure, so that a violation against one individual of the family is tantamount to a violation against everyone in the family. So, when in the early sixties a member of my family, meaning my father, had difficulties with law enforcement and others, there was no question in my mind what obligations were. No one had to tell me what I had to do... Here was a city [New York] that just simply had mountains of steel and concrete. I found myself embroiled in a controversy much the same as what took place in the hills of Sicily over who stole whose chicken, you know? I mean it really at times became nonsensical to me as to what the heck I was doing there."

New Jersey crime boss Sam (The Plumber) DeCavalcante would dismiss the younger Bonanno as a "bedbug," while Bill Bonanno's godfather, Gaspar DiGregorio, was even less charitable. Eleven months before Bill Bonanno's arrest in Montreal, at eleven o 'clock on a freezing January night, gunmen with murderous intentions and Keystone Kop methods tried to gun down young Bonanno and two others in Brooklyn. The murder attempt backfired, and DiGregorio was judged by the Commission to be too much a bungler to head a crime family. Stripped of his power and declining in health, DiGregorio faded into obscurity and isolation.

But Joe Bonanno's cousin Stefano Magaddino continued his plotting, and worked, with some success, to pull defectors away from the Bonanno organization. Thrown into the guerrilla war with little experience, Bill Bonanno appealed to long-time family loyalists, including those Cotroni members he met in Montreal in November 1966. When Magaddino heard of Vic Cotroni's meeting with young Bonanno, he turned "mad like a beast," in the words of one mobster. The Undertaker felt Cotroni had no right to meet the New Yorkers without his permission. Vic Cotroni sent word to Magaddino that the meeting with Bonanno had not been planned, but declined to go to Buffalo to meet Magaddino. Vic Cotroni valued his American markets and his life; so he sat tight, quietly hoping things would blow over...rather than blow up.

Chapter Seven

Western Ties

*"People are much easier to cheat
here than in Italy."*
— Hamilton mobster Giacomo Luppino
praises his new homeland

T he Cotroni saga might have ended there, with Vic Cotroni on the wrong end of a pistol blast, were it not for a wise old man from Hamilton who was rumoured to carry a human ear in his wallet. Bonanno's rival, Stefano Magaddino, was livid over what he considered to be Cotroni's betrayal: meeting Bill Bonanno without seeking permission from Magaddino first. Vic Cotroni was warned that the Bonannos were a lost people and that he, Cotroni, was replaceable. Magaddino's emotions were partly those of a businessman fearing a hostile takeover from the competition and partly those of someone consumed by a medieval family feud.

To the rescue came Giacomo Luppino, the old don of the southern Ontario underworld. Luppino managed to confuse, downplay and otherwise stifle Magaddino's murderous rage. The reason Luppino cared so much about the fortunes of the Montrealers was a basic one: his daughter Grazia (Grace) was married to Paolo Violi, a former Hamiltonian who was rising fast in the Vic Cotroni mob.

Any setback for Vic Cotroni would be a family tragedy for

Giacomo Luppino, and Luppino valued nothing more in the world than his family.

Paolo Violi wasn't considered a major player in the Montreal Mafia when he was spotted by police meeting with Bill Bonanno's men in November 1966. He hadn't been seen meeting with Vic Cotroni before August 1964. The two most significant things Violi had done before the meeting with Bonanno were to murder a man to settle a Calabrian vendetta and to choose the right wife — pretty, dark-haired Grazia Luppino. Which act was more significant is a moot point, but a wedding such as the one that united the Violi and Luppino families is not something to be taken lightly. Mafia nuptuals have all the political nuance of an Elizabethan state wedding. And by simply saying "I do," Grazia Luppino did her groom's career immeasurable good.

Paolo Violi's new father-in-law was an old-style Calabrian mafioso who eschewed the gaudy materialism of young entrepreneurial criminals. He preferred something much more basic and difficult to quantify: respect.

A wiretap once caught Luppino telling Magaddino, "I, Don Stefano, do things for my own dignity." As sociologist Pino Arlacchi writes in his excellent book *Mafia Business,* traditional mafiosi like Luppino...

> "... had no love of ostentation. His power, like his consumption, was characteristically discreet and reserved. To say little, to keep a low profile, to disparage the extent of one's influence — these were the rules the mafia followed in its appearance in public life. The mafioso felt his superior and exceptional position to be sufficiently established by the fact that he led a life of leisure: even when he was not rich, the traditional mafioso lived like a gentleman in that he did no work and depended on nobody. In a world where the great majority of the population had to work hard every day, this freedom to use one's own time in one's . . . way is the clearest symbol of honour and power. His courteous manner, the breadth of his social circle, the mystery and secrecy that veiled his private life: all made it quietly clear that the mafioso belonged to world of gentle folk.
>
> "The mafia made no display of superfluous consumption, because none was necessary to establish his respectability. Indeed, he would have found conspicuous consumption

counterproductive, because it would have contradicted his other, populist image as 'everyman.'"

There's a lot of Vic Cotroni in this description. But Cotroni also liked the finer material things in life, like his summer retreat, his Cadillacs and his shiny cufflinks, which boldly announced they were the property of "VC." Giacomo Luppino fit Arlacchi's traditional Mafia everyman definition perfectly. He discussed murder and extortion in the backyard of his house on Ottawa Street South in Hamilton while the family laundry flapped on the clothesline near his tomato plants. His home was what a school teacher or police officer might expect to buy: a solid but unprepossessing two-and-a-half-storey red-brick box in Hamilton's east end at the foot of more monied Hamilton Mountain and three blocks from his church. His only known source of income was a $175-a-month veteran's pension from his First World War service in the Italian army. And, it is said, he picked fruit for $5 a day when he arrived in Ontario in 1956. He was not, however, too proud to also cheat on the Unemployment Insurance system, something he later feared would land him in jail.

Luppino bemoaned the changes that were transforming his world and society in general. Born in 1900, he was raised in a culture where respect and spending power were not interchangeable. But postwar materialism gave conspicuous consumption more respect than leisure in the eyes of many, including some members of the ranks of the Mafia. The emerging mass media captured the glitter of materialism more easily than it did the subtle ties of leisure. The promise of enormous wealth offered by the drug trade only heightened this, and mafiosi soon began to look beyond the borders of their neighbourhoods to huge potential profits on a world market. The quick decisions, violence and glitter of the drug trade also made the new Mafia more appealing to the young than it had been to their elders.

Like fathers everywhere and throughout time, Luppiono lamented that children today were not respectful enough. He complained that a son did not always consult him before committing crimes. He was also upset that one of his sons was living common-law, and Luppino refused to allow the woman in his house although the son could visit if he came alone. But in his new son-in-law, Paolo Violi, Giacomo Luppino found a sympathetic ear. Together the two men laughed at how the mob was portrayed on

North American television and, taking a break from crime talk, worried about injuries to Eddie "The Entertainer" Shack of hockey's Toronto Maple Leafs.

Paolo Violi's views on the family were traditional. A wiretap once captured him threatening to beat and perhaps kill an associate who was having an affair with a mother of three. A police wiretap also recorded Luppino's disgust with new attitudes, which he found more pronounced and offensive in North America than in his native Calabria: "You know what my uncle Michelino told me? ...he said he gets great satisfaction in talking with me because I know and talk to him in the same way as if we were in our own town. But the rest, he said they do it the American way...it appears that here in America things can only be fixed with money."

Violi's views were welcome in his father-in-law's home. A police wiretap from the mid-1960s also caught a furious Luppino telling Violi about a man who had beaten a woman for another man: "I told him what kind of half man he is. If I have to do something in fear I'll go and drown myself in the lake. I told him, that if a man is weak and has to do these things because of fear and these things are wrong, then it's better for him to kill himself... I told him if they want to kill me, because I say this, and if they should kill me I'll always spit in their faces and tell them they are dishonerate [sic]."

But not all Luppino's observations of Canadians were so negative. One tape revealed he found some facets of North American culture an improvement on the Old World and that he wished his English was better so he could set up a business as "people here are much easier to cheat than in Italy."

Before the old don came to Canada in 1956, he had been investigated in connection with two murders in Calabria. Legend has it, his wallet held what appeared to be a piece of shrivelled leather. Mob lore said it was the ear of a man who dared to refuse to commit a crime for him. Luppino was said to have punished the insubordination by hacking the man's ear off in public — a grisly variation of the manner in which a bullfighter carves the ears from a vanquished bull.

Extortion, loan-sharking and involvement in construction unions helped pay the bills, but Luppino's real joy came through the exercise of power, not from the monetary rewards that exercise yielded. A police officer who observed him in action noted, with a touch of hyperbole, "Power and prestige, that's what it's all about. Really, that's what the man's about. The key to the whole thing is prestige.

The fear he can lay on people just because he is there. He'd rather have someone call him Mr. Luppino than give him $10,000."

A police bug picked up Luppino discussing his cherished role as the wise man of the southern Ontario underworld: "It is the same as saying there is a company at Hamilton, at Toronto and there is a head of each. Toronto represents the centre and Hamilton represents the commanding point. In Oakville, there are two, but all these *abboccatos* [regions] are represented by one. In other words, we have to play the way I say."

Part of the reason Luppino could dictate how others "played" was his connection with Bonanno's cousin and bitter rival, Stefano Magaddino of Buffalo. Magaddino respected Luppino, and Luppino liked to talk of how the bovine old Buffalo don sat beside him at a Magaddino family wedding for a twenty-minute chat. Such a tie helped give Luppino inroads into the United States, although he always felt closer to the languid flow of life in his native Calabria than the business-like frenzy of his new home.

The Violis came to Canada from Sinopoli, just a short hike through the Aspromonte mountains of Calabria from Luppino's hometown, Castellace di Oppido. Sinopoli was once the centre of a rich Greek colony, but prosperous days were long behind it. Like the Luppinos, they showed no signs of wealth when they arrived in Canada in the 1950s, and Paolo Violi's first decade in Canada was as a low-level, petty criminal in the Toronto-Welland-Hamilton triangle. Pictures of him taken at the time show an intense, skinny young man in his early twenties, just 5'5" and perhaps 130 pounds. Four years after his arrival, he set out to settle a vendetta that began in Calabria and ended on a rainy night in a parking lot in the west end of Toronto. On May 24, 1955, Violi and recent Calabrian immigrant Natale Brigante argued. Moments later, Brigante lay on the pavement at the corner of Dundas Street West and Howard Park Avenue, his stiletto near his palm and his life draining into the gutter through a torn artery in his hip. Nearby were four shells from Violi's .32-calibre automatic pistol. Violi tucked the gun away and fled to Welland where he was picked up for manslaughter. Police were told the two men were arguing over who had control of a prostitute. But the prosecution's case died when Violi calmly told a court that the killing was in self defence and offered a knife wound as evidence.

A police officer who has specialized in the Mafia says he's sure the dispute was about more than control of a hooker, that it was ordered from Italy. "I'm sure [Violi] was told… 'Take care of this problem for us.' Otherwise he never would have shot up [in status] the way he did…The key to the whole thing is that hit…That's the key. The marriage was probably contracted, too."

By the early 1960s, Violi had moved to Montreal to work for the Cotronis, but he maintained ties to Hamilton. Magaddino had hoped that Violi would give him a beachhead in Bonanno territory. In 1965, Magaddino was overheard boasting that he had planted his own people in Montreal and that he would be aware at all times of what was happening; that he had been in Montreal for forty-five years with "family" members; and that there would not be a Mafia family in Montreal without Magaddino at the top.

Paolo Violi clearly had his own ideas. He privately told Luppino that the Cotroni family should strike out on its own and should be subordinate to neither the Magaddino nor the Bonanno family. Violi displayed dangerous signs of hubris as he belittled the abilities and judgment of Vic Cotroni and his close associate Louis Greco. He told Giacomo Luppino, "I already know that Cotroni is weak…I told him, 'Compare, I am with you 100 per cent but only if…you are sincere. Otherwise I won't be 100 per cent with you.'" And Violi was not in awe of Bill Bonanno either, as shown by a conversation with Violi's brother-in-law Jimmy: "I told you that if I was to know that Bonanno was coming up again I would tell him what a dishonest man he is. I would have gone myself and shown him what I thought of him…I would have told him, 'I'm not with you nor with him. I'm by myself. I don't want to have anything to do with anyone, because you're all a bunch of bastards.' The way things stand today that the *abboccatos* [regions] will split and everyone will be on their own. I'm telling you that, in Montreal, we will be alone by ourselves."

A police officer who listened to wiretaps of Violi says, "What he didn't realize was those guys [Vic Cotroni and Louis Greco] realized what the hell was going on and he didn't. . . . He was a little fat-headed, a little swell-headed."

By the mid-1960s, Paoli Violi was a rising star in the Montreal mob and was headed towards a murderous clash with his superiors, if his opinions didn't soften. After he arrived in Montreal, Violi quickly became an associate of Vic Cotroni's younger brother Frank and seized control of extortion rackets in the Italian district. He was nicknamed "The Don of St. Leonard." He also became involved in counterfeiting and ran bootleg whisky from Montreal to southern

Ontario. When he was arrested in 1960 in Toronto for bootlegging, police discovered an interesting phone number in his pocket: that of Rocco Zito, a short, stocky Toronto waiter known to police for his ugly temper and extensive crime connections. Violi's bootlegging trial dragged on into 1961 before he was finally convicted. And whenever he had a Toronto court date, he brought with him a load of whisky blanc.

Paolo Violi had twin brothers, Rocco and Giuseppe, who were also in trouble with the law in Montreal. Rocco was jailed for carving a rival with a knife, and Giuseppe was found guilty of leaving the scene of an accident. The twins faced deportation for their crimes, but then their case became a *cause célèbre*. The controversy arose after Ottawa flip-flopped on what to do with the brothers. It first ordered them deported, then said they could stay, then ordered them out of the country. No lesser figure than Opposition leader John Diefenbaker protested that the Immigration department didn't have unlimited powers to order their deportations. As Diefenbaker demanded a wholesale probe of immigration practices, the Supreme Court ordered the twins released after eight months in dank Bordeaux Jail. Their lawyer hailed the case as proof that "the little fellow is not pushed around." The Violi twins said they just wanted to celebrate Christmas with their family, and then work with their brother Paolo at his north-end ice-cream shop making pastries and rich coffees.

Their father, Dominico, wasn't so lucky. The Canadian Immigration department banned him as an undesirable, noting that top American and Italian mobsters regularly visited his home in Parma near Cleveland. His mob ties began long before his family moved to North America as part of a wave of immigration in the 1950s. As a young shepherd in Calabria, he had been exiled from his village to an isolated region of southern Sicily for allowing his sheep to graze on another shepherd's field. While exiled in Sicily, Dominico Violi exhibited a rough side that would be passed on to his sons, and he was once confined in an isolation cell for what was later described as pronounced anti-social behaviour.

Paolo Violi married Grazia Luppino in Hamilton, on July 10, 1965, and their personal day of joy did far more than unite two people or two families. Police noted with interest that Violi's best man wasn't one of his brothers but Vic Cotroni of Montreal.

Also making the trip down from Montreal were Vic Cotroni's valued confidantes, Louis Greco and Joe DiMaulo, and one of the family's financial experts, Michel Pozza.

And when the happy couple began to have children, Violi's connections multiplied accordingly. Over the next few years, Vic Cotroni stood as godfather for one of their children. Vile-tempered Hamilton heroin smuggler John Papalia and Toronto mob leader Paul Volpe were godparents of another two. And when Violi's new in-laws married into the Commisso family of Toronto, yet another avenue into the Ontario underworld was opened.

Paolo Violi brought new opportunities and new tensions to Vic Cotroni. Violi was arrogant, brash and dangerous. But he also gave Vic Cotroni better links to Ontario and Calabria. Cotroni planned to cash in on those links, but he couldn't afford to be blinded by them. The most important connections in the North American underworld remained those that ran into New York City. They were dominated by Sicilians, not Calabrians like Violi. Mobsters who ignored these realities could expect to be ignored or shot. This was a lesson Violi had yet to learn.

Chapter Eight

The Minister Who Died

*"The Liberal Party's victory was
nothing but the victory of the
election riggers, Simard-Cotroni."*
— FLQ Manifesto

There was a crazy, hostile wind blowing over Quebec in the fall of 1970. It was the wind of revolution, of murderous dissatisfaction, and it gusted through St. Leonard where the Cotroni power was at its greatest. Any political change was of interest to men like Vic Cotroni, since you can't have organized crime without compliant politicians.

This turbulence had a thousand origins, but none was stronger than those in a South Shore riding where a small band of disaffected Quebec nationalists decided that the machinery of democracy was irreparably fouled up by men like Vic Cotroni. Paul Rose, a failed teacher-turned-revolutionary, was said to have learned of patronage deals involving Liberal provincial cabinet minister Pierre Laporte in the construction of a hospital in Chambly, Rose's home riding and Laporte's constituency. Rose, his brother Jacques and labourer Francis Simard had another souring experience with mainstream politics in 1970. The Parti Québécois, which they supported, was racked by an electoral scandal in Taillon riding, next door to Chambly. The candidate they supported, Pierre Bourgault, was defeated at a party nominating convention by Pierre Laporte's cousin. The shocking defeat took place amidst charges that hundreds of non-separatists packed the meeting.

Suspect election practices were nothing new in 1970. Decades before, Vic Cotroni, Napoleon Dubois (father of the fearsome Dubois brothers gang) and countless other young criminals served their crime apprenticeships providing muscle for politicians during elections. They supplied the criminals, the politicians supplied the organizations, and organized crime was born. The idealistic young men and women of Rose's circle were disillusioned when their party seemed to be buying into the same tradition.

As Simard later recalled:

"Where we come from, politics is something else! It takes more than mind, you need muscle too. When things were slack, between elections (municipal, provincial or federal, it didn't matter), our musclemen worked as waiters or bouncers or looked after the different rackets that somehow make up the sideshow of our democracy: protection, gambling, prostitution, etc. Wherever you'd look you'd find them: things are rotten all over. With their contracts, their friends, the kind who can't refuse when you make an offer, they can always find a few hundred souls. When election time came around, they crawled out of the woodwork. You couldn't have an election without them, and nobody ever tried. If somebody got elected from the South Shore of Montreal, it wasn't because he was a Liberal, a Unioniste or a PC — that part was bullshit. It was because he had the musclemen on his side. And just because they had muscles didn't mean they didn't have brains. On the contrary. They never forgot number one. Elections were profitable. They got respectable around election time. They became consultants, people came to ask their advice.

"That wasn't our idea of politics. We couldn't believe that somebody from the Parti Québécois, an indépendantiste, could associate with those kind of people...Before we knew it the whole thing had turned into some kind of gangster movie."

Meanwhile, angry South Shore housewives were complaining to police that their husbands were losing their paycheques at a notorious gambling den controlled by the Cotroni family. Police began a project code-named "Operation Vegas." They planted more than twenty bugs in gangland haunts throughout Montreal. To their surprise, mixed in with talk of gambling and drug-dealing came the frequent mention of someone quite unexpected — the second-most important member of the provincial government, Pierre Laporte.

According to the wiretaps, Vic and Frank Cotroni and their senior associate, Nicolas Di Iorio, actively supported several candidates in the 1970 provincial election. Cotroni family member Frank D'Asti had contributed heavily to Laporte's unsuccessful bid for the Liberal leadership in fall 1969; he contributed again in the April 1970 provincial election. On May 3, 1970, police eavesdropped on a meeting between D'Asti, di Iorio and associates Angelo Lanzo and Romeo Bucci, as they speculated on who would get key cabinet positions for the victorious Liberals. The topic of discussion was the need to have the appropriate person appointed justice minister. An RCMP report dated September 17, 1970 noted: "They [D'Asti and di Iorio] foresaw that they would be able to get favors from Laporte. ...They were very hopeful that Laporte would be appointed justice minister. At that time, René Gagnon and Jean-Jacques Côté [Laporte's chief campaign aides] were working hard to assure them that prospects were good and this would come about. Their aim was to obtain financial contributions for the campaign. ...They were very disappointed when Laporte was named minister of labour and immigration instead of minister of justice. However, they have been assured since then, mainly by Côté, that they would have no problem with Justice minister Jérôme Choquette."

But Choquette disappointed the mobsters by quickly earning a reputation as a fervent law-and-order man. Cotroni enterprises were hit by a series of raids, and the Quebec Liquor Control Board shut down a nightclub owned by di Iorio. Police overheard di Iorio and D'Asti appealing to Gagnon and Côté, who was a tavern-owner, to urge the government to end the "harassment" of their clubs.

None of the conversations before or after the election suggested Laporte had anything to do with heroin-trafficking or any Cotroni crime enterprises. But it had been common knowledge that di Iorio's Victoria Sporting Club was a popular gambling den. Laporte should have known this, since the Victoria Club was in his own riding. However the Mounties chose to look at it, it was an explosive situation. After the election Laporte was a key man in the provincial government, filling in for Premier Robert Bourassa as the province's head when the premier was out of the province, and the Quebec Liberals were a bulwark of confederation at a time when the separatist movement was on the ascent. A public connection between these defenders of confederation and Canada's most notorious crime family would be politically catastrophic. But a confidential police report suggests that Laporte himself may have met with the mobsters. On April 16, 1970, less than two weeks before the election, Laporte, Gagnon and Côté met with di Iorio and D'Asti in an apartment building on Sherbrooke Street. The next day, three police surveillance officers wrote a report for the co-ordinator of the Quebec Bureau of Research on Organized Crime. They described the incident:

1) On April 16, 1970, we were informed that a meeting was to take place the same day at 1800 hours at the apartment of René Gagnon, the secretary of Pierre Laporte, between the former and Nicola De Iorio [sic] (FPS 484485) and Frank D'Asti (FPS 570148). Jean-Jacques Côté was also to take part in the meeting.

2) According to information received this apartment was situated on Sherbrooke St. E. in Montreal in a large apartment building near the Montreal Municipal Library. The number of the apartment was 1503.

3) A preliminary verification was carried out at the building at 1150 Sherbrooke St. E. and no name appeared on the lobby directory for 1503. It was confirmed that the apartment was situated on the top floor.

4) The same day at 1740 hours, in the presence of Corporal Andre George (3743), we observed MV [motor vehicle] Oldsmobile 1970, blue in color, bearing vehicle license number 2P-8899, registered to Pierre Laporte, parked opposite 1150 Sherbrooke St. E., Montreal. The MV was driven by an unidentified man. Mr. Laporte stepped out of it and went into the building at 1150 Sherbrooke St. E.

5) At 1800 hours we observed Jean-Jacques Côté entering the building at 1150 Sherbrooke St. E. Photos of the subjects were taken.

6) At 1810 hours we observed MV Cadillac 1969, gray in color with black vinyl roof, bearing motor vehicle license number IM-0731, registered to Nicola di Iorio. The latter, accompanied by Frank D'Asti, entered the building at 1150 Sherbrooke St. E. Photos of the subjects were taken.

7) At 1850 hours we observed Pierre Laporte leaving the building at 1150 Sherbrooke St. E. He was alone and entered his car and left.

8) At 1900 hours surveillance terminated.

9) N.B.: A telephone was installed 14/4/70 in apartment 1503 and its use will terminate May 1, 1970. The number is 523-3774.

Côté later argued that Laporte didn't know who he would be meeting that afternoon, and that the "notoriety" later achieved by D'Asti and di Iorio was "unsuspected by everyone at that time." Côté protested that he organized the meeting only because he learned that D'Asti and di Iorio had information on a vote-stealing plot being organized for the upcoming provincial election. The plot involved Liberal adversaries using a mobile trailer to transport teams through suburban ridings south of Montreal where Laporte was head of Liberal election operations. Côté argued that the meeting on April 16 was called because of Laporte's "disbelief" that such a plot was possible. Upon hearing D'Asti and di Iorio's charges, Laporte immediately left the meeting, asking the underworld night-club owners to "please keep Mr. Côté informed of developments in this affair."

Pierre Laporte surely wasn't too shocked by what he heard in-side Côté's apartment. Smart, personable and a devoted family man, Laporte was no political innocent. He had two decades of experi-ence in the political trenches, both as a critic and as a participant. He graduated from the Université de Montréal law school in 1950, and went to work for the daily newspaper *Le Devoir* which was sharply critical of the kickbacks and patronage of the Union Nationale government. He wrote acidic commentary on the govern-ment of Premier Maurice Duplessis for the paper, but also moon-lighted as a writer of campaign material for some of Duplessis's cabinet. He wrote an exposé of corruption at a provincial hydro-electric project. In response, the premier damned Laporte as "a man without a heart, a pig, a snake and a slothy individual" whose work pandered to "the vilest instincts of yellow journalism and the most ignoble sentiments." After another exposé, this time on insider trad-ing in the sale of a government-owned gas company, Duplessis can-celled press conferences for a month and a half rather than face questions from Laporte, who worked for "a Bolshevik journal," according to Duplessis.

Laporte's observation of corruption didn't deter him from trying to get closer to the centre of power. In 1961, after a close and bitter by-election, he won a seat in the Legislature as a Liberal representing Chambly. His Union Nationale rival noted that, while Laporte had covered the Legislature for *Le Devoir,* he had also been involved in renting heavy construction equipment to the Liberal government. A cartoonist marked his entry into government with a drawing of Caterpillar tracks leading to the provincial government, with the caption "Pierre Laporte's arrival at the Quebec Parliament." But within a year of his election victory, Laporte was being touted as a possible candidate for premier. His appeal grew as he warned that the average man mustn't be forgotten in a time of high unemployment: "Otherwise, the masses, like those of France in 1789 and Germany in 1933, will be swept away in an undoubtedly unacceptable excess, one that has been sown by our faults and our omissions."

Meanwhile, the opposition dubbed him *"Monsieur Dix Pour Cent"* ("Mr. Ten Per Cent") and charged that he was collecting kickbacks. Daniel Johnson, former Union Nationale premier, labelled him *"le patroneux des patroneux,"* or "the all-time king of the porkbarrel."

In 1970, Laporte drew the ire of critics on the fringe of the separatist movement who were then infinitely more anonymous and dangerous. He had become a staunch foe of separatism, and he feared his new opponents sufficiently that his house was placed under police guard.

That autumn, Canadians were yanked forever out of their cocoon of security. On October 5, 1970, a cell of a group called the Front de Libération du Québec kidnapped senior British trade commissioner James R. Cross from his home on Redpath Crescent in Montreal's diplomat row. The cell demanded publication and broadcast of what they grandly called their manifesto. The sixth paragraph was particularly troublesome to the underworld of Vic Cotroni: *"We once believed that perhaps it would be worth it to channel our energy and or impatience, as René Levésque said so well, in the Parti Québécois, but the Liberal victory showed us clearly that that which we call democracy in Quebec is nothing but the democracy of the rich. The Liberal party's victory was nothing but the victory of the election riggers, Simard-Cotroni. As a result, the British parliamentary system is finished and the Front de Libération du Québec will never allow itself to be distracted by the pseudoelections that the Anglo-Saxon capitalists toss to the people of Quebec every four years."*

The "Cotroni" of that phrase was obviously Vic, who had been involved in election misdeeds for five decades. The "Simard" was the wealthy Simard shipbuilding family, Premier Robert Bourassa's wealthy in-laws, who lived in Sorel.

Pierre Laporte described the abduction as "a wind of madness temporarily blowing across Canada." But five days later that wind blew in his direction. It was about six on a Saturday evening, and Laporte planned to dine out with his wife, Françoise, and son Jean. Two decades of marriage hadn't lessened his fondness for Françoise. "Pierre was the type of guy who went fishing with his wife," a friend recalled. "When he went travelling, he would always think how he could take his wife. He wouldn't go to a stag party. And he would introduce his wife with eyes that big — the way a young fellow would introduce his girl to the relatives."

Laporte had just heard the province's Justice minister Jérôme Choquette on television, telling Cross's abductors, "No society can expect that the decisions of its governments, or of the courts of law, can be erased by the use of blackmail, because this signifies the end of all social order." Then he went out to play catch in a field opposite his Chambly home with his eighteen-year-old nephew, Claude, and one of Claude's friends. An errant pass bounced near the road, and Laporte bent down to retrieve it. A blue Chevrolet Biscayne stopped abruptly alongside him. Looking up, Laporte saw a hooded man with a machine gun who motioned for him to get into the car. The gunman's companion, also hooded, shoved Laporte inside, where two other men were waiting. All wore wigs, false moustaches and makeup.

One of those men, Francis Simard, would later say that Laporte's fate was sealed as much by having his number listed in the phonebook as it was by his dubious connections to the world of Vic Cotroni: "I don't know how we thought of Pierre Laporte, or who thought of him. ...He had to live close by. We looked in the telephone book. A Pierre Laporte lived in Saint-Lambert. ...We called; his wife answered. I forgot what we told her. Yes, Pierre Laporte was there but he couldn't come to the phone right now. ...It seemed impossible to us...'Too easy,' we thought. Given the context, for a minister to be at home, nice and secure — we couldn't get over it."

Friday, October 16, was the cruellest day in a hellish week for Laporte. His eyes were taped shut, his hands shackled and his legs chained to a bed. Then he heard what must have seemed like the sound of freedom. The siren of a police car wailed down Armstrong

Street near the rundown bungalow where he was held captive. His three captors were out of the bedroom, and Laporte made a frantic bid to escape. He hurled his upper body out the window. But halfway to freedom, he felt the jolt of his leg chains, which trapped him midway through the pane of shattered glass. Blood gushed from the muscle and main artery of his left wrist, right thumb and chest. His captors yanked him back into the bungalow as the police car drove on to investigate a minor house fire.

A source close to the terrorists would tell Robert McKenzie and Ronald Lebel of the *Toronto Star* that the kidnappers were planning to force Laporte to write out a detailed "confession" that would read like a "Magna Carta of [political] corruption." The plan was abandoned after the cabinet minister's futile and bloody attempt to free himself. Laporte was weak from loss of blood, and his spirit was unimaginably shattered. Early in the ordeal, he had bouts of euphoria, during which he told his captors, "It'll all work out. I know it. Don't worry. It'll all work out perfectly." Now he was a zombie. "He didn't move," Simard would recall. "No reaction. We took off his blindfold. He didn't even look at us... It was, like Laporte was already dead. He was like somebody stripped of all life. He looked totally empty. You could feel that he'd already received the death blow."

Across town in the Queen Elizabeth Hotel, Françoise and family friends were frantic. At about 9:30 that night, René Gagnon, Laporte's aide, said he was visited by mobster Frank D'Asti who "...said he could help us rescue Pierre Laporte...he said, 'René, we can find him. We know where he is.' I said, 'Fine. Make the necessary arrangements.'"

But the kidnappers and mobsters were from different worlds — the far left and the far right. Gagnon would try to explain the meeting by saying, "Wrongly, I admit, [I had] lost faith in the authorities in power. Faced with the confusion within the police forces we decided to seek D'Asti and [Nicolo] di Iorio's help."

In confidential police reports, di Iorio was called "pimp" and "bumboy." He moved up in the Cotroni organization on the strength of his political contacts.

It's not unusual for the mob to be sympathetic to politicians. The Mafia traditionally distrusts reformers and revolutionaries. It wants to profit from hypocrisies and poor legislation, not clean them up.

Paul Rose would later reportedly tell police that on Friday, October 16, 1970 he returned to the clapboard bungalow at 5630

Armstrong where his brother Jacques and Francis Simard told him of Laporte's frantic lunge for freedom. In what police would say was an unsigned statement by Rose, Rose was quoted as recalling, "On Saturday, October 17, 1970, we talked about the War Measures Act, the speech by Bourassa the night before…and we´also discussed the mechanics of Laporte's execution and the measures to complete the operation, that is, the disposal of the body. All three of us were in the house at 5630 Armstrong when Laporte was executed. Two of us were holding him while the third tightened the chain that he wore around his neck."

Laporte's life was extinguished and his body was stuffed into the trunk of a green Chevrolet and left at a nearby air base. Gagnon received news of Laporte's death just moments after hearing D'Asti's offer to help find the kidnap victm.

Chapter Nine

Reputations

*"My client may be an illiterate man,
but he is nevertheless a man of heart."*
— Vic Cotroni's lawyer

Vic Cotroni regarded publicity with the same unease with which he was said to view dentists' needles or subpoenas. But his youngest brother Frank had a different style, one more in tune with the beat of the streets of Montreal than of the old world. Not only was Frank more comfortable speaking French than Italian, he had married into a French-Canadian family with more than its share of criminals. When Frank ran into legal troubles in the winter of 1971, he didn't retreat into silence. Instead he called a press conference and summoned scores of journalists to explain what a bum rap he faced.

As reports came north that he had been arrested in Mexico for car and credit-card theft, Frank Cotroni felt the need to make sure the story was told from his point of view. He was fighting for his reputation, something infinitely more valuable than any piece of turf he controlled. For reasons known best to himself, he thought that the relatively minor charges were an affront to his dignity. Although he was now an international-level criminal, he was attempting to craft a public image of himself as a respectable businessman. But wire-service accounts of the Mexican arrest made him appear like a petty thief, which explained why he felt the need for the bizarre news conference.

Just because the Cotronis were making their fortune through heroin-trafficking, prostitution, pornography and extortion didn't mean they didn't care about their name. On the contrary, in the world of Vic and Frank Cotroni a reputation was a life-or-death thing, something jealously guarded as a portable commodity that could be won or lost.

The Cotronis were constantly surrounded by thieves and killers. They had no written contracts, no recourse to police or the courts. With Carmine Galante on ice and the Bonanno name under attack, there must have been a heightened awareness that things could not be taken for granted, that their name couldn't be sullied without a fight.

So, on February 18, 1971, Frank Cotroni appeared in a luxury suite at the downtown Montreal Holiday Inn, his squat, muscular frame elegantly holstered in a tailored black business suit set off by black patent leather shoes, a white Italian silk shirt and a navy tie striped with maroon. His sullen stare could still cause a heart to stop at twenty paces, but his tightly curled black hair was neatly coiffed and his mod sideburns had a sharp, tidy edge. The fingernails on his powerful hands were neatly manicured. Assembled reporters where told that he had recently been jailed in Mexico because of an enormous misunderstanding. To make the story easier to swallow, it was served up with hors d'oeuvres and washed down with free drinks which were served to the press by solicitous family lawyers.

"It was simply a case of mistaken identity," Cotroni explained of his fifteen days in a Mexican jail cell. "It wasn't a frame-up." He went on to say that he and his family didn't appreciate the attention given the case and added that he had no plans to return to Mexico, because "there's no justice there."

Undercover policemen who were posing as reporters had to laugh when a member of the press jokingly opened the questioning with the words, "Well then, Mr. Prime Minister..." The mobster laughed too, then described the folly of the Mexican government which had detained him for supposedly stealing a Cadillac and buying jewellery with a stolen credit card. His lawyer, Sydney Leithman, presented journalists with documents showing that his client had been officially released without charges by Mexican authorities. They were told that the Mexican arrest was merely a case of mistaken identity, as Cotroni wasn't even in Acapulco at the time of the purchases in question. No one asked about a meeting in Acapulco in February 1970 between underworld money-laundering genius Meyer Lansky, Paolo Violi and Frank's older brother Vic. Lansky, a close confederate of Lucky Luciano and a mob legend, didn't sit down with just anybody. Police suspected the Mexico meeting was called to discuss the possibility of legalized casinos in Quebec.

Frank Cotroni's presence in Mexico in 1971 showed he had moved up from days of providing muscle and bullets to buttress his brothers' rackets. Also unmentioned amidst the drinks and denials of the press conference was the fact that heroin-traffickers alternated their traffic through Montreal and Acapulco, to make their moves less noticeable to police. Criminals, like other businessmen, need to be able to adapt constantly to change, and the old French Connection of Carmine Galante was in shambles. As for the accusation that Cotroni stole a new Cadillac, the media was told that the car was borrowed from a friend who, in turn, had borrowed it from a pudgy encyclopedia salesman from Laval. In case there were any diehard skeptics in the room, the salesman was present to say there was nothing the matter with Cotroni borrowing his new Cadillac. The salesman said he had only known Frank Cotroni for a month, "But I've heard of him."

The spectacle of an international drug-runner calling a press conference to attack piddling charges was too much for one policeman in the room who muttered, "It's incredible. The world has turned upside down."

There's no record of what Mexico City drug-trafficker Giuseppe (Pino) Catania and his confederate Tommaso Buscetta said about the press conference. But it's clear what Catania thought; fearful of increased police attention, he temporarily suspended all drug deals with the Cotroni organization.

Also less than convincing was Frank Cotroni's acquittal in the summer of 1971 in a trial concerning a failed attempt to tunnel into a bank vault. Police had discovered a fifty-three-foot tunnel from the basement of a Montreal duplex to a vault in a bank on Decarie Boulevard. There were drill holes in several spots in the bank wall, and the vault's alarm system had been tampered with by a complex diversion of wires. The case began with what was perhaps Frank Cotroni's greatest public humiliation as he was paraded in leg irons into the courtroom by police. News photographers sent wire-service photos of the spectacle across the country. Further theatre was provided by Judge Gerard Lagniere, who moved his court to the lower duplex and crawled into the tunnel in the presence of the accused and the press.

Frank Cotroni's bail was set at $100,000. An unidentified man, escorted by a solidly-built male companion, marched into the Montreal courthouse with a large brown envelope and purchased Cotroni's freedom with $1,000 and $100 bills. What had been a public embarrassment for Frank Cotroni ended as a show of power as five underlings took the fall while ensuring that the case stopped with themselves, just as their tunnelling had stopped short of the millions of dollars in cash and securities in the bank vault. The underlings refused to point their fingers at Frank Cotroni, his father-in-law or his two brothers-in-law. This meant enhanced status in the underworld for the underlings and freedom for Cotroni.

Frank Cotroni was back in court in 1972, this time facing extortion charges. Dionysos Chionis had been under twenty-four-hour guard for more than a month since he had complained that thugs used strong-arm tactics to sell "protection" for him and his prosperous steakhouse. The Greek immigrant's testimony described an old-time extortion technique. Recent immigrants such as Chionis were always the most vulnerable to underworld protection schemes, since they weren't familiar with Canada's customs and often lacked faith in the police. Chionis testified that three men had demanded $250 a week in protection money and that one of the men "told me that he worked for Frank Cotroni." He added that the fee was negotiated down to $150 weekly. "They told me they would break everything and demolish the restaurant. I promised I would make the first payment the following Monday. They said they were killers and if I didn't they would cut off my head with a knife." There was also talk of breaking legs. Chionis made three payments, he said, then the men told him they wanted half of his business. At that point he decided to seek a meeting with Frank Cotroni, who told him "he hadn't sent those men to see me and that he didn't have anything to do with them."

But when Chionis returned to court for his second day on the stand, his testimony was suddenly contradictory and disjointed. He chainsmoked and paced nervously under police guard during breaks, looking just like countless other witnesses against the Mafia in North America and Italy. Judge Belanger threatened to lock Chionis up if his memory didn't improve immediately. The restaurateur balked at the suggestion that he testify behind closed doors. With no star witness, the case was dead, and charges against Frank Cotroni were withdrawn. As Cotroni prepared to leave the courtroom, the judge congratulated him on "two victories in the same day." The second victory had come with the culmination of a nine-year libel battle by Cotroni's older brother, Vic. At best it was a Pyrrhic triumph or a protracted joke, but it provided a glimpse into a seldom-seen aspect of the underworld. And for a proud man like Vic Cotroni, who valued a low profile and high respect, it was a gross and rare miscalculation.

Vic Cotroni liked to be treated like a godfather, but he hated being called one in the press. When *Maclean's* magazine did just that, Cotroni sued for $1.25 million in damages, a dollar for each of the readers his lawyer claimed had seen the article. Cotroni's lawyer knew much about the Cotroni family and its reputation. He was Jean-Paul Ste. Marie, the man who had feverishly and successfully prosecuted Vic's younger brother Giuseppe for drug-trafficking and securities theft. Vic Cotroni explained his choice of counsel by saying that Ste. Marie was the only lawyer who truly knew he was an innocent man.

Ste. Marie noted that Vic Cotroni had no criminal record after 1938 when, at the age of twenty-eight, he abandoned his career as a professional wrestler to go into the nightclub business. "He is just a simple illiterate citizen who had problems with justice, who came out of it, against whom from 1938 to 1972 no criminal accusation was proven." And while Ste. Marie acknowledged that Cotroni had owned a gambling house on de Bullion Street, he argued there was no moral difference between this indiscretion and the fact that staid McGill University owned brothels in the 1940s. "Of course, my client, when he was a nightclub owner, let people dance on Sundays. But that was a misdemeanour. It certainly does not prove that he was king of the underworld."

Ste. Marie beatified Vic Cotroni with the same zeal with which he had imprisoned Vic's younger brother, Giuseppe. He brought in three prominent members of the Italian community in Montreal, all of whom testified that they held Cotroni in the highest esteem and weren't aware that he might have any Mafia connections. Vic Cotroni was described as a community benefactor, with a particularly soft spot for needy children. "Everyone was soliciting him for philanthropic causes," said Alfred Gagliardi, a former member of the Montreal city executive committee. Gagliardi described Cotroni's reputation in the Italian community as that of a "generous business-man." He noted the huge turnout for the funeral of Cotroni's mother in 1964, an occasion described by a newspaper as "the biggest funeral in Montreal since that of [former mayor] Camillien Houde." He continued: "There were many celebrities, artists, people from the business world, politicians, even clergy. But the little people, the Italian people, were still in the majority."

Ste. Marie argued his client wasn't a fearsome mobster but, rather, a humble victim. *"Maclean's* seems to say: 'What! A man who does not know how to read or write, an immigrant, a nightclub owner daring to sue us! He must be punished!'"

In a dramatic flourish, Ste. Marie mocked the assumption that movies like *The Godfather* should be taken seriously: "Well, there was an old movie called *King Kong,* but that did not prove that gorillas were as tall as skyscrapers. And Bela Lugosi did not prove the existence of vampires, no more than the Quebec film, *Deux Femmes en Or,* proves that every suburban housewife sleeps with the plumber and the telephone repair man."

But Vic Cotroni's libel action backfired, proving that it's wiser for mafiosi to settle their difficulties out of court. Rather than issue a retraction, the magazine took the offensive. *Maclean's* lawyer A.J. Campbell, an avuncular sixty-nine-year-old, told of Cotroni's visits from Joe and Bill Bonanno in the 1960s. American organized-crime expert Ralph Salerno testified that in 1963, when the *Maclean's* article was published, Vic Cotroni was "active in organized crime directly related to the Joe Bonanno organized crime group in New York." Salerno, former head of the New York City police intelligence unit and an adviser on crime to two American presidents, said that Cotroni's reputation since 1963 had not changed, while that of Joseph Bonanno had gotten worse.

Vic Cotroni was suspiciously vague when questioned about a long-distance telephone conversation he had with Bonanno from a telephone booth at the corner of Jean-Talon and Pie-IX Boulevard. He argued that the chat with the underworld boss consisted simply of "…'How are you?'…and things like that." And Cotroni's credibility was further sullied when Campbell probed his association with a Quebec trucking firm. Campbell noted that Cotroni had denied having heard of Ace Trucking Co., a subsidiary of Maislin Transport Inc., even though Ace Trucking Co. had paid Cotroni $15,900 in 1960, $15,300 in 1961 and $15,900 in 1962.

Trucking executive Sam Maislin said Vic Cotroni became a trucking official because he went to the right barber shop and knew the right people.

> CAMPBELL: Now, what were Mr. Cotroni's duties at such time as he was employed by Ace Trucking?
> MAISLIN: Primarily, if I'm correct, we brought Mr. Cotroni in to see if we could bring him in as a sales representative for the Italian trade at that time.
> CAMPBELL: How did he come to be employed, did you make the arrangements?
> CAMPBELL: Yes?
> MAISLIN: And he asked if there was any position he could fill over there.
> CAMPBELL: Right?
> MAISLIN: I don't normally look after sales but I told him, "Come down to the office and see what they could find." And he came down and some arrangements were made to see what he could do to get the Italian trade for our organization.
> CAMPBELL: I see. Before you met him in the barber shop, had you known him?
> MAISLIN: No sir.
> CAMPBELL: Had you made any inquiries as to what business experience he previously had?
> MAISLIN: No sir. I didn't personally,
> CAMPBELL: No. You just told him to go and see your man, is that right?
> MAISLIN: Well, before he could see anybody he'd have to come back and apply for the job.
> CAMPBELL: Yes, but when he did come down to the job did he see you?
> MAISLIN: There was Mr. Parago who was looking after it at the time, not myself; and after speaking to him they decided to take him on.
> CAMPBELL: And what business experience did he indicate to you that he had?
> MAISLIN: Just, "know the people."

The case offered a rare and embarrassing glimpse into Vic Cotroni's private life. The public saw that a mob godfather, like any other man, gets nervous when his wife catches him cheating on her.

The court heard that Vic Cotroni desperately tried to bribe a police officer with $50,000 to keep his mistress's name quiet after police arrested American fugitive Joseph Asaro at her home. Asaro had been sipping martinis with his father, Vincenzo, and with Vic and Frank Cotroni on the patio at the home of Ghislaine Turgeon, Vic Cotroni's long-time mistress and the mother of his son, Nick. Joseph Asaro was no ordinary criminal. He had been on the run for thirteen years since he had gone underground in the 1950s to escape the Kefauver organized-crime hearings. His father knew all about organized crime from his days in the Al Capone mob. Vincenzo Asaro feared his son was dead when, in fact, Joseph was working under the name "Joe Amato" at one of the many Montreal night-clubs under Cotroni control.

It was worth $50,000 to Vic for police to place the arrest of Joseph Asaro anywhere but at Turgeon's home. "Money, that's not the question," he pleaded. "Fix your price and you will be paid. My wife is in the hospital. She is very sick. If she learns of this arrest, at the home of my mistress, she could die. Everyone is going to say that Vic Vincent [Cotroni's old wrestling nickname] is a stoolpigeon. My wife's going to know. The newspapers are going to talk about it and it will be a scandal." Now the topic was in the public eye again, through Cotroni's own doing.

Also related in open court were details of Vic Cotroni's visit to Acapulco in 1970. Moses Polakoff, the brilliant New York lawyer for such mob notables as Meyer Lansky and Lucky Luciano, testified that Cotroni and Lansky were together in Mexico at a large social gathering at the home of former Montreal restaurater Leo Bercovitch. Vic Cotroni's feeble response was to deny ever hearing of the internationally notorious Lansky, let alone meeting him.

As the case wound down, Ste. Marie tried to demonstrate that Cotroni wasn't driven by a desire for money in his lawsuit. "My client may be an illiterate man, but he is nevertheless a man of heart," said Ste. Marie. "Should he win the case, the money will go to charitable works. ...He may not express himself well, but he's a man with a heart."

Judge St. Germain chided *Maclean's* for publishing the article without having personal knowledge of the facts, instead basing it on hearsay from policemen, informers and the writings of other people: "They should have realized that if the police authorities had not seen fit to undertake criminal proceedings, it was because in their opinion the evidence necessary to obtain a conviction in court did not justify it."

But St. Germain also told the court that Cotroni's reputation was "tainted" and didn't justify the full sum of $1.25 million in damages sought. Instead, he awarded Vic Cotroni $2 in damages, plus court costs, giving him a dollar for being libelled in English and another dollar for the French version of *Maclean's*. The humiliation must have been enormous for Vic Cotroni. There's no record of anyone asking him which charity received the $2 cash award.

Ironically, at the time Vic Cotroni was being exposed as an underworld boss, he was transferring power to the young Paolo Violi. Cotroni's old confederate, Louis Greco, had suddenly died. True to his everyman role, Greco was working on the floor of his pizzeria near Jarry Park on December 7, 1972 when a solvent caught fire and he was fatally burned. It seemed too bland a death for a top mobster, and rumours smouldered that it must have been suicide or murder. Greco had given Vic Cotroni strong bonds to New York and Boston, and his Sicilian heritage protected Cotroni's flank from Sicilian opposition inside Montreal.

Paolo Violi lacked Greco's strong ties with the Sicilians who ran the New York mobs. His strongest North American ties were to lesser criminals in the Philadelphia and Cleveland areas. Sicilian mobsters fancy themselves as more worldly and cultured than their counterparts from the isolated Calabrian hills. "[Violi] forgot what his background was," a former police organized-crime expert says. "His background was out of the backwoods of Calabria and [Sicilians] don't like those kind of people trying to be uppity."

Meanwhile, a public crime inquiry was threatening to shine a floodlight on family operations. And on the streets, there was a new and particularly fearsome rival, French-Canadian gangs who were considered even more violent than the Mafia. None generated more terror than the Dubois brothers who once worked in Cotroni nightclubs. The name of Vic Cotroni's heir apparent didn't command any respect from them. They blithely dismissed Paolo Violi as "a punk" and poised themselves to back their tough words with bloody actions.

Chapter Ten

Paolo Under Attack

*"He should have gone into the club...lined
everybody up against the wall and
rat-a-tat-tat."*
—Paolo Violi explains how he would
have dealt with rival bikers

It was just before the 3:00 a.m. closing time on July 22, 1973 at
the small bar on north St. Michel Boulevard, and a singer was
entertaining the crowd with *"Les Portes du Pénitencier."* The
song had been dedicated to Frank Cotroni's brother-in-law, Richard
Desormiers, and while Desormiers listened from his barstool, he
sipped a cognac. He probably didn't notice two men who walked in
quietly, wearing wigs and false moustaches, their fingers taped so
they wouldn't leave any fingerprints. They sat at the bar and each
downed a drink, then one of them suddenly stood beside Desormiers.
Within seconds, he had pumped five blasts from his .38 special into
Desormiers. The night manager jumped from his barstool and was
cut down just as quickly by the other stranger's .32 revolver. It was
the hitmen's third try at killing Desormiers, and this time they finished the job.

Claude Dubois wasn't in the bar that morning, but his presence
was unmistakable. There wasn't any doubt that he was behind the
murders. A roughly handsome, failed nightclub singer with an electric smile and no apparent conscience, Dubois and his eight brothers had been introduced into the nightclub protection rackets by the
Cotronis. Now they were striking out on their own, carrying night-

club extortion a step further than the Cotronis. Employees and employers had to pay for the right to operate. Failure to do so meant broken bones and bloodshed, and the Dubois brothers bragged they were afraid of no one, not even the family of Vic Cotroni. Desormiers had angered Claude Dubois by threatening one of Dubois's men in a Dubois-owned nightclub. Donald Lavoie, one of the hitmen, later recalled that Dubois had warned Frank Cotroni that Desormiers had "better stop horsing around or somebody will fix his clock." Claude Dubois made it clear he wouldn't tolerate any trouble from Richard Desormiers, even if Desormiers was the brother of Frank Cotroni's wife, Pauline.

The Duboises weren't the only Québécois showing a blunt lack of respect for Vic Cotroni's family. Two weeks before Desormiers' murder, on July 10, 1973, two Cotroni soldiers were gunned down after selling poor-quality heroin to Angelo Faquino, an Italian intermediary acting on behalf of French-Canadian bikers. The murders of Mario Ciambrone and Salvatore Sergi sparked a meeting between Paolo Violi and Vic Cotroni to, in Violi's words, "figure out what the hell we're going to do with these Frenchmen."

"The French guys took the stock [heroin] and then shot them," Vic Cotroni explained. "We have to find out what those...Frenchmen are up to... They take two *picciotti* [soldiers] from us and are preparing to shoot another."

Violi agreed the situation was grave. "They shot up some Italian *picciotto* and that's no good for any of us."

But three weeks later the mafiosi were still dithering. On July 31, Violi sat down with Frank Cotroni, whose gang moved in the milieu of French-Canadian gangs. Frank Cotroni said he knew the French-Canadians involved and that they were "crazy, crazy, crazy... They've killed something like ten guys already."

They decided that Frank Cotroni should handle the bikers, and Violi, who preferred to earn his money in the immigrant St. Leonard district, would straighten out Angelo Faquino. "I'm going to take care of that Angelo... I can get him. His brother-in-law, the watchmaker, is near here."

Faquino was driving by stately St. Louis Square on September 2 when he was gunned down by two hoods who frequented the coffee bar that doubled as Violi's headquarters. The two Violi henchmen, Tony Venelli and Moreno Gallo, were arrested for the murder, and while they were in jail, Violi sent them word through a pliant prison guard that he preferred guilty pleas over a trial which would open the family operations to public scrutiny. It was a sign of Violi's might that they complied. Venelli and Gallo were sentenced to four years and life respectively. While Violi couldn't save the obedient triggermen from jail, he did make their stay more comfortable, smuggling cognac and hashish to them inside the Parthenais Detention Centre via an amenable jailer.

Frank Cotroni hadn't followed through with his assignment to handle the bikers, but the war was thought to be over because the Ciambrone-Sergi slayings had been avenged. Then, on September 14, a third *picciotto,* Toni Di Genova, was shot dead in a bar. The Cotroni soldiers were enraged and called for an ocean of blood to wash away the insult, which would, in the words of one family member, "take care of the Frenchmen once and for all."

The family called a summit at the Windsor Hotel. Vic Cotroni, Violi and lieutenant Joe DiMaulo were present. Violi played the role of "the boss . . . the Godfather or the padrone," one mafioso would recall, while Vic Cotroni acted as adviser or chairman of the board. It was decided that the war had gone on long enough and that it was time to return to business. Soldiers were forbidden from taking further revenge. "The order was given not to carry out the planned massacre, but the young soldiers, who were hungry for blood, weren't happy with the decision to bury the hatchet," a family member would recall. "...although the decision looked a bit gutless to the soldiers, it was obeyed."

Violi grumbled that Di Genova would never have been killed if Frank Cotroni had done his job. He thought Frank wasted too much time trying to plot the perfect attack, one in which no mafiosi would have been arrested. Even the turncoat Faquino might have been spared had Frank Cotroni been more decisive, Violi told underlings at his espresso bar. "I told Frankie to leave the Italian [Faquino] to me and to hit the Frenchmen first. When the Italian saw the Frenchmen getting it, he would have come to me and maybe we could have saved him." Violi's offer to help Faquino mustn't be mistaken for pacifism. A police wiretap caught him explaining to his soldiers how he would have handled Frank Cotroni's assignment: "He [Frank Cotroni] should have gone into the club [where the bikers hung out], clients or no clients, lined everybody up against the wall and rat-a-tat-tat."

Another threat to the Cotronis came from inside their family, in the person of Nick Rizzuto, a thick-chested native of the tiny village of

Cattolica Eraclea, Sicily. Rizzuto followed the tradition that honoured men greeted each other with kisses on both cheeks, pushed their sons to marry women of Sicilian heritage and looked disdainfully upon Calabrians such as Vic Cotroni and Paolo Violi — mountain folk who were best for dirty jobs, not decision-making. Rizzuto snubbed Vic Cotroni and Paolo Violi routinely by ignoring family meetings and discussions. Cotroni and Violi bristled, since they wanted to be treated with dignity as well as be given a cut of the money they suspected Rizzuto was making through heroin-trafficking.

Rizzuto was probably the most powerful of a number of Sicilians who were on the scene in Montreal. Cotroni and Violi hoped that tensions between Sicilians and Calabrians could be cooled through a high-level meeting of about two dozen mobsters in a cottage in L'Epiphanie, north of Montreal, in December 1971. The summit was headed by Paolo Violi and his brothers Rocco and Francesco. From the Sicilian side, there was Giuseppe Cuffaro, believed to be a major money-launderer for the Caruana crime family; Leonardo Caruana, a member of the Sicilian Mafia's Commission in Agrigento; and Pietro Sciara, another high-level Sicilian mafioso living in Montreal. Vic Cotroni did not attend, a point of lingering curiosity for police. "He was apparently on his way," a police Mafia expert says, "and all of a sudden, he doesn't show up. We always wondered."

Despite the summit, hostilities festered. On September 15, 1972, police wiretaps overheard Vic Cotroni saying that Rizzuto might be kicked out of the family. "Me, I'm *capo decina* [head of the Montreal wing of the Bonanno group]. I got the right to expel." That month, Bonanno family members came up from the eastern seaboard in hopes of settling the Rizzuto affair. Final decisions on major matters concerning Montreal were still made on the eastern seaboard of the United States. In Montreal, acting as peacemakers, were Nicky Alfano and Nicola Buttofuoco of New Jersey, ostensibly in the country as shoemakers visiting friends. After a discussion with one of the Americans, Violi tried to explain his problems with Rizzuto: "I told him he goes from one thing to the other, here and there, and says nothing to nobody. He does things and nobody knows nothing."

Tensions worsened. Vic Cotroni and Violi began to discuss "getting rid of " Rizzuto and making him "disappear." Another peacemaker, Giuseppe Settecase, was sent up to Montreal. He had so much experience in Mafia relations that his name appeared in underworld files for Agrigento magistrates in 1936. A series of parallel meetings were held in New York, also dealing with Violi and Rizzuto. At one point, two would-be mediators at Violi's Jean-Talon Street espresso bar took a break from the case to nostalgically reminisce about old times and crimes. Police listened in on a wiretap and were stunned. Former police anti-gang head Mario Latraverse recalls, "They came out with all the latest murders that occurred in New York City. They explained everything, everything. 'What happened to such and such?' 'Well, he died because...' And they painted a whole picture of organized crime in New York. Well, we called New York authorities and they were flabbergasted. ...But they were here to mediate the request of Violi to kill Rizzuto. In that conversation, there was proof...that the Montreal family was a subfamily of the Bonanno family...and it was said then that money on a weekly basis was leaving Montreal...every Monday to go to New York."

Violi couldn't kill Rizzuto without permission from New York, and that permission was denied. However, just before he was called before a crime probe on organized crime, Rizzuto quietly slipped out of Montreal for Venezuela, which was then attracting a number of Corsican drug-traffickers from the old French Connection drug ring. Rizzuto would be seen meeting in South America with a bodyguard for Toronto's Paul Volpe, and a major Vancouver mobster. Later, Rizzuto became a Venezuelan citizen, along with two Sicilian brothers also fleeing Montreal, Pasquale and Gaspare Cuntrera. The three couldn't be extradited to face charges outside Venezuela. In Caracas, Rizzuto controlled interests in the construction industry and also ran a nightclub called Il Padrone.

No one could ever accuse the Mafia of being a hotbed of democracy. But leadership could be won through ballots as well as by bloodshed, and Paolo Violi's new responsibilities included voting for the Bonanno family's leader in the Volcano of New York. A vote was necessary after boss Natale (Joe Diamond) Evole died of cancer on August 20, 1973. Joe Bonanno was operating in the shadows of the organized-crime world at this point, having been banished to Arizona for his failed plot to murder three Cosa Nostra Commission leaders.

Paolo Violi led a Montreal contingent to the Americana Hotel in downtown Manhattan, where he was met by leadership hopeful Philip (Rusty) Rastelli. Rastelli and his underboss-to-be Nick (Nicky Glasses) Marangello lobbied the Montrealers in the hotel's Jockey

Bar for their votes. In return, the Canadians were promised they'd get more soldiers from New York to compensate for members lost to prison and the grave. Violi also liked the fact that Rastelli had lived briefly in Montreal during the 1960s.

When Violi heard that the Rastelli-Marangello ticket had won, he was overjoyed. A police wiretap picked up Violi's voice saying, "Mike [Rastelli's Montreal code name] knows Montreal. He's got friends here."

Violi wasn't so happy with the attention the election received from police. He had been trailed from the airport in Montreal to New York, to the Americana and back to Montreal. At one point, he attempted to frustrate his shadows at the Americana by wandering the hotel in a seemingly aimless pattern. "They even took a room down the hall from here to see who would come. When I was in the lobby [of the Americana] I look around and I see these two cops and one starts to take a picture of me, which I don't like very much."

Questioned by police about the trip, Violi said he was in New York to buy new equipment for his ice-cream parlour. His lieutenant Joe DiMaulo had been checking into a pizza franchise, Violi added. For his part, DiMaulo was less coy but no more forthcoming. He said he had no desire to tell a police commission behind closed doors about the trip, for both career and personal reasons: "I'd have to wear a suit of armor if I testified, or I'd be shot."

Paolo Violi had been a young man of twenty when he moved to Canada, and he was still more comfortable in the hills of Calabria than between the concrete-and-steel towers of Manhattan. But he understood the importance of New York and the dangers of losing touch with the New York power base that Vic Cotroni had cultivated. New York had allowed the Cotronis to become strong, but it could easily transfer that strength to someone like Nick Rizzuto. In the early 1970s, however, Violi was willing to run that risk as he looked overseas to Italy, the site of the most famous kidnapping of the decade.

Calabria at the time was in the midst of an upsurge of ugly murders and kidnappings. Oddly enough, some of the blame was laid on the government's efforts to improve the economy of Italy's south through industrial development. Entrepreneurial mafiosi used ransom payments as investment capital as they fought for monopolies in the burgeoning construction industry. One of these capital-raising forays may be the reason that, on a sweltering July afternoon in 1973, a seventeen-year-old hippie was abducted from the streets of

Rome. The youth's name was John Paul Getty III, and his grandfather was American billionaire oilman John Paul Getty. The disappearance was first dismissed as a youthful hoax — until young Getty's mother received her son's severed right ear in the mail.

"We are not interested in cutting up your son piece by piece," the kidnappers wrote. "We are not sadists. We are sending this letter to show the shame of this family which is the richest in the world. ...If the family does not pay according to our conditions we will send another piece of him."

Observers were further horrified that the kidnappers had chosen to use the notoriously poor Italian postal system to express their demands. It had taken the ear nineteen days to travel just 150 miles, and it was feared that other body parts might get stuck in the mail along with countless other wayward packages.

The key underworld figures in Getty's disappearance were Sera Mommolitti, an underboss in the Piromalli Mafia family of the Plain of Gioia Tauro, and Domenico Barbino of Rome. Barbino was a first cousin of Paolo Violi, and his crime family represented the dark side of an increasingly competitive, consumer-based urban society. Their ranks were no longer drawn from the lowest rural classes; they included university graduates who preferred submachine guns to the lupara, the shotgun that was a traditional favourite of Italian mafiosi.

Just how much Violi knew about the Getty kidnapping is a mystery, but there's reason to suspect that he was far more than a curious bystander. Violi and Barbino had grown up together in Sinopoli, and Barbino's mother and Violi's father were siblings. Violi and Barbino met in an apartment in a suburb of Rome shortly before the Getty abduction, and calls were made from that apartment to Violi's father, Domenico, in Parma, Ohio..

Young Getty's ordeal lasted five months, until his grandfather paid the billion-lire ransom and the youth was set free on a road near Naples. A negligible amount of the ransom was recovered, and the rest is believed to have been used to buy trucks needed in the building of the Plain of Gioia Tauro's industrial port. How much, if any of it, ended up in Montreal with the Cotroni family will never be known.

Chapter Eleven

Cocaine Blues

*"I'm no saint, but I swear to you
that I'm no bum either."*
— Frank Cotroni

There's no record of Frank Cotroni's being jealous of Paolo Violi's rapid rise in the organization. Perhaps Frank Cotroni was too consumed with his own problems to entertain the prospect of greater responsibilities. The old French Connection had been smashed, and the Bonanno link had been frayed by problems in New York. Frank Cotroni was trying to move drugs out of South America, and he was experiencing the headaches any businessman suffers when he launches a new venture in difficult times.

His worries were somewhat softened, though, by his ability to buy some of the better things in life, not the least of which was the cuisine of some of Montreal's best restaurants. His favourite places were busy, aggressive marble-and-brass shrines to red meat and middleaged, masculine chic; *arriviste* steakhouses where there was respect for Rolexes and expensive toupées, where patrons could hear chatter about mega-deals in one ear and robust reviews of table-dancers in the other. It was at one such spot on rue St. Laurent on November 8, 1974, during a meeting with his brother Vic, that Frank Cotroni was arrested and threatened with the first significant prison time in a career which included gambling, travel junkets, loan-sharking, extortion, counterfeiting, softcore pornography and narcotics. He and associate Frank D'Asti were each charged by the United States with conspiracy and trafficking in a plot to bring 19.8 pounds (nine kilos) of cocaine with a street value of $3 million into New York. Each man faced a possible sentence of forty years in prison. It hadn't been a good month for D'Asti; three weeks earlier, he had been sentenced in New Jersey to twenty years in prison for his role in a heroin-smuggling ring.

The U.S. government had requested Frank Cotroni's arrest, but he took his fight to avoid extradition all the way to the Supreme Court and enlisted the services of top mob lawyer Moses Polakoff. A conviction in Canada would have meant it would at least be easier for his family to visit him. But he lost the case and was shipped south to a Brooklyn courthouse. On January 7, 1975, assistant U.S. district attorney Thomas Puccio told a jury that Cotroni and D'Asti were "the middlemen" in a major international drug plot. "They were the ones who brought the buyers and sellers together," Puccio said. He described his opening remarks as "only the skeleton which you can fill in as each witness testifies." Cotroni's lawyer, John Iannuzzi, hijacked the imagery and countered ominously that Puccio risked finding a "jumble of bones at his feet."

The prosecution's star witness was Giuseppe (Pino) Catania, a haberdasher and high-level international drug mover who had been indicted in August 1973 as a central figure in the movement of 330 kilos of nearly pure heroin and 9 kilos of cocaine into the United States and Canada. Catania, a one-time Toronto resident and forty-one-year-old father of five, used a cold, matter-of-fact tone to explain why Frank Cotroni had spent so much time in Mexico recently. But Catania bruised his credibility by claiming he hadn't profited from moving a half-billion dollars in drugs: "All I got for it was an old used car."

As a front behind which to deal drugs, Catania had a boutique in Mexico City. It was an appropriate cover since, in the argot of the underworld, drugs are frequently referred to as "shirts" and "suits." He admitted he was testifying in cooperation with U.S. authorities in exchange for a ten-year sentence on pending heroin charges, and he also said he had lived in "relative comfort in a secret location" as he awaited trial, hidden from potential and probable harm. While he had been in a Mexican jail, he said, his bribes brought him a colour television, carpeted floors and servants. When his money for favours had dried up, Catania said, he was placed on the plane for what he believed was Palermo. Instead, the plane touched down in Houston, where he was arrested by Drug Enforcement Agency officers.

Catania testified that Cotroni agreed to pay $99,000 for nine kilos of heroin, if the delivery was made to New York City. But Catania said that when a messenger called him to a Mexico City hotel, he was handed a shoebox that contained only $43,000. He was later paid another $21,000, but said he never got the full amount because Cotroni said the narcotic was poor quality and difficult to sell.

The prosecution's case was buttressed by seventeen different wiretapped recordings from Operation Vegas, the same tapes that had highlighted Cotroni family ties to South Shore politicians. The recordings were made at Frank D'Asti's Victoria Sporting Club, at a Ste. Catherine Street East barber shop, and at a pay telephone in the lobby of the Laurentian Hotel. In the tapes, Frank Cotroni was called "Le Gros" or "The Big Guy."

But not all the prosecution's case was so damning. One witness failed to recognize Cotroni in the courtroom, saying, "I can only remember he had hairy arms." At this point, the witness and the accused were introduced, and Cotroni rolled up his sleeves to show the hair on his arms.

Iannuzzi rode a moral high horse while attacking Catania, saying, "He's laughing in our faces. He wasn't concerned about how many kids got their brains scrambled or were bent in pain and in a cold sweat in some dark alley because they needed a fix. ...He knows that if the prosecution went ahead and charged him with all the drug offences they have on him, he'd rot in jail for the rest of his life."

And D'Asti's lawyer disputed the police interpretation that "shirts" and "suits" were really code words for drugs. Groping for a convincing argument and a metaphor to attack the haberdasher Catania, he called the prosecution's case just "a bunch of loose ends until Catania came along with the thread."

The lawyer's argument lulled one juror to sleep. When he awoke, he marched from the courtroom with his eleven associates and deliberated for ten hours. Frank Cotroni knew that a lengthy prison term for drug-trafficking had broken his older brother Giuseppe's mental and physical health. If he was sent to prison, too, Vic would be left alone in a world where a person desperately needed a family. Frank Cotroni tugged nervously at his socks, then paled as he heard the verdict. He and D'Asti had been found guilty and faced the possibility of spending the rest of their lives in prison.

Cotroni protested to the judge that he was innocent, saying, "I had nothing to do with the transaction." Then he gave a rare public glimpse into his private life. Even those who understood that he was a seasoned criminal knew he was telling the truth when he spoke of his love for his young children. He described himself as a good father, the strongest defence he knew for a man's character. At the same time, he admitted that his work was hurting his children: "I'm no saint, but I swear to you that I'm no bum either. I never took part in drug trafficking. I'm a good father of a family and if I'm sent to prison my family could break up. I've been married for twenty-two years and I'm a good father of a family. I have six children, three of them still very young. The older ones, two boys and a girl, had to quit school because of all the bad publicity about me. My oldest boy [Nicodemo] is getting married soon and I'd like to be there to stand up with him as his father. I've been kept in prison for seventeen months already and in my case that's as hard as five or six years in prison. If you decide to put me in jail, I wish you would order that they put me in a prison near the Canadian border so I can be closer to my family. In closing, if I didn't testify, it was because I wanted to avoid problems with the income tax guys."

D'Asti hinted he could bring highly-placed people down with him. But he must have known his political clout had waned, since members of the Cotroni organization had not had any success when they vigorously lobbied Ottawa to prevent his extradition.

Judge Jacob Mishler said he put little credence in either a pre-sentence report, which described Cotroni as an organized crime figure, or in forty letters from Quebec businessmen, religious groups and a journalist telling of Frank Cotroni's charitable nature. With that, he sentenced each man to fifteen years in prison.

All things considered, it could have been much worse for Frank Cotroni. He was sent to Lewisburg, Pennsylvania, just four hundred miles from his family. And Lewisburg wasn't the worst place to be if you were in Frank Cotroni's line of work since it had a long history as a meeting place, providing the mob equivalent of a postdoctoral seminar for top North American criminals.

Chapter Twelve

The Money-Mover

"I'm telling you, it's murder."
— Cotroni family money-launderer
Willie Obront complains
about police scrutiny

Vic Cotroni liked to describe himself as a humble, illiterate pepperoni salesman. Paolo Violi maintained that he earned a modest living selling espresso coffee and spumoni ice cream. But any doubt about the extent of their financial empire can be quickly erased by looking at the financial holdings of a key underling in the Cotroni group, William (Willie Obie) Obront. Willie Obie was a man with connections through all strata of Quebec society in addition to money ties to the United States and abroad. Willie Obie sat at the head of thirty-eight companies, one of which was responsible for feeding diseased horsemeat to tourists from around the world at fast-food booths at Expo 67. Although Obront's annual declared income was $38,000, he somehow moved at least $83 million through his bank accounts during his association with Vic Cotroni and Paolo Violi, allowing himself the occasional luxury of $50,000 wagers on U.S. football games.

The 1960s had been a time of growth for conglomerates in mainstream business, and Vic Cotroni's world was no different. Obront ran a myriad of different ventures including, appropriately enough, a laundry. His job was to hide the true ownership of funds raised through gambling, loan-sharking, drug-smuggling and other enterprises, and also to put these millions of dollars to work generating further revenues.

For all the intrigue, Willie Obie looked about as exotic as one of the carcasses of beef hanging in his meat coolers. His was the story of cold meat and cold cash, of quietly laundering the money wrung from the streets by the Cotronis. He played a high-stakes shell game, misleading police, the tax department, customers and suppliers about his real worth. His access to interest-free financing and Cotroni muscle put his legitimate competitors at a daunting disadvantage as they tried to stay alive financially in the restaurant, investments, laundry, home-improvements, meat-packing and construction industries. Despite his enormous wealth, there was no doubt that Obront answered to Vic Cotroni and Paolo Violi. Obront would say that his relations with men of the Cotroni gang were business, not friendship, and that other meetings were nothing more than accidents. But an intercepted conversation between Obront and Cotroni associate Angelo Lanzo, who was at a pay phone in the Sirloin Barn Restaurant in Montreal, suggests things were far more structured.

> OBRONT: Going to see the Egg [Vic Cotroni] tonight?
> LANZO: Yeah. That's why I called you. He wants to see you.
> OBRONT: Eh?
> LANZO: He wants to see you.
> OBRONT: He?
> LANZO: Yeah. He told me to reach you.
> OBRONT: You know, calling me on the phone, you know, it's like the worst, worst possible thing, eh, Angie. This phone is like one hundred per cent tapped.
> LANZO: So, what the fuck, I'm not entitled to call you and see you?
> OBRONT: Well, I don't know...
> LANZO: Well, Jesus Christ, Willie.
> OBRONT: Well, what do you want me to tell you? I'm not going to have an argument with you.
> LANZO: Okay.
> OBRONT: I'm telling you, it's murder. I want to meet you...to wait...and, if you have something to say, you tell me, but it's no good this way.
> LANZO: I just found out this second, Willie.

OBRONT: It's no good, you've got to send somebody over here.

The conversation clearly shows Obront had a sense of foreboding about the future, perhaps understanding that the Cotroni family in the early 1970s had yet to appreciate fully the dangers of increasing police use of wiretaps and electronic bugs.

Born in Montreal on March 27, 1924, Obront liked to describe himself as a rags-to-riches success story. He was in his mid-twenties when he first came to police attention. And by the 1970s, former police crusader Pax Plante called Obront and Vic Cotroni "the untouchables" of the Montreal underworld because of their excellent political connections. Obront was a meat-packer and also a shareholder in the Hi-Ho Cafe and *Bal Tabarin* Nightclub, hangouts for such underworld figures as Nicholas Di Iorio and Vic Cotroni. His friends included drug-smuggler Lucien Rivard and Salvatore Giglio, the last New Yorker to oversee the Montreal interests of the Bonanno family before Vic Cotroni took charge.

But the most intriguing stories about the fat meatman concern his relationship with Gerda Munsinger, a German immigrant who worked her way from waiting on tables at Montreal's Chic'n Coop Restaurant to dining, dancing and bedding members of Prime Minister John Diefenbaker's cabinet. When Mounties investigated Munsinger's role in a major sex-security scandal, they constantly came across Obront's name. A Royal Canadian Mounted Police intelligence report states that Munsinger was deeply involved with the Cotroni family and that mobsters sometimes used hidden cameras to get comprimising shots of her well-placed clients. An underworld figure who sounds suspiciously like Obront was mentioned in a secret police report as having lobbied with police for Munsinger to be released from jail in February 1961. And the same racketeer, the report says, persuaded a department store to drop bad-cheque charges against Munsinger, and then immediately paid for her flight to Germany. Obront admitted that he often sent a chauffeured limousine to pick up former cabinet minister Pierre Sévigny at the Dorval airport while he was receiving Defence department contracts for supplying meat. The high-flying hooker, located in Germany by the *Toronto Star,* said that she feared a Montreal meat-broker named Obie who knew about her relationship with a cabinet minister.

Obront had the power to make a lot of people nervous. He was one of a group of Montreal underworld figures who tried to get drug dealer Lucien Rivard freed on parole by offering large bribes. And Claude Wagner, who unsuccessfully fought for the leadership of the Quebec Liberal Party, created a political scandal by noting that Obront and two associates suspiciously managed to have the only meat-storage facilities on the Expo 67 fair site, as well as 500 vending machines on the property. Obront was questioned after the murders of two men, one of whom allegedly borrowed money from him before he was shot dead by a hooded man during a card game in 1968.

Obront gave the Cotronis a conduit between the streets and mainstream business, and between the Italian gangs of St. Leonard and the Montreal Jewish community, of which Obront was a member in poor standing. Carmine Galante had given the Italian mob ascendancy over Jewish gangs in the mid-1950s, and Obront was living proof that the relationship endured. When a Montreal Jew wanted to run junkets into Las Vegas, he asked Obront for the go-ahead from the Cotroni group, since their associate Louis Greco was already running gamblers into Nevada.

Obront's loan-shark clients ranged from the tiny to major movers and shakers, from shepherds to multi-millionaires. The Cotroni men sometimes assigned him the duties of a banker, other times those of an arbitrator. When a humble immigrant shepherd asked Paolo Violi for financing to bring a shipment of goats and lambs north from Texas, he was told, "The best thing is to call Willie Obront and ask him to make a cheque for $5,000." Then Violi called the money-mover and told him "that his friend who deals with goats and lambs is over here and that he needs a cheque of $5,000."

"Send him over here and he will have it," Obront replied.

There was more than goats and lambs at stake when Abe Isaif, proprietor of Marquis Converter Sofas Ltd., walked into Violi's Reggio Bar. Isaif complained that a man named Louis Stoll had cost him $50,000. Violi assured Isaif that Stoll wouldn't bother him any more. For this service, Violi took a 20 per cent cut of the money he saved Isaif.

Obront was dispatched by Vic Cotroni and Violi to sort things out with Stoll. But Violi was stunned to learn that, rather than shrink away, Stoll "started to give Abe shit...He told me, 'I'm a big man. I do $11 million business.'"

Obront was sent back with a sterner message. "This guy lost his temper and honor toward me and I was only there to discuss business," Violi told Vic Cotroni. "So I will tell Obie that the fucker does not know who the people are and I am surprised at you because you had to prepare him of [sic] my visit. Now for this respect which he didn't have toward me... I don't want to do a grave thing but I have to show him something and for this he will have to pay me $50,000. So he will learn for the next time."

How this drama ended is a mystery but what was obvious from it was Obront's role in the pecking order of the Cotroni family: despite his wealth, he was a functionary for Vic Cotroni and his heir apparent, Paolo Violi. He was the mob's version of a warm-up act, preparing the public for the arrival of the headliners. When someone dared to refuse to jump at the mention of the Cotroni or Violi names, it was Obront's job to set them straight. It was beneath Cotroni or Violi's dignity to say they were big men: that was Willie Obie's job.

Mitchell Bronfman was in a higher financial league. He was born into the wealthy Bronfman family, the grandson of Harry Bronfman, whose brother was bootlegger Sam Bronfman. Rich on paper and in pedigree, Mitchell Bronfman was poor in liquid capital in the early 1960s, when he struggled to start up an executive air service. So he turned to Willie Obront. Over a decade and a half, investigators calculated, he wrote out at least 1,199 cheques to pay back Obront. Capital payments were at least $1,417,250, while another $1,056,066 went towards interest.

Closer to home, Obront helped the Cotroni group in its take-over of gambling in the Ottawa-Hull area in late 1973. Police estimated that "Paolo Violi of the Cotroni group" pulled in 25 per cent of a bookmaking operation that handled $50,000 daily.

A series of Quebec police probes into organized crime began in the late 1960s and carried through into the early 1980s, their existence a tacit admission that the legal system had failed miserably in dealing with men like Vic Cotroni and Paolo Violi.

It was only natural that investigators wanted a peek at Willie Obront's enterprises, and equally natural that Obront wanted no part of such scrutiny. In 1974 he bolted from Montreal to south Florida, where he owned an interest in the Pagoda North restaurant, a hangout for major players in the Miami-area underworld and a drop-off point for illegal money transfers. Florida wasn't under the control of any of the New York crime families, and was ripe for expansion, offering the Cotronis some diversity in their holdings beyond their powerful New York link.

Just a year after he arrived in Florida, Obront became a naturalized American citizen. The normal waiting period was five years — yet another mystery in the life of the portly meat wholesaler. Hearing that there were plans afoot to have him extradited from Florida, Obront fled again, first to Costa Rica, then Puerto Rico. During three weeks in Costa Rica, Obront met several times with fugitive financier Robert Vesco and his associate, former Montrealer Normand Leblanc, who were under indictment for a $224-million fraud. Obront didn't seem worried when Puerto Rican police placed him under house arrest. He told a Montreal radio station, "They [Costa Rican authorities] just want to know what I'm doing here and where I'm going."

But he was soon in handcuffs and on a plane north to Montreal to face charges of fraud, forgery, conspiracy to commit forgery and issuing false documents, and to answer questions about the bombing of the home of a Steinbergs supermarket official. The grocery-store chain had dropped one of Obront's meat companies from its list of suppliers. Obront's lawyer, Claude-Armand Sheppard, fumed that the Mounties had no right to make the arrest in Costa Rica, and threatened to sue the Canadian and Costa Rican governments and police. "Obront was, in effect, kidnapped in what amounts to a conspiracy between Canada and Costa Rica to kidnap an American citizen," Sheppard protested.

During his exile from Montreal, Obront had continued to deal with Canadian banks, demonstrating how money has a power separate from geographic borders or morality. None of this came as any surprise to the underworld; as their banker, Obront had long enjoyed a privileged relationship with legitimate bankers. The fact that Obront was a mobster and had fled the country didn't stop the Banque Canadienne Nationale from lending him $15,000 at a lower rate of interest than that charged the average customer. While the general public paid 13.5 per cent interest, Banque Canadienne Nationale charged the fugitive 12.5 per cent.

Valmore Delisle, former manager of the bank's major branch at 500 Place d'Armes in Montreal, treated Obront as a valued customer, and was unapologetic as he told the Quebec police crime probe of his bank's dealings with the gangland money-mover.

PROBE: Did you take any steps, as a result of certain statements made before this commission, describing Mr. Obront as a banker for the underworld or organized crime? Did you at any time take measures to change your relationship with Mr. Obront?
DELISLE: My relations with Mr. William Obront have always been strictly business relations.
PROBE: But all the same, did you take steps to change even your business relations with Mr. Obront?
DELISLE: I didn't think it appropriate at that time, since I considered him financially solvent.

Delisle's bank wasn't the only legitimate financial institution to realize that profits could be made through a connection with the underworld. A banker named Jean-Yves Grégoire said he was very reluctant to accept the post of manager at a Bank of Montreal branch favoured by the Montreal underworld.

GRÉGOIRE: It was known at the bank that 637 Decarie was the Mafia branch.
PROBE: When you say at the bank, you mean the employees and officials of the Bank of Montreal?
GRÉGOIRE: That's right.

Grégoire's testimony was confirmed by one of his superiors at the Bank of Montreal who gave his testimony behind closed doors to protect his identity.

PROBE: And the branch at 637 Decarie, it was whose branch?
BANKER: It was Obront's and his gang.
PROBE: Was this generally known, let's say within...Bank of Montreal circles?
BANKER: Everybody knew about it.
PROBE: Within the bank?
BANKER: Absolutely...

Grégoire said he had told his head office about his concerns that the bank was helping fund loan-sharking, which preyed on low-income people who had scant hope of gaining credit through regular channels. In effect, the bank was playing both sides against the middle. Poor people turned to loan-sharks because they were denied credit from the same banks that encouraged loan-sharks through generous lines of credit. While certain of the "Mafia branch's" customers lacked honesty, they had plenty of money and a certain sense of humour. Phony names were signed to cheques deposited into their accounts: "Simon Templar," a dashing character on the television series *The Saint;* "Judge Marc Codeau," a commissioner with the crime inquiry; and "Pierre Trudeau," the prime minister.

Vic Cotroni and Paolo Violi tried to halt the crime inquiry with judiciously-placed bribes. But times had changed since the 1940s and 1950s. While politicians and police could still be bought, they could no longer be purchased by the dozen, and the probe pressed ahead. Nonetheless, Obront appeared confident on May 27, 1976, when he peered over his glasses at commission chairman Judge Jean (Bulldog) Dutil and announced, "I refuse to be sworn in." His lawyer, Claude-Armand Sheppard, told the commission that Obront had been illegally spirited from Costa Rica: "In fact, he was the victim of a scandalous kidnapping." The Bulldog bit back by sentencing Obront to a year in jail for contempt.

A year behind bars later, Obront was given a second chance to testify. This time, his voice was shaky. But, again, he refused to answer questions. "I don't know why you called me here. I don't feel like I'm a witness. I'm an accused. All the one-sided stories you get here, that's not justice."

His lawyer, Michel Proulx, made a dramatic, passionate plea for mercy. "You have his head. What do you want? Why do you still wish to threaten him?"

Obront was sentenced to a second year in jail for contempt, which was to be served after he completed a four-year sentence for defrauding Obie's Meat Market and its creditors of $515,991. Obront's twenty-two-year-old son, Alan, protested that his father had suffered unusually cruel treatment at the maximum-security Laval Institute: "He's living in a small cell with no windows and a pan on the floor for a toilet. He spends twenty-three-and-a-half hours a day in his cell. He has absolutely no contact with people and his meals are passed through a little slit in the door. And he doesn't even see the guard who feeds him. It's torture. There's no excuse for it for a man charged with a white-collar crime."

Just a few years ago, the Cotroni mob had sneered at the crime commissions. Now police had been able to take down Obront, a man who was intelligent, discreet and well connected politically: a sign that challenging times were ahead for Vic Cotroni.

Chapter Thirteen

Sneak Attack

"I check you out and you're a good boy."
— Paolo Violi praises a young man
who rents an apartment over
his headquarters

Vic Cotroni's and Paolo Violi's most dangerous enemy of the mid-1970s wasn't Nick Rizzuto or the French-Canadian bikers, but a bespectacled loner named Bob Wilson who ran a tiny firm called ACME Electronics. Wilson showed up at Violi's office after Violi advertised that there was a vacancy in the apartment above the ice-cream parlour and coffee shop that doubled as his crime headquarters. Paolo Violi had never really stopped being the poor young man who escaped the hills of Calabria, and he couldn't pass up a chance to make money, however little. Despite the vast amounts he made through extortion, securities fraud and ice cream, Violi wasn't about to miss the opportunity to make a bit more each month in rent.

When Wilson and an attractive blonde woman entered Violi's ice-cream bar on Jean-Talon East to answer the apartment advertisement, everybody stopped what they were doing and stared. The reaction was based partly on a natural suspicion of outsiders, partly in appreciation of the appearance of Wilson's female companion. Violi sat Buddha-like at the back of his ice-cream bar, flanked by bodyguards. The newcomers sat in the opposite corner, and for the next few hours they haggled over the cost of rent for the apartment.

Violi tried to remove himself from the dickering by using a third party to act as an intermediary, relaying offers and counter-offers across the shop. The couple apparently did not know the landlord's identity. They did not seem afraid to argue with him over the rent, although it was impossible for them not to notice Violi's piercing eyes or the reverential treatment he received. Finally, a deal was reached. The rent would be $125 a month. For a long time, whenever Wilson walked through the gelateria, voices dropped and suspicious eyes followed him. Then, two years later, a chance encounter at a neighbourhood pizzeria helped thaw the relationship between landlord and tenant. It was after six in the evening, and Wilson was hungry when he stopped by to order a small pizza to go.

"Hey, Wilson, come here," someone called.

It was Violi, who was enjoying wine and pizza in the company of two of his bodyguards.

"Hi, Mr. Violi, how are you doing?"

"Come over here."

"I'll be over in a second. I want to order a pizza."

"Come over here!"

Wilson obeyed, noting his landlord was tipsy and, for a change, loquacious. The restaurant's owner also visited the Violi table, wringing his hands, bowing and scraping in respect or, perhaps more accurately, fear.

"Sit down. Have some wine," Violi commanded his tenant.

"No, I don't drink. I just finished work and I'm tired."

"Have a drink!"

"No, I don't drink."

"Have a Coke."

"Ya, that I'll have."

Wilson was uncomfortable. His landlord hadn't spoken to him for two years.

"How do you like the apartment?"

"I like it."

"Is there anything…?"

"Well, I wonder, could I paint the apartment?"

"Sure."

"Are you going to give me money for paint?"

"Buy your paint and we'll deduct it off the rent."

"Fair enough. You buy the paint and I'll supply the paint and the painter."

"Okay, have some pizza."

"No, I just ordered one. I want to eat it upstairs."

The mild rebuff pleased Violi.

"You know what I like about you? You're not nosy. You don't hang around my gelateria and sniff around. And you're a hard-working boy. I check you out and you're a good boy."

Wilson rose from the table and went to collect his pizza. Violi had no idea that Bob Wilson was really Bob Menard, a Montreal police undercover officer who had electronically bugged Violi's headquarters. (Before his career was over, Menard acquired seventeen separate sets of identification and a pronounced limp from three near-fatal, close-range rifle blasts.)

Imagine Gene Hackman with twelve cups of coffee in his system and you have got a pretty good picture of Bob Menard. You would never catch Menard saying he liked Paolo Violi, although it is clear he had a certain respect for him. We are all defined to some extent by our enemies, and if you're a street cop like Bob Menard, it's far better to match wits with the likes of Vic Cotroni and Paolo Violi than to spend time with drugged low-lifes like those who blasted Menard in the leg in a botched bank robbery. Menard could scarcely contain his contempt when he tried to compare the old Mafia order of Montreal with homegrown bank robbers. He pointed to mug-shots of the Québécois bank robbers who shot him. "Look in their eyes. What do you see? You see hatred. You see no fucking soul. You know what I see? I see animal."

Violi's eyes were threatening, but in a colder, more businesslike way. They weren't clouded by chemicals or superfluous emotions.Instead they displayed what Menard described as "intelligence but ruthlessness. Total ruthlessness. Paolo would kill but he'd do it in a much more intelligent way... You want to know the difference? They [bank robbers] will kill you indiscriminately, for no reason, while Paolo would kill you if he had to for power and for position and for advantage. That's the difference. ...They'll [French-Canadian bank robbers] kill because they don't like you having a toothpick in your mouth. That's the difference here. Goddamn animals. Nothing else... Paolo will use killing as a means to an end, a method. If you kill someone that you're trying to gather money from — unless you want to use him as an example — what the hell's the use of killing a source of revenue?...That's not businesslike. Real smart guys don't kill until it absolutely has to be done."

When Violi commented that he had "checked out" Menard, he

was likely referring to the minor criminal record the Montreal police had created for Menard's fake police file.

Figuring it was wise to leave well-enough alone, Menard reached for his wallet to pay for his pizza. The owner had seen Menard's conversation with Violi, and he refused to accept the money.

Violi and Menard moved on to polite speaking terms as Violi acknowledged Menard's presence. Violi's men followed their leader's cue and began to relax around the seemingly dull-witted Ontarian. Menard felt fewer eyes follow him as he walked through the building.

The relationship took another step forward when Menard discarded his battered old car. He asked Violi for a loan to buy a new one. Violi reached into his pocket and peeled off a wad of ten $100 (U.S.) bills. Menard took the money to police headquarters, but a check with the FBI turned up no known criminal history to the bills. Another check showed they weren't counterfeit. Menard deliberately stalled on repaying the loan, hoping to catch Violi on loan-sharking, but Violi stayed cool and made no hostile demands for repayment. He also refused to take interest on the loan, although he happily accepted a bottle of expensive cognac.

Menard learned this was routine behaviour for Violi. He was supremely conscious of his image in the community and often was willing to forgo a profit in order to create a debt, which he could cash in for favours in the future. He was a soft touch when neighbourhood kids hinted they would like a free ice cream, and he forbade any swearing in front of youngsters. He was also confident enough to give a St. Leonard businessman a blank cheque and allow him to estimate what he thought Violi owed him. Violi frequently played the role of mediator in a string of neighbourhood problems ranging from personal conflicts to business disagreements. Never was Violi's authority to act as judge questioned, and never, ever — not even once — did anyone raise his voice to him.

Violi's face was a common sight in the neighbourhood press. Photos were taken of him donating money to community events like bicycle races. These favours were returned in small and large ways. Menard noted it was impossible for a reporter or police officer — with the notable exception of himself — to get within a few blocks of the gelateria without word being relayed to Violi. In classic mafioso fashion, Violi could package himself both as a problem and as the solution to the problem. Some things that happened left Mario Latraverse, the head of the Montreal police anti-gang squad, shaking his head. "Loads of times, Violi was in his office [and] some Italian merchant would come in, with no problem in the world. But he would come into his office and say, 'Look, Mr. Violi, I know who you are. I need a special favor from you.'

"And then Violi would use the situation and say, 'Okay, you won't have any problems, nothing to worry. But it will cost you such and such.' The guy was looking to pay...he was looking for a protector and Paolo would seize the opportunity and start collecting from this guy.'"

Violi put in twelve-hour work-days, mostly at the gelateria, dividing his time among visitors who ranged from the powerless to the fearsome. Menard recalls how Violi was treated by neighbourhood people: "There was some fear. He was like the don. He was like the godfather. I can remember some old people going over and kissing his hand... I guess [it was] a mark of respect. He was always bowed to. I'm not saying it was grandiose. It was little things. Little things. They'd go up and shake hands and bow a little bit. Just a tiny nod of the head, but you could see it, if you looked for that sort of stuff."

Guests included Violi's in-laws, the Luppinos of Hamilton, and Bill Bonanno, son of aging American don Joseph (Joe Bananas) Bonanno. Menard recalls, "There would always be some big cars from the States and there would always be somebody there. All the time. It was like a parade. It was like a doctor's office with patients. You know, he'd be receiving in the afternoons. A car from New York. A car from New Jersey. A car from Ontario. God, all kinds of big, huge cars. They'd be parked. The guys would come in. Sometimes he'd greet them at the door. And they'd be on their way after a bit."

Menard quietly took in the sights from his balcony, sipping coffee and making a record of licence-plate numbers. He didn't have to eavesdrop on Violi, since that was being done electronically through a bug in the leg of his chest of drawers. "After a while, I became part of the woodwork," he recalls.

Menard had to pass certain tests before he was allowed to fade into that woodwork. The gangster checked his new car for a telltale identification number Montreal police had on all their cars. But the number had been expertly filed away. Menard was also certain his room was searched. Violi once called on Menard, who claimed to be an electrician, to fix a light that wasn't working.

"I didn't know the first thing about being an electrician," he recalls. "So, I delayed the job until the following morning by telling him I didn't have my tools."

He rushed out and got a quick electronics course that evening. "I was nervous, especially after I had inspected the wiring and connections and found nothing wrong. But the damn light still wouldn't work." Violi held the ladder as Menard sweated, fumbled and worried that his cover was blown. Then the undercover officer had a revelation. "It should have occurred to me before to check the lightbulb, and as it turned out, the bulb was burned out. I was relieved, but Paolo must have been thinking I wasn't very good because I did everything backwards."

Saturday mornings were quiet times at the coffee bar. Menard and Violi often sat together on the front steps and discussed everything except organized crime. Menard made it a policy to never discuss anything Violi had not previously mentioned, and the mafioso made a point not to discuss crime. Their conversations were in English, and often became spirited when they discussed politics and, in particular, the changes René Lévesque planned to bring to the province. Like many other immigrants of his generation, Violi resented the Quebec nationalists' push to educate the immigrants' children in French. The residents of St. Leonard were a minority within a minority, and many felt they were made scapegoats for Québécois frustrations and muted ambitions. Rioting broke out when the St. Leonard school board tried to phase out English-language education in the late 1960s. When some English-language educators in the district received death threats, Violi fought back by placing carloads of bodyguards around-the-clock at the door of at least one English-language instructor until tensions cooled.

Menard had an insider's view of separatist politics: he had infiltrated a radical separatist cell in the early 1960s. For that disguise, Menard ate rice, lost weight, listened to jazz and read volumes of Baudelaire. "I hate that fucking stuff," he says of the poetry.

Violi's distaste for the politics of separatism was far stronger. "God, he hated the PQ party!" Menard recalls, laughing at the fury of Violi's political rants. "I think he hated them more than the cops. He just hated them! He thought they were destroying Canada… He was very nationalistic. He spoke English a lot."

The strain on Menard was inevitable. What was originally planned as a two- or three-month operation stretched on for years. The assignment meant he missed the birth of his son, and his wife was left to raise their family alone. He would steal some time on weekends to see her, and occasionally he visited at night. But he had to return early to avoid being spotted by Violi's sentinels who worked at a neighboring gas station. On snowy mornings, Menard had to allow time for the hood of his car to cool. Then he'd sprinkle it with snow to mask his absence. And whenever Menard ventured out of the apartment, there was the omnipresent fear that he'd be spotted by another policeman and referred to as Bob Menard rather than Bob Wilson. He realized a slip-up or a betrayal meant he could be shot, while success for Menard would mean disaster for the Cotroni empire.

Things were even worse for the blonde posing as his wife. She was a civilian volunteer, this being before the days when the force sought female officers. She had a real-life boyfriend, but seldom saw him. Understandably, her nerves became frayed and finally she had to leave the project. This event evoked a particularly fine piece of acting from Menard who feigned drunkenness and told Violi a depressing tale of bitterness and woe, of how his wife had walked out on him for another man. Later, other women were brought in for short sojourns so that Violi would think that the depression hadn't rendered his upstairs tenant non-functional.

Chapter Fourteen

Paolo Exposed

"Paolo Violi is a thousand men."
— Underworld member describes
the power of Paolo Violi

T he mid-1970s were rough years for Vic Cotroni and his crime
family. He had hoped to transfer power slowly to the younger,
healthier Paolo Violi. Instead he found his organization under siege from police commission hearings and going through an
assortment of trials. The Cotroni crime family knew they were in
trouble but did not know how bad things were. Soon they would
learn about the Menard undercover operation and about a vast range
of related wiretapping operations. Suddenly Cotroni businesses and
lives would be laid bare and vulnerable.

The police commission called Vic Cotroni to the stand before it
called Violi, and he took 1,078 pages of testimony to say absolutely
nothing beyond an admission that he sometimes got his hair cut at a
tiny barber shop on Guy Street. Vic Cotroni was as impassive as
the Sphinx and acted only marginally more intelligent, hoping the
trouble would pass if he sat still and gave away nothing. Commission lawyer Guy Dupre referred to a lengthy list of dates from wiretapped conversations but could pry no information from the small,
sullen man. Cotroni said he couldn't understand wiretapped conversations in which he and his younger brother Giuseppe talked
about financial dealings with a Quebec cabinet minister. Vic

Cotroni said he was baffled by a tape taken from his meat-packing plant in which he suggested that an underling fabricate a police-corruption story and implicate members of the Quebec Liberal Party. He went blank when asked if he had suggested someone "break the legs" of a maker of spicy Italian sausages who refused to raise his prices. He flat-out denied the testimony of one of his underlings that he tried to frame a police inspector in order to undermine Jean Drapeau's crime drive in the late 1950s. Dupre kept reading names and dates and Vic Cotroni remained impassive, professing ignorance. "I have no authority... There were no meetings. These people are simply friends." But, when it was suggested that he was acting dumb, Cotroni snapped to attention and bristled, glaring at Dupre and asking, "Do I look like a dummy?"

Cotroni's 1974 testimony brought him a one-year contempt sentence. During the crisis, Paolo Violi looked to Brooklyn for help, evidence that his dreams of breaking away and setting up an independent crime family had not yet materialized. Violi sent his associate, Pietro Sciara, to the Bonanno family headquarters in Brooklyn, asking the New Yorkers to send up an assistant to "help control" his Montreal soldiers. Violi also needed confirmation that he was the boss of the Montreal underworld. To Sciara, he said, "Tell them that when Vincenzo went to jail, he didn't have a chance to talk to anyone, to give them the responsibility [for the Montreal family] and that I've taken the responsibility... Someone had to."

Paolo Violi was the next centre of attention at the crime probe, and things looked even worse for him than for Vic Cotroni, thanks to the Menard bug. A mystery witness, hidden from sight behind a canvas screen, told the inquiry how the spumoni-vendor was an "all-powerful God. Paolo Violi is 1,000 men." The comments were backed in Violi's own words, recorded in confidential police reports. In them, Violi was quoted as saying twenty-five crime family members reported directly to him, and another thousand were employed by family businesses.

The mystery witness was described by inquiry lawyer Pierre Paradis as "well-placed in the underworld." His voice was distorted to prevent anyone divining his identity and, as an added precaution, journalists were forbidden to record it. The witness explained that the Cotroni family was still a branch plant controlled by New York. The crime inquiry was told that Violi had contacts in New York

City, Buffalo, Toronto and Italy and that Violi "sometimes gets orders from out of town" but that he also had enough authority to command some outside gangsters. A tape from Menard's bugging operation underscored Violi's international connections. In it, Violi spoke with a man who was going to Italy on "business." The man was arrested in Italy shortly afterwards for the murder of a provincial attorney general there.

The probe was also told that Violi's authority extended to municipal politics. Frank Tutino, an independent candidate in a municipal election in St. Leonard in 1974, said he was threatened repeatedly after announcing that he was running for alderman. Tutino said that Violi's adviser, Pietro Sciara, cryptically told him that "...I was exposing myself to danger." Shortly before the balloting, Tutino said he went to Violi's Reggio Bar to meet Sciara and Violi, whom he hadn't met before. Violi was upset, Tutino recalled, asking, "how come he wasn't informed that I was running for election? I said if I had known I needed permission, I would have asked, but now it was too late."

Violi's attitude wasn't that of an outlaw, but rather that of an indignant lawmaker. His life was, in fact, regulated by unwritten codes more confining than any laws ever written in Ottawa, and the intensity of his rages seemed almost biblical, if one can forget that at their core was greed — both for respect and for money. Violi decreed that the proper and honourable thing was for Tutino to withdraw from the race; Violi agreed to reimburse his election expenses. But Tutino called his candidacy a matter of principle. Violi was outraged.

"He spoke about my family," Tutino recalled. "I understood I was playing with fire. I understood my candidacy had upset someone." Tutino braved the campaign, but notified police and hired private guards to protect his family. While his courage was commendable, he finished last in the three-candidate race.

The inquiry also heard the fate of a St. Leonard businessman who dared to try to open a poolroom within 400 feet of the Reggio Bar. Mauro Marchettini was told by Francesco Violi that he could expect to have few customers. In the underworld, there were some who feared Francesco even more than his older brother Paolo. Francesco Violi had his older brother's broad, powerful face, but Francesco's eyes were deeper, darker and wilder.

But Marchettini, unable to break his five-year lease, soldiered on, even when all his suppliers but Coca-Cola stopped making deliveries. His partner sought out Pep Cotroni's son-in-law, Tony Masserelli, to try to reach some sort of accord with the Violis. A meeting was arranged, but Francesco Violi drove the business-man to an abandoned building in St. Michel and demanded once again that the poolroom not be opened. Marchettini tried to ex-plain about the lease, and Francesco Violi turned ugly.

"Franco...began slapping me in the face," Marchettini said. "He did it in a very calm way, without too much force. All the while he was giving me advice about how I shouldn't open there. Then he started hitting me on the shoulders with a four-foot-long stick used to mix ice cream. And he kicked me in the face. I was bleeding from the mouth and I had a broken tooth and both eyes were blackened."

Francesco Violi returned Marchettini to the new poolroom, where Masserelli was waiting. Masserelli bought the bar from the owner and released Marchettini from his lease. Thus he freed the Violis of any threat of competition in the espresso and ice-cream trade.

Slowly Violi's image was changing from that of St. Leonard strongman to neighbourhood bully. It was a dangerous shift for Violi, but one he was powerless to stop. Another crime-probe wit-ness, whose identity was also hidden, told of being forced at gun-point in the basement of the Reggio Bar to sign over protection money to Violi: "I was suffering. We were making sacrifices, my wife more than I. Sometimes there were days when we had nothing to eat. I didn't want to sign them [the cheques]. Paolo had a cigar in his mouth. He told me: 'Sign.' I cried like a child. I had worked on my business for fifteen years and they ate it all." The businessman made a desperate plea for mercy, pretending he had children when in fact he was childless: "I was crying. I said, 'Paolo, I've got kids, like you. My kids have the right to live like yours!'" Violi was un-moved and the man's business soon collapsed.

Another businessman told how Paolo Violi visited him in 1971, promising to take care of all his problems. Lino Simaglia, who ran a north-end food-packaging firm with his brother, said he had no particular problems at the time, and understood Violi's message to mean, "I would be allowed to continue to 'pack' under my name." In effect Violi was selling the immigrant brothers protection against himself. Violi set the fee for his "service" at $2,000 annually, but, being a reasonable man, allowed Lino Simaglia to negotiate him down to $1,000.

"At Christmas, Violi called saying I had to give him a gift...

$1,000 in cash," Lino Simaglia recalled. "My business wasn't that good. I couldn't afford to pay my debts or buy Christmas presents for my wife and children."

Simaglia's brother Quinto told of the frustrations of having to abide by the laws of two forms of government, that of the state and that of Violi: "We pay $1,000 to have peace at work, not to come to court... We're not General Foods. We're just a little company and we're trying to build it up."

Perhaps the testimony that hurt Violi's reputation the most came from his own ranks. Two of his young soldiers told how they would steal wedding presents while the bride and groom were at church.

"We mostly did Italian weddings," Peter Bianco admitted. "We cleaned out the house while the people were at the church." Bianco tried to downplay Violi's role in the thefts but was contradicted by a tape from Menard's bug which caught Violi chastising Bianco and his partner, Tony Teoli. Violi verbally lashed the twosome for slacking off for three days, calling them a "pair of no-goods" who had brought him "nothing but cheap stuff." Then he told the young thieves about a neighbour who left town each weekend, and suggested his home might be easy pickings.

Violi was brought down by his own bragging as much as by his greed. Menard's bug recorded him boasting to Vic Cotroni of an attack on a man who had threatened to murder Violi in 1973. Laughing like a schoolboy, Violi told Cotroni that he had shot the man as he lay sleeping: "I shot the asshole three times. The papers didn't say so but I'm telling you it was me, with another soldier, who went into the apartment. He was sleeping and boom, boom, I shot him three times." The tape captured Violi bemoaning the fact the victim wasn't killed, adding, "They say he's...still got two [bullets in the head] and they can't get them out...but he'll remain crippled... It's worse than being dead." Violi went on to complain that his 9-millimetre handgun was too small, and that he'd prefer a .22-calibre pistol. "Those damned pieces are so hard to find, so could you find me some?"

"I can find you a couple," Cotroni replied.

Police knew Violi was lying to Vic Cotroni on the tape, says former Montreal anti-gang police officer Mario Latraverse. "We know that Paolo was lying when he said that. We know because we have other conversations that prove that...he was trying to impress Vic."

Violi was caught in a double bind. He could either be misrepresented as shooting a sleeping man, or straighten things out and be exposed as a braggart. He chose to be portrayed as brutal rather than as a blowhard. But he still looked foolish. Menard's undercover work threatened to topple Violi by undermining the respect he commanded. A tape made from Menard's bug on December 5, 1973, showed that Violi was totally unaware of the fact that his organization had been penetrated. He ridiculed the inquiry, saying, "They're running around, butting in, and their balls are in an uproar because they don't know anything."

At the crime probe, Violi was silent. He sat on the stand, looking like a proud Roman emperor. He carried a considerable girth on his stocky frame. While the weight bothered him, its effect was to make him look powerful, not flabby. He ran through a range of facial expressions and hand gestures but, like Vic Cotroni before him, refused to say anything of substance, choosing instead a year in jail on a contempt charge. "I don't refuse to testify, but I have absolutely nothing to say to this court," Violi said.

A Reggio Bar employee, Vincenzo DeSantis, took the same tack. Breaking laws of fashion as well as of the state, DeSantis wore a purple velvet suit and two-tone green-and-black shoes to the commission where he announced he wouldn't testify because the inquiry "discriminates against the Italians and we French Canadians."

Judge Jean Dutil wasn't impressed by the speech of the silver-haired DeSantis, known in the north end as "Jimmy Rent-A-Gun," saying the inquiry was trying to "free the Italian community from this small band which holds it hostage." Like Violi, DeSantis was sentenced to a year behind bars for contempt.

Paolo Violi's legal woes weren't confined to the crime commission. He was arrested in late November 1975 while dining in the outdoor café of a hotel in downtown Toronto, a favourite spot of his where he was known to tip bellhops generously. That afternoon he sat with his Montreal lawyer, Maurice Hébert, and his brother-in-law, John Luppino of Hamilton. The charge was conspiracy to commit grievous assault while mediating a neighbourhood dispute in the summer of 1972, and it was just one more worry for a man already under considerable stress.

The Violi party grumbled at the timing of the arrest, since he wasn't even allowed to complete his repast. He was led from the dinner table in handcuffs somewhere between the entrée and dessert. Police allowed him to shed the handcuffs for the flight home. A bomb threat that delayed the flight seemed an omen of trouble to come.

Violi had anticipated legal woes for his group. Earlier in 1975, he had called for a special Mafia defence fund to handle legal bills, but it's not known if he was successful in setting up the plan. Violi thought it was beneath the family's dignity to pass a hat to handle the legal bills for Frank Cotroni's cocaine-smuggling trial.

"Vincenzo never did it before," Violi told Vic Cotroni and associate Joe DiMaulo. "But now we have to do it because every family everywhere has a bankroll. No matter what happens to us or to the family, we've got to have money ready for that. Nobody can say they never made a cent out of family matters, so they can't refuse to pay to the bankroll."

A month before Violi's arrest in Toronto, he had had to appear before a Superior Court justice to appeal a one-year jail term and $25,000 fine for conspiring to manipulate Buffalo Oil and Gas stock on the Canadian Stock Exchange. The case showed the dangers of dealing with non-Italians, unschooled in the ways of *omertà,* or silence. One of Violi's accomplices, an American fugitive named James Danielson, gave a full confession to police, exposing Violi as what Sessions Court Judge D. Reilly Watson called the "essential personage in the conspiracy." It wasn't Violi's first foray into the world of stock manipulation. He and Vic Cotroni had a profitable racket involving "boiler room" stock salesmen — con men who used high-pressure tactics to sell worthless stocks. Violi and Cotroni had been extorting salesmen in Montreal and Toronto and profiting from their services, secure in the knowledge the criminals wouldn't run to police for help. In the Buffalo Oil and Gas case, Judge Watson hadn't been impressed when Violi described incriminating entries in a notebook as "formula for ice cream."

"This is virtually an insult," the judge replied.

With that, Vic Cotroni's heir apparent was dispatched to jail to begin a one-year term for conspiring to rig stock prices. And, more important, the aura of power surrounding Violi was further stripped away, something not lost on his murderous rivals.

Chapter Fifteen

Nabbed

*"Compare, be aware that we don't
like crooked things."*
— Paolo Violi

V
ic Cotroni didn't look like a man to be feared when he presented himself at a Toronto courtroom in the fall of 1976
complaining of a urinary-tract infection, diabetes, hyper-
tension, spinal arthritis, cardiac enlargement, coronary thrombosis,
myocardial infarction, iritis in both eyes, angina, swollen ankles
and a rectal polyp. As Italian Mafia expert Vincenzo Macri notes,
debilitating illnesses arising during court cases are a time-honoured
tradition of Vic Cotroni's crime society: "No prominent Mafia boss
is without his sheaf of impressive-looking medical documents, con-
firming that he suffers from very serious illnesses — illnesses that
prevent him travelling to the place where he is supposed to be held
in detention, or coping with the rigors of...imprisonment, or attending a court hearing. In most cases, the illnesses are either non-exis-
tent, or they are common ailments (such as arthritis, diabetes, or
liver disorders) which suddenly become severe. ...Several Mafia
bosses have been suffering for years from incurable diseases, according to their medical certificates: we must expect their imminent
demise."

But even mob bosses cannot intimidate germs and aging, and
there is reason to believe Vic Cotroni really was sick, although

probably not as sick as his portfolio of medical documents suggested.

The ailing Cotroni faced charges stemming from what police codenamed "Operation Benoit." Montreal police wiretaps had recorded an extortion plot involving Cotroni, Paolo Violi, Hamilton mobster John Papalia, and Sheldon Swartz of Toronto. As he went to face charges, Cotroni appeared so frail that police had to help him out of a squad car at police headquarters in Toronto.

The trial centred on charges by Toronto money-lender Stanley Bader that he became involved in a $300,000 extortion payoff in 1973 because he believed that the Cotronis had a contract out on him to be beaten. This contract, John Papalia told him, would leave him so injured he would never work again. But Bader soon came to believe that he was actually the victim of a swindle by his close friend and fellow loan-shark, Sheldon Swartz. Cotroni and Violi were not the authors of the hoax, but they also were not about to let an opportunity pass them by. They demanded a cut of the profits because their crime family's fearsome reputation was the main reason Bader turned over the money.

Cotroni and Violi were incensed to learn that Papalia had approached someone and threatened, "If you don't pay the people from Montreal...they will put you away."

A wiretapped conversation from April 30, 1974, in Calabrese, at Cotroni's place of business, Reggio Foods at 10090 Paris Street in Montreal, picked up Cotroni and Violi planning their strategy for extracting a cut of the money. In typical mafioso fashion, Violi wouldn't let the slightest insult go unanswered, nor would he pass up a chance to make a profit.

> VIOLI: We will tell [Papalia], "Look here, Johnny. You don't use our name for this type of thing.
> COTRONI: He already knows that.
> VIOLI: "You, Johnny, know these things, that you have to work all together, but instead you did it alone. You used our names. Didn't you want us to be friends? Bring the one hundred and fifty thousand and no one will know anything."

Later that day, the microphone in Bob Menard's apartment overheard a conversation in Calabrese and English from the Reggio Bar.

COTRONI: I don't want chicken feed. Let's talk. He wasn't
talking for me... He said the people in Montreal played dirty...
VIOLI: We'd better try it, or else we will not get anything.
COTRONI: So he has to give one hundred and fifty?
VIOLI: Eh, no, oh, yes…half.
COTRONI: Half.
VIOLI: Half.
COTRONI: Because he used your name, *compare.*

Later that day, in the Reggio Bar, the two Montrealers confronted
Papalia, who protested that he only made $40,000 out of the scam.
The meek tone of Papalia's comments made it clear who was considered the lowest in stature of the threesome. The Cotronis may not
have broken free of the Bonannos, but they were clearly big enough
to scare Papalia, widely considered Ontario's top mafioso.

PAPALIA: He's got two-sixty. Believe me. If he took three hun-
dred, he's got two-sixty.
COTRONI: Yeah! But you see the guy, he gonna say, "I gave
this money to Johnny."
PAPALIA: He can say he gave it to Jesus Christ! I don't care
what he says. He didn't give it to me, Vic.
COTRONI: Let's hope because, eh, we'll kill you.
PAPALIA: I know you'll kill me, Vic. I believe you'll kill me...
I'll tell him in my own way. In my own backyard. Not up here,
Vic.
COTRONI: This way, we never, we never reach that guy.
PAPALIA: Then you come, you come to Toronto then.
VIOLI: Any place. As long as we gonna straight up this things
[sic].

But on May 13, 1974, the Montrealers still hadn't gotten what
they considered to be their money. A conversation at Reggio Foods,
in Calabrese, was punctuated by a loud banging, as apparently Violi
lost control of his emotions and pounded wildly on furniture. He
considered his name almost as a tangible commodity, like a handgun, and threatened dire consequences to those who dared use it
without authorization or due payment.

COTRONI: You'll have to say to him, "Johnny, you walk but
walk a bit more straight." That's all.

VIOLI: No. No. I say to him, *"Compare,* be aware that we don't like crooked things. Besides our friendship, and what we say, we respect each other. But with us you have to come straight. This guy made use of our name. He is close to you. And this guy gave him the money because he made use of our name, and that he's supposed to bring it to you and you're supposed to bring it to us. Now this guy got the money...we want." Yes! I'll tell him, we want our share, if this guy is with you. If he is not with you then you leave it in my hands. I'll tell him, and I will look after it myself with this guy.

COTRONI: Eh, no. We could get him. We could get him ourselves... If that guy starts to scream, when you start to talk, you tell him, "Here. We have to talk. But very slowly and not loud."

VIOLI: Yes. Yes. Don't worry.

COTRONI: You tell these things to Johnny. You tell him, "Here, it's not a question of one trying to scare the other." Here, we will talk slowly, slowly... This is an easy fuck, you see.

John Papalia was a particularly vulgar and edgy man, even for his chosen line of work, and his nerves were particularly bad on the final day of the trial. Montreal police anti-gang head Mario Latraverse was on the witness stand that morning. During a break, Papalia and another man followed Latraverse to the men's room and started to insult him. Latraverse recalls replying, "You fucking bastard. You might be King Shit here but you're not going to run me around."

At this point, Vic Cotroni's son-in-law, Tino Baldelli, entered the men's room and tried to mollify things by saying, "No, no, no, Mr. Latraverse."

The altercation ended for the moment. But during the next recess, it was Latravese who followed Papalia into the men's room. Latraverse recalls, "I closed the door and I said, 'You want to do something about it? There's only the two of us now.' And he backed down." When Latraverse left the toilet, he was approached by Vic Cotroni. "Mr. Latraverse, I just found out what happened," Cotroni said. "Don't worry about it. I'll talk to him. I know you're a gentleman and he's not going to treat you like that."

Vic Cotroni might have been physically frail, but his family name and connections radiated power, and Papalia didn't utter another rude peep to the detective. But during the lunch break, Papalia vented his frustrations on a CBC cameraman who was photographing the

Hamilton hood and his entourage for the *Connections* series on organized crime. Papalia was perfect for television, dressing the part of a B-movie hoodlum in a shiny suit, fedora and wraparound sunglasses.

"You fucking degenerate motherfucker!" Papalia told the cameraman. "Drop the camera and come with me alone, you cocksucker, bastard! I'll tear your fucking eyes out of your head, you degenerate, you, you...go suck your mother's cunt, you cocksucker!"

At a loss for something even more vile to say, the little hood spat at the lensman, and then wound down his soliloquy with one final "Cocksucker!"

A Papalia underling, even less articulate, then delivered a vicious kick to the photographer.

Presumably Papalia was in an uglier mood later that day, when Mr. Justice Peter Wright passed judgement. The judge told the foursome he was disgusted; he called the evidence "grim and appalling" and "about as bad as it can be." Wright continued, "Nor do I detect any real hope for the rehabilitation of any of you, or any remorse. You are hardened and successful criminals. You have lived on the terror and fear and vices of others. You have used the weapons of threat and extortion in a section of society in which murder and violence are the servants of greed and power."

Wright sentenced each of the accused to six years in prison.

Paolo Violi and Vic Cotroni had their convictions overturned on appeal after serving only six months. For his part, Stanley Bader fled to Florida and appeared to be turning his life around as an executive in a firm that dealt in precious gems. But around two in the morning of March 16, 1982, he was shot dead answering the door of his luxury townhouse. Earlier that year he had received a string of threatening phone calls, including one that warned, "Look over your shoulder. You won't live out the week... This is in revenge for five years ago."

Chapter Sixteen

Paolo Hunted

*"The church is here to care for
everyone in death."*
— A priest at the church of
Vic Cotroni and Paolo Violi

Paolo Violi had a reputation for his intense rages, but when he learned of Bob Menard's deception, police heard that he smiled faintly and shrugged. Some of Violi's top soldiers pressed Vic Cotroni to have Menard killed as an example and to restore some of the honour lost by the deception. Vic Cotroni's reaction was a simple, "Ask Paolo," and Violi's response was, surprisingly, not one of rage but one of respect; what one might expect from a coach for the spirited performance of an athlete on an opposing and triumphant team.

"He's a stand-up guy," Violi told Reggio Bar regulars, then added, "He's a better fucking soldier than the rest of you."

Violi must have realized that things could have been worse. When Menard left St. Leonard, he told Violi he was heading to Ontario because he was sick of the rising tide of Quebec nationalism. Violi could appreciate the sentiment and volunteered to put him in touch with his in-laws, the Luppinos of Hamilton, saying, "They'll take care of you."

But, to the undercover officer's eternal frustration, police decided it was time to wrap up Menard's operation. Violi must have felt at least some relief that his in-laws were not also in danger.

Violi had obeyed the code of silence and refused to testify before the Quebec police crime commission, but it wasn't nearly enough to restore his former position of respect. The wiretap conversations had shown that Violi didn't measure up to the traditional Mafia standards of leadership. He was clearly a braggart and was indiscreet. Perhaps worst of all, he showed himself to be a petty criminal who didn't balk at having his soldiers steal from Little Italy brides as he attended their weddings, a man whose actions deprived St. Leonard children of gifts at Christmas.

Loss of respect carried with it physical consequences. Now the Calabrese and others around him were vulnerable to attack from the Sicilian flank of the Cotroni organization whose ambitions had been previously suppressed. Violi granted Menard a reprieve, but there were doubts that Violi's underworld confrères would be so forgiving of Violi.

Violi's adviser, Pietro Sciara, chose Valentine's Day, 1976, to take his wife to see the Italian-language version of *The Godfather,* a feel-good movie for mobsters with its depiction of heroism and old values amidst a corrupt world. Even though Sciara was Sicilian, he and Violi were so close that Violi called him "Uncle Petrino." The two men were drawn together and to crime for the power, not the money, as Violi explained in a taped conversation. "Uncle Petrino, we're here to do the thinking, to arrange things for this one and that one...and our job all the time is to straighten things out."

The tiny north-end theatre featuring *The Godfather* was owned by Vic Cotroni's sister, Palmina Puliafito. Accessible from all directions, it sat in the shadow of a major overpass and beside an equally busy underpass. When Sciara left the theatre arm-in-arm with his wife, they were approached by a man whose face was hidden by a hood. Sciara had a second, perhaps two, before he was knocked out of his wife's arms by the force of a 12-gauge shotgun blast. It was a stylized Mafia execution worthy of the prose of Mario Puzo, and it ended Sciara's life in its sixty-first year with suddeness and irony. Back in the 1960s in his native Italy, Sciara had been sentenced to preventative detention on an island after being found to be a member of the Mafia under Italian anti-Mafia laws. To the end, Sciara remained loyal to Mafia codes such as *omertà,* or silence, even when the results were patently absurd. Just two months before his stylized murder, Sciara testified in Italian at the Quebec crime commission that he didn't know the meaning of either "Mafia" or "anti-Mafia."

There are two possible explanations for "Uncle Petrino's" murder. The first stems from rumours that he talked behind closed doors to the crime probe. This suspicion arose from the fact that although he was sentenced to fifteen months in jail for being illegally in Canada, he wasn't kept in jail. Or was Sciara's murder part of something much bigger: the opening volley in a war against Paolo Violi himself? Violi must have at least considered the possibility. He knew he was vulnerable, and there were certainly those in the Sicilian wing of the Cotroni family who would have liked to see him dead.

But there was no sign that Sciara's murder frightened Violi's brother Francesco. He was apparently alone in his office at Violi Importing and Distributing Co. Ltd. at 11530-4th Avenue in the industrial section of Rivière des Prairies on February 8, 1977. Francesco was talking on the phone when the man on the other end of the line heard what sounded like gunshots. Next there was the sound of footsteps running away, and then there was nothing at all. Police found Francesco's body sprawled on his office floor. They speculated that at least two hitmen were involved, since he had been caught with a shotgun blast to the face and revolver shots to the body.

The theory that Paolo Violi was targeted for murder grew in credibility. If there was a hit planned against Paolo, it was logical to kill Francesco first. "[Francesco Violi] had the mean streak in him," says former Montreal anti-gang squad head Mario Latraverse. Adds Detective Sergeant Normand Ostiguy of the anti-gang squad: "He was even worse than Paolo... He would do anything."

When he heard the news of his brother's death, Paolo Violi was behind bars serving a contempt term for refusing to testify at the crime probe and awaiting his sentence in the Bader extortion case. His grief must have been mixed with at least some fear, but he took pride in denying such emotions. A photo taken at the time shows him lounging in his cabana suit beside a jailhouse pool, flanked by grinning cohorts. Days in jail were spent sipping smuggled cognac, enjoying the company of many of his associates, directing his business operations, and corresponding daily with his wife, Grazia. They had been married a decade now, but Violi still appeared lovestruck. He sent her hundreds of letters, sometimes writing her five times a day. Sometimes the beautifully scripted missives were in verse, and often their borders were adorned with sketches of hearts and flowers and birds. Grazia pasted them into a scrapbook and marvelled at how he kept his poise. Later she told journalist Ann Charney,

"When I visited him in prison, he always cheered me up. He didn't want me to worry... He treated me like I was his baby."

But nights, when the shadows merged, were different. Violi knew this was the time when killers preferred to do their grim chores. Word was that he was allowed to lock his own cell from the inside. A Mafia associate recalled, "You know, Paolo Violi, that was a guy who was afraid of everybody inside the jail. He was afraid somebody was going to kill him all the time. During the day he was happy. He sees the night coming, he's afraid. You know in jail you got no trouble during the daytime. The trouble is at night."

When Paolo Violi was freed from jail that fall, it was no secret on the street that there was an open contract on his head, with amounts of up to $50,000 mentioned to police. A more nervous, less proud man would have escaped north Montreal, but Paolo Violi would have rather died in his world than flee it. Certainly Nick Rizzuto had quickly left for Venezuela after Violi had made it clear he wanted the Sicilian dead. But Paolo Violi was uncharacteristically passive, and there was no counteroffensive against the Sicilians, the most obvious suspects in the murders. His organization had splintered into factions while Violi was in jail. And in the words of one police officer, "The protection was off him."

But even if it meant the difference between life and death, Violi refused to seek police help. "He did not cooperate with us and we did not offer him any form of physical protection if he cooperated," a police official said. "He made it clear to us that he was not interested in helping."

Paolo Violi kept going to his regular haunts: his ice-cream parlour and Violi Importing, which he ran with his brother Rocco. He also frequently visited his old espresso bar adjoining the ice-cream parlour, which he had recently sold to the Sicilian Randisi brothers, Giuseppe and Vincenzo. The Randisis were no strangers to Violi's world as their father, Giuseppe, was a reputed mafioso who had recently been deported from Canada. The Randisis' was the type of place where a man could be shot in the face in a roomful of regular customers and police would have little hope of finding a witness. Violi felt comfortable there.

Police began to hear reports that three men had been hired to commit a murder, and they trailed Montreal Sicilians who they suspected were mob killers. But on January 22, 1978, after three weeks of continual surveillance, police took the day off. A ranking officer later explained: "The policemen were to resume the surveillance

Monday morning on several suspects we had information were hired to kill someone. We decided to give the men a day off because they were tired and it looked as if nothing would happen. We took a chance."

Paolo Violi got a call that evening at his home, inviting him to a card party at the Randisis'. He left. Then, just before 7:30, he called his wife, Grazia, telling her he'd be home soon for supper. At 7:32 p.m., his back was to the door as he played cards. Vincenzo Randisi was at the table, while Giuseppe Randisi tended bar. Two armed men wearing ski masks walked through the back door. "Everyone on the floor," one of them ordered. They seemed to know their way around the coffee bar, fuelling the theory that they had been hiding in the basement. The dozen or so customers dived for cover under pool tables, all except Paolo Violi. A gunman levelled a .12-guage shotgun at the back of Violi's head and squeezed the trigger, ending the mobster's life in its forty-seventh year. A second blast into the top of his head followed an instant later, but its purpose was merely symbolic. Paolo Violi's anguished wait was over.

Grazia got another phone call a few minutes after the murder. She was told there was trouble at the espresso bar but was given no details. When she raced to the Randisis', she found her way blocked by police cars and officers. She went home and sat by the window of her white brick house into the early hours of the morning before she was told that her husband would never come home again.

When Bob Menard heard the news, he was jolted but not surprised. He knew that Violi's drop in status had made the mobster a liability, and that liabilities weren't taken lightly in the world of Paolo Violi. Menard also knew that his undercover work played an indirect role in making the killing possible. "I was shocked," he said. "Not sad, but shocked." Menard's voice rises in protest at the suggestion Violi would have been wise to flee Montreal and set up operations elsewhere or turn himself in to the police: "Paolo was not a runner. Paolo was not the type who would run away from anything. He was going to weasel to the cops? Ha! You've got to be kidding. Ha! Paolo weasel to the cops? Not when your balls turn to brick... Not Paolo. Never!... He's just not the type. To him, honour, that was it. I'm not glorifying the sonofabitch. I'm just saying that was the way he was."

The murder also shook Vic Cotroni. Weeks later, he was still holed up in his luxury retreat in Lavaltrie, apparently in mourning, while also taking extra precautions to protect his life. The murder had been a blunt reminder that anyone can be murdered and that one's chances of being shot rise with the length of time one has spent in the Mafia. There had been a rumour that Vic Cotroni might even have ordered the hit, that the aging gangster wasn't ready to give up power yet and considered Violi a liability. More likely, he knew of the plot and gave his grudging approval, knowing a refusal might add his name to the assassin's hit list. Vic Cotroni was not one to buck New York, and any hit on Violi had to be sanctioned from the United States.

"If he look[s] the other way, then he himself is finished. He winds up a nothing," says a police officer who specializes in the Mafia.

There were thirty-one black Cadillacs carrying flowers worth an estimated $18,000 at Violi's funeral, a sign of strong respect and, in some cases, even love. By 9:00 a.m., police had to take special crowd-control measures and block off side-streets. Some of the three hundred ornate tributes had been ordered in the United States; one was signed, "Naples, Italy." One was from Carmine Galante; others were from small business people of St. Leonard. A wreath from his father depicted a huge clock with its hands set at 7:32, the instant of his murder.

By north-end Mafia standards, the funeral was impressive if not spectacular. Mafia funerals were a time-honoured gauge of a man's power and respect. Francesco Violi's body had drawn twenty-six flower-bearing funeral cars; Louis Greco's impressive entourage had been estimated at between thirty-five and forty. The pomp standard by which neighbourhood funerals were judged was set by Vic Cotroni's mother, whose death was marked by a procession of more than sixty flower cars.

Violi's body was carried in an iron and bronze casket worth $3,000 to Madonna della Difesa Church, where he had attended mass about once a month. But the north-end church — which can seat a thousand people beneath a giant ceiling fresco that includes Mussolini on horseback a few feet from Pope Pius XI — was only half-filled with the grief-strickened and the curious. About a dozen young men tried to keep the press out of the ceremony as three priests celebrated requiem high mass backed by a seven-man choir.

"This is not a public place today. It's for the family," an usher told a journalist as he escorted him to the street.

While the flowers were impressive, the mourners were not. There were no top-level mafiosi from the United States, a reminder of Violi's failure to make as strong ties to the United States as to Italy, a factor that helped explain Violi's current condition. High-ranking mafiosi from Toronto, Hamilton, Detroit and Buffalo had been spotted at Dorval Airport and throughout the week at the funeral home where the body lay. But few mobsters of significance were sighted at the funeral. Naturally, Violi's father-in-law, Giacomo Luppino, rushed from Hamilton to Montreal with his family by plane the morning after the slaying. And Violi's old associate, Mike Racco of Toronto's Siderno group, was seen trying to shield his face from camera lenses as he left the funeral home. With him was Cosimo Stalteri, a Toronto-area resident wanted for questioning in Italy for murder. Frank Sylvestro of Guelph was there, although police noted that he tried to disguise his visit and make it appear that he was in town to watch a hockey game. Notably spurning the opportunity to pay respects to Violi were leading members of the Montreal Italian community from organizations such as the Sons of Italy, the National Congress of Italian Canadians and the Federation of Italian Canadians. Said one neighbourhood observer, "This guy's brother even had more cards. Besides, you can tell there are no bosses, there's nobody important here. Everybody's running around. There's no control like there usually is." Through all the commotion, it did not go unnoticed that Vic Cotroni attended the funeral, but did not sit with the Violi family.

What the funeral lacked in gangsters, it more than made up for in photographers from the Montreal police force, the Quebec Provincial Police, the RCMP and the Canadian Immigration department. They tried half-heartedly to pass themselves off as members of the working press, wearing snowmobile suits and ski clothes, but at least one camera still bore the marking "C Division Training." Most of the police photographers shared sidewalk space with more than sixty journalists and technicians, although photographers were grandly perched on a cherry-picker crane, which hoisted them high above the snowy procession. Police used third-floor windows of a nearby school for high-angle still and movie shots. The spectacle was too much for a resident of the Italian quarter in a nearby espresso bar who told a reporter, "You guys are going crazy with this guy. He was a bad man, but there are lots of bad men. The only time you go crazy is when it's a bad Italian who dies and then you make it seem like all Italians are like the one who dies. But he's dead. Why don't you let him go?"

Anonymous callers claiming to be parishioners had jammed the church's phone line that week with questions like, "How can you bury a pig like that out of the Catholic church?" Father Marius De Santis's stock reply was, "I'll quote Christ to you: 'Let he without sin cast the first stone.' Who are you to judge? Judgment, the only one that counts, is given from upstairs. The church is here to care for everyone in death — whether it's you or Paolo Violi."

Violi's widow, Grazia, sat quietly through the forty-minute funeral mass, celebrated without a formal personal eulogy. But she lost her composure as she left the church. She was followed by her father-in-law, a cadaverous man with a skull-like face and burning black coals of eyes. He had made the same grim trip less than a year before for the funeral of his son Francesco. Paolo Violi's widow wept as she climbed into a black Cadillac, surrounded by gawking passers-by, and her condition had worsened by the time she arrived at Notre Dame des Neiges Cemetery. The sight of cameramen in the CBC crane proved too much for mourners at the gravesite, and several made menacing gestures with shovels.

The funeral had been a brave attempt at dignity, but had dissolved into violence — much like Paolo Violi's life.

Who would have had the nerve to shoot Paolo Violi dead? Who was confident enough to do this in St. Leonard and escape retribution? In Violi's prime, no one could get within a block of him without his knowing. On the streets, the shotgun blast that banished Paolo Violi from the world of the living was considered to be the sound of the normally quiet Sicilian arm of the Vic Cotroni organization asserting itself. Police considered the theory that Vic Cotroni's old benefactor, Carmine Galante, had ordered the hit from prison, considering Paolo Violi a liability after his crime-probe débâcle. But a stronger theory zeroed in on the Sicilian Nick Rizzuto, the loner Paolo Violi had wanted killed. That theory gained credibility when police started rounding up suspects. Two of them were related by marriage to Rizzuto, and soon the Sicilian's hand was seen by many to be everywhere behind the murder — everywhere except on the trigger.

Whoever was behind it, Paolo Violi would have approved of the style of the hit, if not its victim. It was done with respect both for planning and tradition — a classic Mafia murder for a man who fancied himself a classic mafioso. The murder weapon was a Zardini shotgun, made only in a small southern Italian village, with equally rare pellets, much larger than the standard shot sold in North America. The weapon was sawed off at the handle, giving it the feel of an oversized pistol, and its two short barrels were mounted one atop the other, rather than side-by-side, the style popular in North America. The lupara had been fired at close range by someone with nerve enough to walk right up to his victim, guaranteeing Violi's death while sparing bystanders.

Before Violi was buried, police arrested three Sicilian immigrants, two in their homes in St. Leonard and another in a nearby bar. They were previously unknown to authorities, although the family name of one of the accused, Agostino Cuntrera, would catch the attention of police over the next decade as power in the old Cotroni family shifted to its Sicilian wing. This transfer of power would bring Montreal more in line with New York, where Sicilians traditionally held an upper hand in the five major crime families.

Before the murder, police had watched the suspects meeting in their St. Leonard homes, in a nearby shopping centre and in a Mike's Submarines of which suspects Giovanni DiMora and Cuntrera were co-proprietors. Police noted with particular interest when the Sicilians visited the combination coffee bar and Italian social club that was Nick Rizzuto's haunt. The suspects were also observed in the neighbourhood of Vic Cotroni's daughter, Rosina Baldelli, with whom Cotroni had lived since his wife's recent death, and at Violi's old espresso bar on Jean-Talon East, now the property of the Sicilian Randisi brothers. Since Nick Rizzuto and Vincenzo Randisi were friends, police watched with particular interest when the three suspicious men repeatedly met with Vincenzo Randisi. At one point, the flurry of meetings was interrupted when police towed away the suspects' Econoline van for illegal parking.

The red Econoline had been rented by Dominico Manno under a false name, and when police peeked into it in late December 1977, they found a double-barrelled shotgun and an M-1 rifle, both of them sawed off. On December 29, police noted DiMora and Manno entering the Randisis' coffee bar by a rear exit, each carrying a plastic bag about the length of a rifle. Police trailed DiMora and noted that he and his associates drove the van to DiMora's car, boarded it, and then cruised slowly by Paolo Violi's home on Comtois Street.

By the time the Paolo Violi murder case got to court, one of the suspects, Nick Rizzuto's son-in-law Paolo Renda, had fled Montreal and was believed to be in Venezuela or Italy. DiMora glared straight ahead in the courthouse, refusing to be intimidated by gawkers and press cameras. DiMora looked the part of a hitman, with greasy hair slicked straight back and a ruddy face framed by unfashionably thick mutton chops. His body was that of a linebacker, although built on a smaller scale, and he exuded power even under his stormtrooper-length black leather coat. If looks could kill, DiMora would not have needed the Zardini. Manno and Cuntrera, on the other hand, looked more like victims, covering their faces with their hands and their leather jackets, and twisting away from prying eyes, like dogs cowering before being kicked. The fourth man, Vincenzo Randisi, was freed for lack of evidence.

The three suspects were allowed to plead guilty to plotting the killing rather than actually executing it, thus guarding the mystery of who fired the deadly blast with the Zardini. Presumably the Crown worried that it didn't have sufficient evidence for a murder conviction.

Mme. Justice Claire Barrette-Jones decided that, aside from their bloody indiscretion, the three authors of Violi's death were exemplary citizens: "They were model immigrants who performed the most modest tasks in an effort to earn a living and to slowly and laboriously build themselves a trade." DiMorra and Manno each got seven years in prison, while Cuntrera was sentenced to five years. The maximum sentence each faced was fourteen years and the Montreal *Gazette* exploded with indignation: "For society to let people off with punishment this light — under a seven-year term, a prisoner is eligible for parole after just two years — is almost to sanction the planning of executions... All his adult life, Paolo Violi worked to undermine respect for the law. Now, even in death, it would appear that he has accomplished the same."

Four Violi boys had emigrated to Canada in the 1950s. Now three of them lay together in Notre Dame des Neiges Cemetery, under a marble arch decorated by a bird of prey standing guard over statues of two angels and Jesus. Two had been murdered, the other killed in a car accident. Only Rocco Violi remained, and he was not considered a major player in the underworld. But he was still a Violi, and he must have worried that his brothers' killers would want to complete the job. There is no record of his thoughts on a July afternoon in 1980 when a motorcyclist pulled up alongside his old grey Oldsmobile at a red light at the corner of Pascal Gagnon Boulevard and Paul-Emile Gamache Street. The biker drew a sawed-off shotgun from his leather jacket and fired a blast at Violi. It missed, and Violi raced away. But before he reached the next intersection, he was trapped again. This time, the gunman caught him in the head.

Miraculously, Rocco Violi survived, despite twelve pellets in the head and a badly injured left eye. If he felt the need to run or hide or talk to police, he didn't show it, protesting that he didn't want uniformed policemen guarding his room at Maisonneuve Hospital. And Rocco Violi refused to help police catch the men who were trying to kill him. As an investigator said, "He's not a very talkative person... at least he isn't with us."

Three months went by with no further attacks, and the crisis seemed to have passed. Then, on October 17, 1980, Rocco Violi sat reading a newspaper in the kitchen of his St. Leonard duplex on Houel Street with his two sons. Suddenly he slumped over, hit by a single shot from a high-powered rifle which left a small, clean but fatal hole. The killer had been perched on the third floor of a nearby commercial building, and he left the .308-calibre Remington with a telescopic lens on the floor of the building, along with a napkin that presumably had been used to wipe away fingerprints.

The murder resembled a political assassination, not a Mafia hit. But then, no one had called Rocco Violi a Mafia don. There was no torture, no proximity to the victim, no regard for the fact that his sons had to watch the slaughter.

There was still no effort by those close to Rocco Violi to help police, something the victim would have understood. "We're getting very little cooperation," an investigator said. "They don't co-operate with the police very much."

Rocco Violi was buried with his brothers at Notre Dame des Neiges Cemetery after a quiet Latin mass at Notre Dame della Difesa Church, where he had attended daily services. Only invited friends were allowed to view the body at the Alfred Dallaire Funeral Home on Jean-Talon East.

Then, at the last minute, the time of the funeral service was moved ahead thirty minutes to 9:30 a.m., apparently to shake off spectators. An imposing man was stationed by the door to keep gawkers at bay. The flower procession was a relatively modest fourteen Cadillacs. No underworld notables attended, although one wreath bore the name of Joe Bonanno, in gratitude for the Violis' hospitality when Bonanno was in Canada in the mid-1960s.

Despite the tribute from Bonanno, the Violis had lacked Vic Cotroni's tight tie to the United States, and in the end they died because of it. Paolo Violi had privately groused that Vic Cotroni should have broken out from under his American bosses, but now all the Violi brothers were dead, while aging Vic Cotroni was being pushed back to power. Vic Cotroni was proven right, but there is no sign that he was gloating.

It was the fourth time Domenico Violi was allowed north from Parma, Ohio, to bury a son. The elder Violi, who had been twice deported from Canada in the early 1920s, was given until nightfall to bury the last of a generation of Violi men in the soil of their new country.

Chapter Seventeen

Carmine's Last Kick

"Between you and me,
all I do is grow tomatoes."
— Carmine Galante

We return now to Carmine (Mr. Lilo) Galante, the intense little man with the smouldering cigar and the flaming ambition who gave Vic Cotroni his link to the big-time underworld of New York City back in the 1950s. Two decades later, Carmine Galante was preparing to burst back into his old world. He had been granted parole for the final years of his twenty-year sentence for heroin-trafficking. To Vic Cotroni, a renewed Carmine Galante was good news. His northern fortunes, shaken with the murder of Paolo Violi and the rise of the Sicilians, needed a boost.

Some might argue that Carmine Galante never really left his old world during his years in Lewisburg. The dirty grey prison, set in what was once the heart of Pennsylvania coal-mining country, was nicknamed "the country club." Its G Block maximum-security wing was called "Mafia Row." There, fresh meats and tasty cheeses were stashed in false ceilings, and for thirty dollars a pint obliging guards would smuggle in Scotch. Galante sat alone at the top of Mafia Row, decreeing there would be no fights, drunkenness or arguments in his presence. If he heard angry words, he'd march over to the offending parties, his cigar in his mouth, and give each combatant a minute to state his argument. Then Galante would close the case for good by turning to one party and ruling, "You're right, he's wrong."

"The warden ruled nothing — Lilo did," mobster Vincent Teresa explained. "At the snap of his finger, he could have turned that prison into a battlefield. Instead he was Mr. Law and Order."

The most privileged prisoners were invited to dine with Galante in "Club Lewisburg," where they played cards, ate steak and sipped spirits stored in after-shave bottles. To determine if a new prisoner was worthy of his company, Galante would drop names of underworld notables, and if the newcomer feigned ignorance, he passed Galante's test for discretion. Those he deigned to speak with included Jimmy Hoffa, president of the International Brotherhood of Teamsters union, behind bars for attempting to bribe a juror in an extortion trial and for misappropriating $1.7 million in union funds. Brash young John Gotti also impressed Galante who attempted to recruit Gotti into the Bonanno group only to be told, "John belongs to Neill" — a reference to Aniello Dellacroce, an underboss in the rival Gambino family. Also enjoying the cheeses and rarefied Mafia company of G Block was Vic Cotroni's younger brother Frank, serving his sentence for cocaine-smuggling and broadening his business connections.

Throughout his years in prison, Galante remained a fierce Bonanno loyalist. He quivered with fury whenever he spoke of Carlo Gambino, the benign-looking, little man with a weak heart who was New York's most powerful Mafia leader. Galante reasoned that Gambino was to blame for the mob's decline in strength since the late 1950s. Gambino had discouraged drug-trafficking, thinking it would ultimately destroy the crime network. Drugs brought with them heavy prison sentences, which increased the chances of informers in the mob's midst. Gambino also froze mob-membership ranks in an effort to prevent police infiltration. But these moves only caused young criminals to look away from the mob and toward the huge expanding open market for narcotics. The crime organization found itself undercut by the very young hoods who could have offered the new blood it badly needed.

Galante wanted to change all this, and he was determined not to atrophy while he waited for his change. In Lewisburg, he kept his squat body trim with regular handball games and bragged, "When I get out, I'm going to make Carlo Gambino shit in the middle of Times Square."

Finally, in 1974, Galante was eligible for parole, which sent ambitious members of the Bonanno family scurrying off in search of fine Cuban cigars to give him as a coming-out present.

Before Galante could carry out his grand plans for expansion, he needed to win back power within the Bonanno family. Blocking his way to the top of the family was Phil (Rusty) Rastelli, who didn't want to step aside but well knew the consequences of angering Galante's group. Years before, in 1962, Rastelli's wife, Connie, was furious at Rastelli for having an affair with a younger woman and sought her revenge by talking to police. Initially ignored, she captured police attention when she supplied the address at which a star federal witness was being hidden in preparation for the trial of Big John Ormento, the same trial that sent Galante to prison. Ormento told her to stop talking, but Connie Rastelli ignored him. Shortly afterwards, she was shot dead.

Perhaps these events were on Phil Rastelli's mind when his son-in-law was gunned down shortly after Galante got out of prison. Rastelli quickly stepped aside, making room at the top for Galante. Galante sought to re-establish old Mafia codes of loyalty and discipline in the Bonanno group, then the weakest of New York's five families, with an estimated 250 members, including the Cotronis, and 180 associates. The role of the Cotronis was to handle heroin brought in from Europe as the old French Connection was reopened. Galante also sought a west-coast beachhead for shipments from Southeast Asia, and he looked for links with South American suppliers. To this end, he allied himself with members of the Genovese and Lucchese crime families. The goal was to improve North American distribution and corner the market from Montreal to Mexico City.

All this activity boded poorly for existing drug-traffickers who didn't get out of his way — for example, Carmine Consalvo and his brother Frank. Carmine Consalvo's heroin network had made him a millionaire by age thirty-nine, and he saw no need for Galante. When he was found under the window of his luxury twenty-fourth-floor apartment in Fort Lee, New Jersey, no one in the underworld believed the police conclusion that it was suicide. Frank Consalvo, a bodyguard for Gambino's underboss, Aniello (Mr. Neil) Dellacroce, vowed revenge. Soon after, he plunged to his death from the roof of a tenement in Little Italy, completing what the tabloid press dubbed "The Case of the Flying Consalvos."

By police count, at least forty other drug-traffickers were murdered as Galante waged war to regain turf lost to black and Hispanic dealers in Harlem, Bedford-Stuyvesant, the Bronx, Newark and Jersey City. He also gained control of family operations for booking and numbers in Brooklyn, Long Island and New Jersey, as well as total control of myriad semi-legitimate and legitimate family enterprises, like loan-sharking, extortion, labour racketeering, garment and trucking firms, restaurants, bars and a Wisconsin cheese company.

Galante moved quietly, since he was on parole until 1981, and police could easily yank him back to jail before then. He travelled with bodyguards but carried no gun, and his dress was often unassuming to the point of sloppiness. While he owned tailored suits, he walked about Greenwich Village in an undershirt, his pants held up by rope. He never discussed business over the phone or in his flat in an ordinary-looking brick apartment house on Waverly Place in Greenwich Village. Business calls were made from phone booths and nothing of importance was ever put in writing. His fear that he was under constant surveillance was a potent brew of paranoia and reality — he was frequently under surveillance by the Drug Enforcement Agency; the FBI; and the narcotics, intelligence and organized-crime divisions of the New York Police Department.

Police were watching as Galante was chauffeured around town in different limousines, none of them registered to him. Sometimes it was the gold Cadillac belonging to his daughter who was so quick with the accelerator and deft with the steering wheel that it was rumoured that Galante had dreams she would someday become a member of the Mafia. Police watched the father and daughter make frequent trips to the East 38th Street apartment of Ann Acquavella, Galante's mistress of twenty years and mother of two of his children. Like Vic Cotroni, Galante considered himself too staunch a Roman Catholic to divorce his wife. Police noted that Galante's favourite eatery was a bar-restaurant on the East River near the old Fulton Fish Market; that he selected his artichokes and tomatoes at Balducci's in Greenwich Village; that he enjoyed the wares of De Roberts pastry shop on First Avenue, the food of the *Tre Amici Ristorante* on Third Avenue, and the ambiance of the Crescent Lounge on Avenue U in Brooklyn. Law officials recorded the fact that Galante liked to jog along the East River near the United Nations Building and that he played handball at the YMCA. Police observed how he was treated in Little Italy, where he was ostensibly a salesman for the rundown L&T Cleaners on Elizabeth Street. Friends in Little Italy were permitted to lightly touch his arm, while the less intimate acknowledged his power with an almost imperceptible bow of the shoulders. Police wrote down the licence-plate numbers of the cars of visitors to his weekend retreat in Hampton Bays, New York, as well as the numbers of his favourite phone booths. Also duly recorded was the fact that the little mobster sometimes carried his own garbage bags to the curb. And in the fall of 1976, police noted with particular interest that Galante sent two associates to Montreal, presumably to meet with his old allies, the Cotronis.

Carmine Galante was spared the need to carry out his murderous threats against Carlo Gambino when the cunning mobster died of natural causes in bed in his waterfront compound in Long Island in the fall of 1976. With his death, the Gambino organization appeared vulnerable to Galante's assault, but Gambino's once-ferocious underboss Aniello Dellacroce thought differently. Dellacroce's name translates into English as "little lamb of the cross" — but there was nothing lamb-like about his methods or reputation. He took extreme pleasure in killing, and a federal agent said, "He likes to peer into a victim's face, like some kind of dark angel, at the moment of death."

He also enjoyed posing as a priest and calling himself Father O'Neil, a play on a common mispronunciation of his first name. Those around him were unnerved by his occasional practice of having a look-alike stand in for him in public.

At the same time that Father O'Neil was moving towards a bloody feud with Galante, Galante lost his parole for "associating with known criminals," and Dellacroce appealed to his fellow commissioners for a contract on Galante's head.

Killers from at least two families wanted the status that would come from the hit. *Time* magazine reported that, through his remarkable influence inside prisons, Galante was soon accompanied inside jail by armed Mafia triggermen, who stood guard outside his door through the night. When Galante was transferred to the medium-security federal prison in Danbury, Connecticut, the gunmen appeared to tuck Lilo in and guard his door. Wiretaps revealed that Galante's fears of being administered last rites by Father O'Neil weren't unfounded. A Manhattan probation officer warned the Danbury warden that he was told by "a highly reliable source that an attempt to murder Mr. Galante will be made in your institution."

Galante was sent into isolation, where he ate and exercised alone and refused to trust prison guards or even the prison chaplain. He felt safer on the streets. In a dizzying series of events, he was released by mistake, rejailed, and then re-released on bail.

In 1977, the FBI investigated a tip that Galante was targeted for murder by legendary mob money-mover, Meyer Lansky, and a year later, they checked out tips that there still was a contract out on Galante.

If Galante, then sixty-seven, was worried, he didn't let on when questioned by freelance journalist John J. Miller: "No one will ever kill me — they wouldn't dare. If they want to call me boss of bosses, that's all right. Between you and me, all I do is grow tomatoes."

Carmine Galante rode back into prominence in the underworld on the wave of "zips," new immigrants from Sicily who were imported because of a shortage of talent in the Italo-American underworld. Zips took their nickname from the quick way they spoke their native language. They moved equally swiftly in the drug underworld, and by the 1980s they controlled the largest share of the drug traffic between Sicily and North America. This was a different strain of mafiosi than what Galante had known when he was sent to prison in 1962. Greater money, or the *narcolire*, brought with it greater autonomy for Sicilian drug barons, along with enormous arrogance and violence. Blood begat blood, money begat money, and no one was safe.

On July 12, 1979, four days after his chat with Miller, Galante had a lunch date at Joe and Mary's Italian Restaurant in Brooklyn with his cousin, Giuseppe (Joe) Turano. Turano was preparing to leave for Sardinia for a holiday with his wife and daughter, and Galante dropped by his modest restaurant on Knickerbocker Avenue to eat a late lunch and say goodbye. It was considered safe turf for Galante and his clannish, secretive brigade of zips, some of whom had been smuggled into New York via Montreal. They were some of the meanest killers in the business, and Galante considered them his.

Galante was chauffeured to Joe and Mary's in a brown stretch Lincoln. He was delayed slightly by the driver of a grey Plymouth, who objected loudly when the Continental double-parked on Knickerbocker. "Hey, move that thing!" the Plymouth's driver shouted. Galante stepped out of the limo's back seat and the Plymouth driver instantly recognized the elderly, hawk-nosed passenger. "Forget it," the driver shouted as his foot hit the gas pedal.

Inside Joe and Mary's, Galante walked to the concrete patio, chatting briefly with Turano's mother, Constance, who sat crocheting under a painting of The Last Supper. He was met by two of his zips, Baldassare (Baldo) Amato and Cesare (Tall Guy) Bonventre, a cousin of Joe Bonanno. The two men wore leather jackets despite the warm July weather. Galante lunched on salad and red wine in the vine-covered courtyard, then began to enjoy a post-prandial cigar. Around 2:45 p.m., a long-time Bonanno family member known as Little Moe suddenly developed stomach pains and rushed out of Joe and Mary's, holding his midsection. "I have pains," he told Galante. "I don't feel good... I should go home."

He was right. Four hooded gunmen entered the restaurant. One intruder guarded the front room, cradling a black machine gun, while the other three marched onto the patio, carrying a pumpaction shotgun, a double-barrelled shotgun and automatic pistols. Turano's sixteen-year-old daughter, Constanza, was in the kitchen when she heard her father's voice asking, "What are you doing?" It was the last time she would hear him, as his question was answered with a volley of gunshots. A man at Galante's table had the back of his head blown off in a gust of double-O buckshot, and Galante was blown backwards off his chair by a twin blast from a shotgun. A gunman walked up to his body and put a .45-calibre bullet into his left eye. Galante's cigar remained clenched between his teeth, burning. The afternoon sun danced off his diamond pinky ring and his Cartier watch ticked on as the gunmen retreated into a blue Mercury. Galante's bodyguards went with them.

Later, on July 12, police observed a party at the Ravenite Social Club in the tenements of Little Italy, just a couple of blocks from the neighbourhood's restaurants, which were a tourist Mecca. Police believed that Galante's killers were among the celebrants, sharing goodwill with his so-called bodyguards. Galante's rival, Philip Rastelli, was in the Manhattan federal correctional centre that summer, but police noted that he had received a steady flow of visits from Bonanno family captains before and after the murder.

In a detective story, the killer is most likely the character you least suspect. But things aren't always so complicated in the underworld. Almost everyone at the Ravenite Social Club had a reason for killing Carmine Galante, and it was believed that a broad range of mobsters conspired against him. Even his old boss, Joe Bonanno, was said to be unhappy with Galante's tight-fisted, hyper-aggressive ways. Galante was shoving his way into Atlantic City casino operations, angering mob interests there.

Fanning the hostilities was Galante's recent emergence as something of a media star. The press attention reached a zenith in February 1977, with portraits of Galante in the *New York Times, Time,* the *New York Daily News* and the *New York Post.* The coverage had a basic theme: that Galante was hell-bent to be the boss of bosses in the Mafia. But Mafia writer Thomas Plate traces the explosion of stories to a government public-relations effort rather than to any machinations by Galante. The Unified Intelligence Division of the Drug Enforcement Agency was under review by the White House and was in danger of losing its funding. So the UID, which collected intelligence for police forces, drew up an impressive fifty-nine-page report called *Major Organized Crime Report Concerning Carmine Galante.* Galante was a fearsome and ambitious hood, but speculation was that the report targeted him because he was a hood the UID knew enough about to describe in detail. After the report was leaked to the media, Galante became an instant celebrity of sorts, and the UID's profile rose accordingly.

But secret FBI files show that Galante did not live up to his press clippings in the eyes of some authorities. A July 7, 1979, memo to the FBI's head office stated, "The press has reported that Galante was killed because he aspired to become Il Capo Di Tutti Capi [the boss of all bosses]... There has not been a boss of all bosses of the Mafia since Charles 'Lucky' Luciano abolished the position in 1931, and created the Ruling Commission. It is our belief that it would have been impossible for Galante to have recreated this position and he would not have attempted such."

The whole episode suggests Galante was a victim of empire-building, both inside and outside the mob.

In death, Galante was shunned by both the mob and the church. No underworld notables showed up at the Provenzano Lanza Funeral Home to pay their respects. Among the sparse gathering were his daughter Nina, his estranged wife and his lawyer, Roy Cohn, who had gained notoriety in the 1950s.

"Even his own people don't like him," a police officer said of Galante. "Funerals tell you a lot about wise guys, and this tells me that now he can't scare them anymore, they don't want nothing to do with him."

Criminals weren't the only ones who wanted nothing to do with Galante. The day before Galante was to be buried, Terence Cardinal Cooke announced, "The Archdiocese of New York cannot permit a public celebration of a funeral liturgy for the late Carmine Galante. We extend our sympathies to the family, but are not able to grant a liturgical service because of the scandal that would ensue."

The last time such an extraordinary denial was made was in 1957, when Albert (The Executioner) Anastasia of the Gambino family was shot dead in a barber's chair in the Park Sheraton Hotel in Manhattan.

Carmine Galante, who took from people all his life, was granted a final act of charity: Cooke permitted a priest to read prayers for him. Galante's daughter Nina wept as a priest sprinkled holy water on the bronze casket and said, "Our prayers are now ended. And we bid our last farewell. There is sadness in the parting, but we shall fill up with new hope, for one day we shall see our brother again and enjoy his love, by God's mercy. I leave the judgment to God."

Carmine Galante could have helped Vic Cotroni in the late 1970s, just as he had two decades before. Instead, Vic Cotroni had lost both his heir apparent, Paolo Violi, and his long-time benefactor, Galante. The Cotroni family was entering a new, violent age at a time when its leader, Vic Cotroni, looked old and vulnerable.

PART THREE

Upheaval

"Monopoly's moments — almost always produced and sustained by governments — would be fewer and shorter. Old dynasties would go down, and newer ones would be shorter lived. There would be less places to hide."
— Michael Bliss, *Northern Enterprise*

Chapter Eighteen

Enter the Eighties

*"You won't find him standing in line
at a manpower centre."*
— A police officer comments on Frank
Cotroni's release from prison

On April 25, 1979, when the youngest of the Cotroni brothers was released on parole after serving just a third of his
fifteen-year sentence for smuggling cocaine, he looked more
like a prince returning from the Crusades than a drug-trafficker
coming home from Lewisburg Prison's Mafia Row. His hair was
worn in a well-groomed, cavalier style, flowing halfway over his
ears. And his eyes shone even brighter than his perfect teeth as he
strode through Dorval Airport in Montreal, his New York lawyer,
John Iannuzzi, in tow. With his black fedora pulled rakishly low,
Iannuzzi looked as much the part of a mob leader as Frank Cotroni,
except that the grinning lawyer deferentially walked a half-step behind Cotroni so as not to block the microphones and camera angles
for press photographers. Cotroni looked more magisterial and less
threatening than he had in his younger days, when his thick hands
were never more than seconds away from a baseball bat or a revolver. Now he was playing the part of the returning saviour of the
Cotroni family name. And his powerful hands, highlighted by a
bullet-sized pinky ring, carried a briefcase and a non-fiction paper-
back on crime.

The procession wasn't just good for his ego. After five years between concrete walls in Lewisburg, he was also offering a blunt warning to the underworld: Frank's back!

The irony was that, before he left, Frank Cotroni had not been considered so noteworthy. He ran his drugs and nightclubs and an assortment of scams, but in those days, Vic Cotroni was the undisputed head of the family and Paolo Violi was the designated boss-in-waiting. From all accounts, at the time Frank Cotroni was happy enough with this scheme of things. But much had changed since he was packed off to Lewisburg. Violi now lay with his bothers in Notre Dame des Neiges Cemetery, a painful testament to the fact that the Calabrian side of the family had been overtaken by the Sicilians. Carmine Galante, who had done so much to tie the family to New York, was also a bloody memory. And Frank's older brothers, Vic and Pepe, were tired after decades of trials, tribulations and convictions.

When Frank Cotroni returned to Montreal, business monopolies, both inside and outside the law, were under siege. Family stability was not what it had been. Even inside the Mafia, that bastion of conservatism, there were divorces, and Frank Cotroni's marriage to Pauline Desormiers was on the rocks.

New business links were needed to the United States, especially since the murder of Galante earlier that year. Improved communications and travel meant the world was a smaller place. Frank Cotroni would have to cope with competition from halfway across the world if he wanted to be a success. Mobsters were looking far outside their old neighbourhoods and shifting from the false humility of men like Paolo Violi's father-in-law, Giacomo Luppino, to the greed and conspicuous consumption of carnivorous venture capitalists.

If Frank was going to succeed, he'd do so with a different style than that of his older brothers or Paolo Violi. It had always been a bit unfair to call him an Italian-style organized criminal, since he was born in Montreal and was a different, distinctly North American man. He had two nicknames on the street, one in French and one in Italian. He was both "Le Gros" — the Big Guy — and "Il Cice" — the tender, life-giving core at the centre of a hard nut. His face was more expressive than the taciturn Vic's was, and on April 25, 1979, he was decidedly happy, despite — or perhaps because of — the dangers and challenges that lay ahead.

There were dark whispers that Frank Cotroni had almost not made it to that joyful day. He had been let out early on parole because he was considered a model prisoner at Lewisburg. One police officer specializing in the Mafia said that Carmine Galante had considered him too much a model prisoner. Word reached jailers that a contract had been put out on Frank Cotroni's head. As the police Mafia expert said, "[Galante] thought that Frank was talking. They put him in protective custody and he said, 'Get me out of here. I'm not some goddamn stool pigeon.'" How things between the two men were resolved remains unclear to this day.

Prisoners leaving Lewisburg were entitled to $100 to help them make the switch to the outside world, but Frank Cotroni didn't bother to ask for the money. Somewhere between Lewisburg and Montreal, he had switched from the brown jacket and pants he had bought in a prison shop to a natty grey suit, with a metallic-grey cravat and crisp white shirt. Two cigars were stuck in the pocket of the coat jacket as a celebratory touch. Frank Cotroni was the first passenger to step off his Eastern Airlines flight from Philadelphia, flashing his teeth in a broad smile. True to his extroverted nature and the code of *omertà,* he waved at reporters and shook their hands, then refused to answer any questions as he was ushered into the back seat of a waiting blue-grey Cadillac.

"I don't know what his plans are," said the mobster's long-time lawyer, Sydney Leithman.

A policeman watching the spectacle added, "One thing is sure. You won't find him standing in line at a manpower centre."

Just five months after Frank Cotroni was released from Lewisburg, his older brother, Pep, died in hospital. Pep Cotroni had been sick a long time. He never really recovered from the years he spent in dank, primitive Stoney Mountain Penitentiary. Once freed, Pep Cotroni never played a top role in family enterprises, although he did keep his hand in extortion, narcotics, gambling, stolen securities and fraud. On the legitimate side, he had interests in a spaghetti house, as well as a company that supplied flour for pizza crusts. He was also a trustee of his mother-in-law's estate, conservatively estimated to be worth more than $500,000. Frank Cotroni is said to have looked up to Pep, so the death must have been painful. His other older brother, Vic, was also in declining health and remained in semi-retirement until his September 1984 death from cancer — another reminder of the declining strength of the Cotronis in the crime underworld.

At Frank Cotroni's side after his release was a vain, handsome, young French Canadian named Réal Simard. Simard fancied himself a yuppie who married an appreciation for the finer material things in life with a sensitivity that included a love for children and a fear of blood.

Others were less charitable, calling Simard a thug in designer clothes, both more violent and less disciplined than his boss.

Simard grew up near the St. Timothée Street rowhouses where the Cotroni empire began. He was the son of an alcoholic child-beater and nephew of Armand Courville, friend and partner-in-crime of Vic Cotroni. Although they didn't meet until later, Frank Cotroni was an impressive figure in Simard's eyes. He was easily the most handsome of the Cotroni brothers and was frequently seen in the city's best steakhouses and behind the wheel of his four-door Lincoln Continental, smoking fine cigars.

Simard served his crime apprenticeship with extortion, weapons offences, and a string of bank robberies, proudly acquiring a criminal record in the process. He displayed the need for a strong father figure, something he hadn't found at home. And when he met Frank Cotroni behind bars in the 1970s, Simard quickly announced that his uncle was Armand Courville.

Frank Cotroni took the twenty-two-year-old under his wing, allowing him sips of the fine cognac he'd had smuggled into the Parthenais detention centre in cigar tubes and counselling him that bank robberies were not a particularly lucrative form of crime. Frank Cotroni also offered Simard a job as driver. Being a chauffeur can put a criminal on the highway to rapid career advancement. Al Capone began his career as a driver for Johnny Torrio, and Carmine Galante was once a chauffeur for Joe Bonanno.

Naturally, Simard's good fortune attracted jealousy from Cotroni underlings who wondered how they could be bypassed for someone with no Italian blood. They were also nervous about outsiders. It's easy to be a mobster when things are going well, but non-Italians have a history of buckling and speaking to police when faced with serious prison time. Simard felt the resentment and relished it. For a man with his ego, being envied was worlds better than being ignored.

His job was to take Frank Cotroni from his Rosemount home to downtown hotels and restaurants where Cotroni would do business, sometimes stopping along the way for mundane chores such as picking up laundry. The mobster displayed little desire for banal conversation or any need to bounce ideas off Simard who would spend his time alone in bars, waiting for his master's next trip. Gradually, Cotroni conversed with him more and Simard relished a concomitant rise in respect. One night, as Simard piloted Cotroni's Lincoln through the darkness, Frank Cotroni turned to Simard and said, "Réal, I want you to make a big step." The direction of that big step was clear: Frank Cotroni wanted Réal Simard to become a killer. Soon, Cotroni was teaching him how to stalk a victim and an important but simple rule: "You never leave a body without giving it a bullet in the head."

Michel (Fatso) Marion was, at thirty-five years of age, a formidable man both in girth and reputation. He was a former associate of holdup-man and escape artist Richard (The Cat) Blass, who had been shot dead by police in a chalet in the Laurentians years before. Since Marion was believed to have murdered some Cotroni family friends, his slaying would serve as a calling-card of sorts for Frank Cotroni, announcing graphically that he was back on the streets and in a serious mood.

The fat man was eating breakfast in a diner in the Laurentian community of Ste. Adèle on January 18, 1980, his back to the window. He didn't notice when Simard calmly walked in and pulled out a revolver from inside a folded newspaper. Marion was probably dead before the third blast, which went to the head.

Simard would recall Cotroni behaving like a proud father that evening when they met for supper at a Ste. Adèle restaurant. "I'm so happy for you. You did a good job," the mobster said, cupping his powerful fingers around Simard's neck and kissing him on both cheeks.

Giuseppe (Joseph) Montegano should have been less of a challenge. A north-end cocaine dealer, he was accused of selling lowgrade cocaine to Frank Cotroni's sons, and it was rumoured that he had been too close to the rival Sicilians as well as an informer for police. Any hope Montegano might have had of living evaporated when he bragged that he made the young Cotronis snort his cocaine at gunpoint.

Simard's plan was to lure Montegano into the Agrigento Social Club, a private club on Belanger Street run by Frank Cotroni's son, Francesco. Then Simard would ambush Montegano and take him for a one-way car ride, since Frank Cotroni did not want blood inside his son's club. But inside the club, Montegano figured out the plot and bolted towards a window. Simard shot him dead, but this time it was a messy job.

Simard fretted, not for the loss of Montegano's life but because of the amateurish manner in which Montegano was dispatched from it. Frank Cotroni told Simard not to worry about police shutting down the bar, since the family had more such establishments, then again kissed him on both cheeks.

There would be more opportunities for Simard to perfect his bloody craft.

Chapter Nineteen

The Sicilian Threat

"Nick came back when
everybody was dead."
— Montreal police officer describes
the return of Nick Rizzuto
to Montreal

If you drive about a mile north of Montreal's old Bordeaux jail, near Gouin Boulevard, you'll find a neighbourhood of new Tudor-style mansions which one Montreal police officer describes as "bigger than our courthouse." This area was the epicentre of the explosion that was rocking Frank Cotroni's world as he tried to regain control of Montreal for the Cotroni family. Rather than win respect in their old neighbourhood through mediation, the Sicilians created a village of Italian marble and wrought iron within Montreal for themselves alone, separated from the old Italian community by expensive leaded glass and silence. In this well-heeled section of the city, one could find Vito Rizzuto, the basset hound-faced son of Nick Rizzuto, in a new, sprawling, cut-stone creation, a medieval fantasy run amuck in suburbia.

Two doors away lived Nick Rizzuto, the man believed by many to be Montreal's top Sicilian mafioso and the prime beneficiary and suspect in Paolo Violi's murder. Also in the neighborhood were a legion of others from Rizzuto's birthplace of Cattolica Eraclea, Sicily, some of whom had been photographed with Cesare (Tall Guy) Bonventre, the gaudy former bodyguard of Carmine Galante who was a key suspect in Galante's murder.

167

Gone were the days when neighbourhood mafiosi such as Violi mediated community disputes while parading as a living embodiment of manly honour. The Sicilian compound-dwellers were heavily into heroin-smuggling, an anti-social activity not designed to endear one to one's neighbours. "There's no link [with the old St. Leonard Italian community]," a police officer said. "They don't want to be touched by anyone. They don't want to see their pictures in the papers. They want to be forgotten."

Police sometimes like to compare fighting organized crime to squeezing a balloon; when you press hard in one spot, it pops up immediately somewhere else. The Sicilians rebounded in force shortly after Paolo Violi was murdered in January 1978. The Cuntrera-Caruana family, who operated quietly under Nick Rizzuto in the Sicilian wing of the Cotroni group, stepped up their operations, which stretched far beyond north Montreal, into New York, Switzerland, England and Venezuela, where they were said to enjoy particularly strong political connections. A few years later, when the Calabrian dominance had waned, Nick Rizzuto slipped back into Montreal.

"Nick came back when everybody was dead," said a Montreal police officer. Pino Arlacchi, an Italian Mafia expert and sociologist, said the fact the Sicilians hailed from minor centres helped them keep their profiles low. "There are other families that nobody pays attention to that internationally are incredibly relevant... But nobody pays attention to them."

The Cuntrera-Caruana group represented the new spirit in the Mafia. They took as their role-model the daring venture capitalists, and as their creed they adopted conspicuous consumption. They lived and travelled on a grandiose international scale, driving BMW 732i's and Mercedes-Benz 500SELs and owning English country mansions with names such as Broomfield Manor and The Hook. The children were kept away from the old neighborhood and attended well-heeled private schools such as Selwyn House with the offspring of more mainstream capitalists. As the 1980s progressed, the split between the Calabrians and Sicilians in Montreal became more definite, leaving the Cotronis prowling the old neighbourhood and downtown haunts, and the Sicilians behind the walls of their mansions, plotting international finance, fuelled by millions in heroin profits.

Police found the Sicilians harder to police than the Calabrians. They stuck to themselves, making it difficult to cultivate informers.

As Detective Sergeant Normand Ostiguy of the Montreal police antigang squad said, "It's getting harder and harder. They're all aware of our electronic devices now." Conversations were tough to decipher, even if intercepted, as people used codes, and referred to things such as "shirts" in place of "drugs." Ostiguy added, "And not only that. They go and take a walk and they talk with whomever they want to talk. They won't talk inside their office or inside their car. They know that we may be there, electronically speaking."

By the early 1980s, Frank Cotroni was hearing reports that one of his family's long-time money-launderers was working for both the Cotronis and rival Sicilians. Michel Corrado Celestino Pozza had been a confidant of Vic Cotroni's friend Louis Greco back when Montreal's Sicilian and Calabrian mobsters were able to work together under Vic Cotroni. Pozza was neither Calabrian nor Sicilian; he had been born in the northern Italian city of Trento, which perhaps explained why he felt no particular loyalty to either side in the feud. University-educated and respected for his first-class financial mind, Pozza was the mob equivalent of a brilliant civil servant, a man with a strong brain but no power base of his own. He had fallen into a swamp of personal gambling problems, but by the late 1970s, he had rebounded and was much — too much, in fact — in demand.

It's not known if the Cotronis were aware of the full scope of Pozza's manipulations. In 1979, Pozza had been a houseguest at the Sicilian seaside resort of Mondello with a major Palmero money-launderer. And on November 16, 1980, Pozza was in New York with three hundred other Sicilians to celebrate the wedding of Giuseppe (Pino) Bono, a portly, nondescript Mafia boss who had been the original heroin-supplier for Montreal's Sicilian Cuntrera-Caruana family, before they began dealing directly with Thai sources. Bono chose no less a site than St. Patrick's Cathedral for his nuptials with the daughter of a Queens pizzeria owner. The wedding was followed by a $64,000 reception at the luxurious Hotel Pierre. Among the guests who partook of fine Italian food and bottomless champagne supplies were Montrealers Nick Rizzuto and his son Vito, Joseph Lo Presti and top drug dealers from New York and Sicily. Like Rizzuto, Bono had transferred some of his operations to Venezuela in the 1970s.

Frank and Vic Cotroni may not have known this. Indeed, even experienced mafiosi must occasionally get confused by the complex webs of relationships and rivalries in the world. Theirs is a paranoid, insular world where rumours are widespread and potentially deadly. Whatever the Cotroni brothers thought they knew about Pozza distressed them greatly. They called a special meeting with Pozza to try to pull him onside, but they appear to have had little success. As he left the meeting, Frank Cotroni was said by police to have muttered to Simard that "something has to be done about him."

Michel Pozza's wife was out of town the night of September 17, 1982, when Simard shared a friendly drink with Pozza. The evening had seemed cordial enough, but the next morning, Simard was waiting outside the accountant's Mont Rolland home. He carried a .22-calibre pistol, having heard it does a victim more internal damage than his usual .38. Pozza had been under police surveillance because of his relationship with the International Ladies Garment Workers Union, but the watch had been called off because police were short of manpower.

When police arrived at Pozza's home, they found much more than Pozza's lifeless body. A search of his home and car revealed a secret Quebec government study on the possibility of legalized gambling in Quebec and phone numbers and addresses in Palermo, some bearing the name Ciancimino, the last name of one of Sicily's best-known politicians.

Vito Ciancimino had been a major power in Sicilian politics for half of his sixty years and had spoken out loudly against the Mafia while he was a senior Christian Democrat and mayor of Palermo. But he also played a central role in granting extremely lucrative building contracts and permits. While Ciancimino was mayor of Palermo in 1971 and 1972, some 4,000 building contracts were awarded; 2,500 of these went to three elderly pensioners who were fronts for Mafia firms. Naturally, people were suspicious. One suspicious person was Sicilian crime-fighting legend Giovanni Falcone who would soon be making a visit to Montreal.

Falcone was going to Canada partly because of Frank Cotroni's old associate, Tommaso Buscetta. Buscetta was in Brazil in 1982, grieving the disappearance of two of his sons and the death of his way of life. No one had to tell him that his boys were victims of the Mafia wars, grabbed up in Sicily because his enemies couldn't get to Buscetta himself. Eventually, fourteen of his family members would be killed in a vicious attempt to goad Buscetta back to Sicily to seek revenge.

Buscetta had allied himself with the wrong side in a bloody Mafia civil war that centred on control of the drug trade. Buscetta's fate was hitched to that of Gaetano Badalamenti, head of the Sicilian Mafia Commission from 1971 to 1978. Badalamenti was one of the men who met with Carmine Galante and Joe Bonanno in Palermo to reorganize the world's heroin trade several lifetimes ago. Buscetta lived in Toronto and Montreal in the late 1960s and early 1970s, then moved south to New York, first working as a construction labourer, then, in Little Italy, running pizza parlours said to be fronts for the drug trade. When he was arrested in New York in 1970 as an illegal alien, Buscetta fled to Brazil, and eventually became proprietor of a cocaine operation which he ran from his luxury villa (called *Rancho Alegre* or the Happy Ranch) near São Paulo,. Brazil had a large community of Calabrians, Sicilians and Corsicans, and shared 10,000 miles of frontier and unpoliced borders with the cocaine-producing mountain countries of Bolivia, Peru, Colombia and Paraguay.

Buscetta's grief that year led him to do an extraordinary thing, something he would have considered unthinkable a few years before; he decided to testify against the Mafia. Buscetta had had an exaggerated view of the Mafia as a second government, with its own sacred principles, which included sparing the wives and children of murder targets. Now this cosmos had been shattered, replaced by a bloody Hobbesian struggle where decisions were based solely on personal need and desire.

"I no longer recognize the Mafia," Buscetta said. "It's not the organization in which I spent my life. I now believe in justice and that is what I want to lend myself to."

Judge Giovanni Falcone of Sicily liked to paraphrase Shakespeare's *Julius Caesar* and say that, "The courageous only die once; the scared die a thousand times a day." Armed with seemingly impenetrable nerves, he had put at least eight hundred mafiosi behind bars. But he impressed interviewers as much with his good humour as with his courage. He managed to joke and wink frequently, something not expected of a man who had a standing contract out on his head and who had been the target of at least a half-dozen murder plots. His assassination was considered inevitable and Sicilians took bets on when the grisly deed would happen.

Naturally, it was under heavy guard that Falcone came to Canada in January 1985 to examine links between the murder of Cotroni money-launderer Michel Pozza and Buscetta's revelations. For three days, on the fifth floor of the *Palais de Justice* in Montreal, Falcone heard the testimony of more than a dozen witnesses, including bankers, notaries and Pozza's widow. The trip was part of an odyssey that brought Falcone from Sicily to the United States to Cotroni territory as he tried to build on Buscetta's massive catalogue of Mafia activity. The significance of Buscetta's information could be fathomed using Machiavellian logic, which Falcone prided himself on understanding.

"Do I have a recipe? I sure do," he said. "I am a Sicilian. Often I ask myself what I would do in the Mafia's place at this or that particular juncture. And I generally am right on target when I come up with an answer."

Canadian authorities studying the Pozza murder would note that Frank Cotroni wasn't the only one with a grudge against Pozza. Pozza had been investing millions of dollars in Quebec for former mayor Ciancimino, but had lost much of it, while at the same time profiting personally. Pozza had been a houseguest at Ciancimino's seaside resort near Palermo, but he apparently had not returned the hospitality. "He was charging them horrible [interest] rates," says a former Canadian police Mafia specialist.

For Frank Cotroni, the Pozza connections were a reminder of how claustrophobically small the world had become; and how violent the underworld remained. Pozza's murder did not solve Frank Cotroni's problems with the Sicilians; their north-south connections into New York were stronger than the power of any one individual, even one with a brain like that of Pozza. For Frank Cotroni, it was a good time to think like a Canadian nationalist and look west towards the growing financial power of Toronto.

Chapter Twenty

Toronto Bound

*"By far our biggest concern must be the
Cotroni family of Montreal."*
— Police intelligence report, 1983

W hen the bullet-torn body of Toronto mobster Paul Volpe
was found stuffed into the trunk of his wife's leased BMW
on November 14, 1983 at the Toronto International Airport, heads turned in the direction of the Cotronis. Cotroni family
hitman Réal Simard was prowling Toronto at the time, and it was
no secret that the family was interested in moving west. The
suspicious would recall that Frank Cotroni had said several times
in 1983 that he planned to move full-time to Toronto, and they
speculated that Volpe was murdered to clear the way. Improving
east-west ties was seen as one way the family could compensate
for its now-shaky connections with New York City.

Frank Cotroni had been heard to grumble more than once
that one of the few bad points about "Toronto the Good" was a
dearth of police officers on the take. Toronto had replaced Montreal
as Canada's largest city, with its growth accelerated by businesses
fleeing Quebec in the wake of the Parti Québécois election victory.
Cynics suggested that the Cotronis were escaping not just a bad
business climate, but the rival Sicilians of Nick Rizzuto as well.

Rumours reached Cecil Kirby, a killer for Toronto's Commisso
family, that Volpe's murder was ordered by Vic Cotroni. For a while,

Kirby and police believed the rumour, but theories blaming the Cotronis for Volpe's murder eventually waned, then died. It was recalled that the Montrealers got along well with Volpe and that Volpe would have been a potential ally for them in a new city. Indeed, Frank Cotroni had gotten along so well with Volpe that Cotroni introduced Volpe to an undercover police officer who claimed to want in on Volpe's real-estate dealings in Atlantic City. Vic Cotroni was also considered on chummy terms with Volpe and was sighted sharing pastries and pleasantries with Volpe and the Luppino brothers at a Swiss restaurant in the monied Bay-Bloor Street area. James Dubro, whose *Mob Rule* was largely a biography of Volpe, notes that it was very important for the Toronto mobster to pay tribute to Vic Cotroni in Montreal, including kissing the Quebecker gently on the knuckles.

Toronto in the early 1980s seemed ripe for fresh blood, both literally and figuratively. Still operating in a relative power vacuum was John Papalia of Hamilton whose rackets included extorting money from Greek gaminghouse operators on Danforth Avenue. But Papalia's best days were behind him. One Toronto police officer specializing in the mob joked that Papalia was afraid to take holidays for fear his rackets would be stolen: "He's a criminal from the dark ages... [He] has a lot of power through what he has done in the past, not what he's doing today."

St. Clair Avenue baker Michele (Mike) Racco had enjoyed great respect, but he died of natural causes in 1980, and his son Domenic lacked the maturity to replace him. His Siderno group included the vital, volatile Commisso brothers, but they were behind bars on an assortment of charges.

So police watched with interest as Frank Cotroni lunched on St. Clair Avenue in Toronto's Little Italy with Rocco Zito, an outwardly modest grandfather who had been a member of the Calabrian *'ndrangheta* before he emigrated to Canada three decades earlier. In the early 1980s, Cotroni had travelled through Europe, ostensibly for his tile business, and it didn't escape police notice that heroin was being smuggled in tiles. Zito had long been suspected of ties to heroin traffickers, including Tommaso Buscetta. By the winter of 1983, Cotroni was coming to Toronto at least once a month, and being chauffeured around the city by pro boxer Eddie (Hurricane) Melo. Police noted Cotroni's movements, which included trips to a billiard parlour on Bloor Street West, a restaurant in trendy Yorkville, an Italian-style barber shop on Danforth Avenue, and Delta's Chelsea

Inn, where he was said to have had a romance with a bar employee.

It didn't escape police notice that Cotroni's driver, Melo, also worked as an organizer for Local 75 of the Hotel and Restaurant Employees International or that Cotroni had shared drinks with union officials. And when Cotroni lieutenant Claude Faber came to Toronto, Local 75 was billed for his room, meals, drinks and closed-circuit movies. The hotel union has a long and sorry association with organized crime and is a source of curiosity, anger and profound embarrassment within mainstream labour. In 1981, it suffered the bleak distinction of becoming the only union ever kicked out of the Quebec Federation of Labour for unethical conduct, amidst charges of too-tight ties with hotel managers and the Cotronis. In the United States, reports by the Senate and Justice department in the 1980s said large portions of the union were under the control of organized crime, most notably Joseph (Joey Doves) Auippa of Chicago. Controlling a hotel union local doesn't just give mobsters access to union dues — it also allows them to put pressure on hotel managers to deal with mob-supported businesses that supply vending machines, linen supplies and other products, and strippers.

Back in 1981, the powerful United Food and Commercial Workers union got a taste of Melo's brand of unionism when it unsuccessfully vied with Local 75 for the right to represent Toronto airport-strip workers. A bartender complained that Melo pulled a gun on him and asked, "You don't want anything to happen to your baby or your wife, do you?" In his own defence, Melo showed his fists to a police officer, saying, "I have my own weapons — these two."

Police were particularly on guard as Christmas 1983 approached. Domenic Racco and lesser-known Vincenzo Cherubino had been slain the same month as Volpe, and there were fears that Frank Cotroni's presence would cause things to erupt further. "I think [Frank] Cotroni was looking at this area as being prime to become the end-all, be-all that Paul Volpe wasn't," says a Metro Toronto police officer specializing in organized crime. Roy McMurtry, then Ontario attorney general, was told in a meeting with southern Ontario police chiefs just before Christmas 1983 that Frank Cotroni was a man to watch. "By far our greatest concern must be the Cotroni family of Montreal... Needless to say, we consider [Frank] Cotroni our most serious threat."

As Frank Cotroni's man in Toronto, Réal Simard cut a confident figure on the bright pink carpet of his thirtieth-floor Bay Street penthouse and at the wheel of his silver Mercedes. His luxurious surroundings were part of his new role as Cotroni's advance man in Toronto. Cotroni was behind two agencies that booked table-dancers into Ontario strip clubs, a business that was dramatically expanding in southern Ontario in the early 1980s. For club owners, the dancers were far cheaper than big-name strippers since they could perform continuously and were paid dramatically less money. Dancers lived mostly off their tips, and clubs paid them only $5 an hour, plus accommodations and one meal a day. Another $40 to $80 weekly went to their agency. Since cocaine use was high among dancers, much of their earnings could be redirected to Cotroni through "candymen" working in the clubs.

At first, the table-dance operations were handled by Cotroni's son Paolo. But after his father had gone to the trouble of travelling to Toronto and clearing his way, Paolo changed his mind. Like many fathers who try to ease their offspring into their work-world, Frank Cotroni was in a potentially embarrassing situation. Simard saved face for his boss and found interesting work for himself by offering to step in to fill the void. Simard now cultivated the appearance of a legitimate high-roller as the head of Prestige Entertainment at 329 St. George Street, but his instincts remained those of the streets.

It was this carnivorous core of his personality that brought Réal Simard to room 345 of the Seaway Hotel on Toronto's waterfront strip on the evening of November 29, 1983. Simard was expanding beyond strip clubs and moving into cocaine-selling in Toronto, and his trip to the Seaway was part of that expansion. He was also using the visit to teach an associate something that Frank Cotroni had taught him a few years earlier: if you want to kill someone, put the final bullet in the head.

Robert Hétu was a drug dealer who had boxed and trained fighters at George Cherry's Champion Boxing Club in Montreal, best known as the home club of the Fighting Hiltons, a boxing family close to Frank Cotroni's heart and with a considerable following in Quebec. Hétu was a small man and a dangerous one. He once boasted he had murdered four men. He was in the Seaway that night with a fellow drug-pedlar, Joseph Héroux, waiting for a cocaine payment for a deal made with Simard and his associate, Richard Clément.

Later, Hétu would replay that surreal evening in his mind "a thousand times," piecing together how only seconds after he opened the door, Héroux lay sprawled out on the floor with four bullets in

On a rainy September afternoon in 1984, twenty-three flower-bearing cars and a seventeen-piece band escorted Canada's most celebrated crime boss through the streets of Montreal on his way to the afterlife. Vincenzo (Vic, The Egg) Cotroni earned that rare Mafia luxury—death by natural causes. The 'Godfather,' as he was known in life, was said to have been watching the papal visit on TV when he succumbed to cancer in 1984. He was 74.

His brother, Frank, was in prison at the time and was denied a day pass to attend the funeral. The authorities offered to allow him to visit the funeral home. But this time it was Frank who rejected the idea. As an associate explained, "Frank's children, and a lot of his friends, will be attending the funeral and Frank's a proud man. Nobody wants his picture in the paper sharing a pair of matching chrome bracelets with some burly screw [guard]."

Editors note: All photos in this section, except for police mug shots, are from The Michel Auger Collection. Mug shots are from various police departments

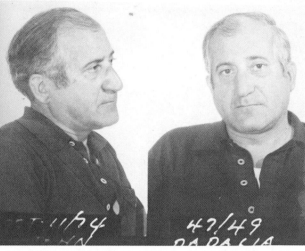

Papalia ruled the Hamilton and Niagara region with the blessing of Buffalo Mafia boss Stefano (The Undertaker) Magaddino. Papalia and Cotroni were considered the most powerful — and deadly — mafiosi in Canada. Gunned down in 1997 near the house in which he was born. Papalia was 73.

Johnny (Pops) Papalia
"The Enforcer"

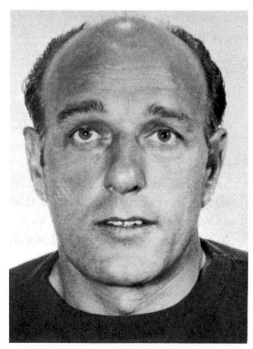

Paul Volpe — Toronto mobster boss and Papalia rival. Murdered in 1983.

Ken Murdock — Contract killer of Papalia and Carmen Barillaro.

Three of the four Violi brothers: Left, Francesco; centre, Paolo; right, Rocco.
All three met with gangland deaths.

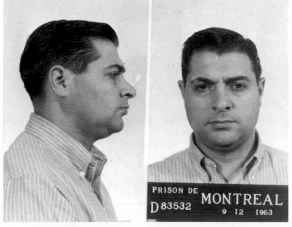

Hamilton-raised Paulo Violi spent several terms behind bars.

Above: In custody: Underboss Paolo Violi, stands at right in flowered shirt
Below: Giuseppe Violi funeral. Paolo, front right, father Domonico to his left. Father-in-law Giacomo Luppino behind Paulo's right shoulder. Brother Francesco behind his left shoulder. Giuseppe died in a 1970 traffic accident.

Top: Paulo Violi outside his Reggio espresso and ice cream bar.
Middle: The Zardini shotgun that killed Violi as he played cards inside the bar. The double-barreled weapon is made only in a small, southern Italian village.
Below: Violi went to jail many times. In the mid-70s, it was for contempt of court

after he refused to testify before a Canadian crime probe. He was sentenced to one year in prison. While behind bars, he lost further control of his soldiers to Sicillian Vito Rizzuto and street territory to the Hells Angels in the battle for the lucrative drug trade in Montreal.

Above: Vito Rizzuto, left, with his Toronto henchman Raymond Fernandez.
Below left: Father Nick Rizzuto spent five years in Venezuelan jail for cocaine trafficking. Remained close to son Vito — alleged Montreal crime boss.

Above: Vito in '73. By 2006, he was in Canadian jail awaiting extradition to the U.S. to face murder charges.

Charles Gagne
Contract killer of Eddy Melo.

Eddie Melo, right, talks with Peter
Scarcella on Toronto street.

Angelo Musitano

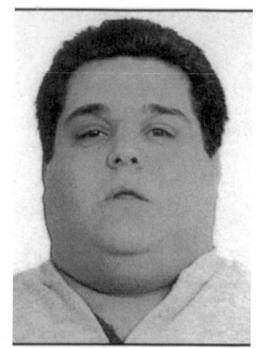

Pat Musitano

The Musitano brothers organized Hamilton and Niagara-area gangland hits.

Hells Angels—Montreal Chapter: *Above:* Maurice (Mom) Boucher (back row left); Walter (Nurget) Stadnick (1st row, 3rd from left). *Below:* Hells Angels hitman of the '70s Yves (Apache) Trudeau (2nd from right in front row).

his head and another in his neck.

Hétu had felt something was wrong about the deal, and squirreled thirty grams of cocaine behind a mirror in the hotel room. Around six that evening, Clément phoned and asked if Hétu and Héroux were alone.

Assured that they were, Clément said he and Simard would be by soon to complete the cocaine deal. Sometime between 6:30 and 7:00 p.m., Hétu and Héroux heard a knock on the door.

"Who's there?" Hétu asked.

"David and Richard," replied Simard who used the name "David" in Toronto.

Héroux remained seated on the bed; Hétu answered the door. Five years later, with bullet fragments still in his head, Hétu would try to patch together the pieces of that evening: how Simard first shot him in the chin, then followed up that blast with a bullet to the back of his head, and how Clément shot him beside his left ear, again somehow missing his brain.

When the three bullets crashed into Robert Hétu's skull, he was blasted into another level of consciousness, a strange new vantage-point, from which he could watch the murderous attack as though through a veil. Later, he would struggle to describe the feeling: "When the shot goes in there is no pain, but you feel your head moving." Then Hétu held his breath and lay as still as his nerves would permit, "So they would think I was dead and would not shoot again." He was facing the bed and could clearly hear Héroux's final words — "Are you crazy, Clément?" — and the "zip, zip, zip" that silenced his companion.

"I felt myself dying," Hétu would recall. "It's difficult when you see the guy who shot you is right there. You're nervous."

Ironically, during a visit to Simard's St. George Street office earlier that month, Hétu had asked him for a gun. Simard pulled a .22 pistol from a false ceiling and handed it to him. That revolver was found by police in Room 345 of the Seaway, unfired and close to Héroux's lifeless body. Simard had worn gloves for the murders, but dispensed with the false beard he usually donned for such grim chores, since it irritated his sensitive skin.

Réal Simard was arrested the day after the killing, spoiling his plans of returning to Montreal to murder boxing-club owner George Cherry. That hit, Simard would say, had been planned for the night of a boxing card and had been sanctioned by Frank Cotroni. Simard admitted shooting Héroux and Hétu, but said Clément was proud of his contribution to the bloodshed: "[Clément] was telling me it was his first time [killing someone] and he was happy. He said, 'I did it. I did it.' We kissed each other on the side of the cheek. It's an old tradition in Italian families when you do something for the godfather."

Clément had escaped from Toronto with his stripper girlfriend, travelling to Hamilton; London, Ontario; back to Toronto; then on to Niagara Falls, Quebec, Calgary, Vancouver, Paris, Cyprus and Lebanon. Metro Toronto police sent wanted posters through Interpol to 146 countries in an effort to catch Clément, but when he was finally found, it was because he had grown tired of running and surrendered himself to police.

Now Frank Cotroni had to worry about Simard's loyalty; would he stay quiet when faced with a major conviction, or would he tell all to spare himself? Cotroni did not know yet that he had a potentially greater problem in his midst. He had become close to a man who introduced himself as a European money-launderer. That friendship would last two and a half years. The two had become so close that the man was a guest at the wedding of Frank Cotroni's daughter, and Cotroni had introduced him to crime associates such as Paul Volpe.

But the man was really a police officer, building a case that could topple the last, best hope of the Cotroni empire.

Chapter Twenty-One

The Cyclone

"We were a piece of shit to him, you know? And he was right."
— Frank Cotroni's hitman
on former world champion
boxer Matthew Hilton

George Cherry has nothing but kind words to say about Frank Cotroni, even though Réal Simard said Cotroni approved of the plot to murder Cherry. At least some of this is good politics; you don't live long in George Cherry's world if you're quoted bad-mouthing the Cotronis. But there also appeared to be real affection when George Cherry spoke of his long professional and personal association with the Cotroni family.

George Cherry was a cherubic-looking man who could easily pass for a brother of singer Mel Torme, and his glossy black business cards featured him smiling in a tuxedo, clearly pleased with himself and his place in the world. His office in the Champion Boxing Club in Montreal's working-class Rosemount district was lined with photos of himself with greats of his favourite sport including former heavyweight champions Joe Frazier and Floyd Patterson. Outside his office, by the boxing ring, was a huge picture of the boyish Hilton brothers back when they were full of promise and untouched by the law or death.

Nearby, a plaque bears the names of club benefactors: it included the name of Vic Cotroni's son Nick.

How George Cherry got to know the Cotronis and achieve what

he considers success was a story worthy of Charles Dickens, as Cherry told it. The story began when Cherry's mother died when he was five. He spent the next several years in orphanages, since his father was in jail. Between the ages of nine and eleven he stayed with his father, who had remarried, but family ties were frayed and couldn't hold. George left home for good at eleven, developing a street sense and connections that would serve him well in adult life. For years, his bed was any car in north Montreal with an unlocked door, and one summer morning he awoke inside an Oldsmobile to see the ruddy face of a stocky, black-haired stranger who was looking at him.

"Hey, what are you doing here?"

"I'm not stealing your car. I'm only sleeping. I'm not stealing your car. I don't know how to drive."

Then something happened that would change the course of Cherry's life. The stranger was Frank Cotroni and he asked if Cherry wanted a job cleaning his country home. Young Cherry spent the summer washing Cotroni's Oldsmobile, cutting the grass, doing dishes and discovering a sense of family. When he returned to Montreal, Cherry became part of a group of friends who would head to the Cotroni country home on weekends: "It was like his little gang that used to come there and play volleyball and eat spaghetti. They used to make a big pot every Sunday, you know, for everybody."

Cherry worked in a nightclub, then sold boxing tickets, then ran the Champion Boxing Club and promoted fights. Cotroni was ringside for the top amateur and pro bouts, and he hosted well-attended post-fight parties. For amateur cards, he would quietly slip promoters fifty-dollar bills and whisper, "Take care of the kids after. Buy them a few hot dogs and Cokes." For pro fights, he'd buy tickets by the dozen. Cherry said he and Cotroni maintained a friendship but nothing more: "I'm not a part of his organization or anything like that."

The Frank Cotroni that Cherry described was a man who was invariably polite, sympathetic to the poor and able to resolve potentially explosive situations with a few quiet words. "He likes to shake hands with everybody. He likes to respect you because he likes to be respected. And I think he's a heck of a gentleman. I've seen him in the gym and many, many times I've seen him with some guy with no money to eat and all that, buy him a lunch, give him a jacket or something... He's got a heart like a house."

But though Cotroni was quiet and gentle, Cherry says, his word carried a great deal of weight in tough circles: "I knew a few guys who had trouble with some tough guy or some dangerous guy. And they didn't want to have trouble. They'd say, 'Frank, that guy can make me trouble.' So Frank would say, 'Oh, well, I could talk to him.'... I've seen him do that often."

This mediator role was accepted as the natural order of north Montreal streets and downtown clubs. Cherry says, "With the name he's got, that's his job, really." But Cherry wasn't so impressed with his driver, Réal Simard. To Cherry he was little more than a bully in designer clothes who traded on the Cotroni name. "He's a guy who's very proud, very fresh. He talks with his nose upstairs, like he owns the world. It was always like that. He likes to give orders and humiliate and all that. I seen him...beat a few guys in nightclubs for nothing, for nothing. And the guy wouldn't defend himself because they knew with who he was hanging around and they knew all that. So, he was walking around downtown in night-clubs like he owned them. That's not Mr. Cotroni's type. He's very quiet. He'd feel embarrassed by those things, you know?"

Why, then, would gentle, polite Frank Cotroni want his long-time friend George Cherry murdered? Simard says that Cotroni okayed a plot to kill Cherry during a December 4, 1983, boxing card. The plan fell through, and Cherry went on living after Simard's arrest for the Seaway Hotel murder in Toronto. As Simard tells the story, it was just business; nothing personal. First, Simard and his partner Richard Clément drove to Toronto to shoot two men whom they believed were out to kill Clément over a debt he owed Cherry. Simard says Cotroni agreed that not just Joseph Héroux and Robert Hétu should be murdered "but also George Cherry when we returned to Montreal. It was a question of showing Montreal a clear message that Cotroni's family was taking [over] Toronto."

George Cherry and Frank Cotroni shared a deep interest in the Fighting Hiltons, a family of boxers with faces like choirboys and bodies like anvils. Cherry says he built his Champion Boxing Club so the Hilton brothers would have somewhere to train. The gesture must have pleased Frank Cotroni, since the Hiltons' emergence on the professional boxing scene provided a bright spot during this troubled time for him.

The Hilton boys are the offspring of Dave Hilton, Sr. — a long-time friend of Frank Cotroni — and Frank Cotroni clearly enjoyed their company; his former wife Pauline says he was a sports maniac. "One of his most cherished desires was that one of his sons would be a hockey or boxing champion," she told the now defunct newspaper, *La Patrie.* "Especially boxing. [He wanted that] much more than if he became a doctor or lawyer."

Not only did Frank Cotroni enjoy watching grown men pummel each other, he also realized there was money and prestige to be gained by getting close to the boxing world, just as his brother Vic had benefited from his association with Québécois folk musicians at Vic's clubs. As well as money and prestige, the boxing world also offered masculine camaraderie. In 1981, when Sugar Ray Leonard fought Thomas Hearns in Las Vegas for the world welterweight title, Cotroni had the cable feed of the fight tapped and directed into a Montreal hotel ballroom. Then he invited a *Who's Who* of the Montreal underworld and, unwittingly, an undercover police officer in to watch the bout. He got the thrill of the fight, companionship — and his friends' admission fees.

Frank Cotroni understood well he could make money through boxing without ever having to feel the crunch of leather against his face. Boxers offered cash and muscle and, in some cases, willing couriers of heroin. The "Borgia" police operation concluded that Cotroni had links to forty boxers, promoters and trainers in Toronto, Hull, Winnipeg, Cornwall, Montreal and Boston, while another police operation, dubbed "Uptown," noted Cotroni's interest in popular Toronto boxers Eddie Melo and Nicky Furlano, both of whom were tied to trainer Travis Sugden. Some bouts were, in the opinion of police in the stands, clearly rigged. "Sometimes they missed the guy and he still fell down," an anti-Mafia police specialist who's also a boxing fan said. Ontario Provincial Police intelligence heard that promoters fixed a fight for Furlano in April 1984 in order to set up a title match with world champion Aaron Pryor. Toronto bookmaker and loan-shark Joe Natale was said to be in on the scam in which Pryor, who had a serious drug dependency, was cheated of his purse.

But there was certainly no chance of a quick return on his money in the late 1950s when Frank Cotroni befriended Dave Hilton, Sr. and drove from Montreal to Quebec to watch his friend win the national 126-pound title. Cotroni liked to talk of how he did a little "rassling" himself, not explaining that his strengths were operating outside the ring and the Marquess of Queensbury Rules, where he was free to use baseball bats and pistols as well as uppercuts and jabs. Cotroni was also a champion of sorts; his prowess in the street-fighting arena earned him the nickname "Cyclone" in the tabloid press.

Hilton, Sr.'s title was tarnished by the frustrations of being a small man when big crowds and big paydays seemed reserved for heavyweights. His skills and savage fighting style scared away most top-level opponents. Fighters would choose to shift weight divisions rather than suffer his relentless body blows, which were inevitably followed with a left hook to the head, delivered with the force of a mule-kick. His sparring partners included young Cassius Clay, who later changed his name to Muhammad Ali. A proud, shy man, Hilton was forced to fight in heavier divisions for paycheques that, when they didn't bounce, never exceeded $500. Soon he was having more trouble with the bottle than with anyone he faced inside the ropes. Sometimes he battled both foes at the same time: he would arrive drunk for fights and still win. Through his troubles, Hilton says he found support from his friend Frank Cotroni: "I was a heavy drinker. He'd be the one that would tell me, 'Come on, Dave. Don't get yourself drunk... You hurt your health.' Frank's pretty quiet...I don't think I've ever heard him say a cross word to anyone...I've never seen him abuse anybody in my life. I've known him for quite a long time and I've never seen him have an argument with anybody... I was kind of wild. If I got drinking, I wouldn't let nobody get away with anything. He's the one that would tell me, 'Cool it. Don't get yourself any problems.'"

Dave, Sr., left boxing in 1976 at age thirty-six with a pro record of 138-15 with 70 knockouts. His sons seemed to have a chance to make a breakthrough to the world title and the riches that had been denied to their father. The brothers' genes were programmed for boxing; bare-knuckle boxers went back at least two generations on both sides of the family. The Hilton boys quickly tenderized the competition in Montreal. They made long road trips with their father, five of them sharing one cheap hotel room and blankets, as well as the dream of the respect and riches of a world title. Their marketability was enhanced by their white skin, a strong selling point in a sport ever-desperate for the next Great White Hope.

Cotroni offered loans for groceries and rent as well as moral support, Dave Hilton, Sr., says. "Many's the time I had to look for a dollar for a quart of milk... It was never 'no,' always 'yes.' And no questions asked."

But Hilton argues the loans were always repaid, contrary to a police report which said Cotroni spent at least $100,000 on the family. Hilton says his friendship with Cotroni was paralleled by that of their children, adding, "They never tried to turn my kids...in wrong ways or anything." Hilton remains loyal to his old friend, despite the notoriety Cotroni attained in the 1970s. "The only god-father I know is the one I've seen on TV," Hilton, Sr., says, pausing to chuckle at his joke. Then he turns serious: "I don't know nothing about anything that they [the press] wrote. I'm certainly sure if he ever did something, why would he come and tell me? He wouldn't want me to know. That would be his business. He's not that kind of man."

Frank Cotroni was a ringside fixture at professional and amateur fights, and a welcome guest at the Champion Boxing Club. But until Matthew Hilton won the International Boxing Federation junior middleweight championship at the Montreal Forum on June 27, 1987, Montreal boxers were not particularly big money-makers. Frank Cotroni was not able to attend when Matthew Hilton won the title, pounding out a unanimous decision over Buster Drayton to become Canada's first native-born professional world champion in forty-four years. "He was very happy," Hilton, Sr., says. "He [Cotroni] was inside [jail on drug charges]. He never seen the fight but he sent word from somebody... He was very happy about it."

Promoter Henri Spitzer dismisses the suggestion that Frank Cotroni's frequent presence at boxing events somehow made the sport dirty. Spitzer argues that Cotroni was also a familiar face at Canadiens' hockey games at the Forum and Expo baseball games at Olympic Stadium: "He's a sports fan... When he's at boxing matches, he usually buys ringside tickets. Whoever buys the front-row tickets are more noticeable than people sitting maybe up in the blues or the reds." Frank Cotroni certainly did not seem ashamed of anything, Spitzer adds: "He was seen all over town. Big hotels, big restaurants. Anywhere... He was always in big hotels in broad daylight in the middle of the dining-room. So he wasn't hiding anything from anybody. Neither were the Hiltons or me or anybody else around him."

The promoter scoffs at the suggestion that Cotroni's interest in boxing in Montreal extended to money-making: "As far as I'm concerned, he's never had any connections [with boxing] or any ties. Why would he? There's no money. There's nothing. Why would he be interested financially? It just doesn't make sense. Even with the Hiltons. There never was any money here. The money is there now with Matthew Hilton because he's world champion, but he's signed up with [American promoter] Don King for the past two or three years anyway... What's happening in the States, between Cotroni and King and other people, nobody knows."

But Réal Simard, Frank Cotroni's *Gentleman's Quarterly*-issue hitman, was more suspicious. Nobody outside the underworld knew exactly why the Hiltons' business manager, Frank Shoofey, was gunned down outside his Cherrier Street office late on the night of October 15, 1985. But it was clearly a professional hit, a topic about which Simard has some expertise. Shoofey was considered in some circles "the people's lawyer" and he had a client list that read like a police most-wanted list; it included Frank Cotroni's infamous rivals, the Dubois brothers.

Simard has two theories about the Shoofey murder: "The first one is the boxers. The second one is about a lawyer who was involved in some, well, love affair. Who apparently put a contract on Shoofey's life." In Simard's first theory, "the boxers" translates into the Hiltons. Back in 1984, Simard says, Frank Cotroni was taking a cut from the purses won by the Hiltons. Frank Cotroni was convinced that he would soon be extradited to the United States to face drug-trafficking charges in Connecticut. The mobster was open to selling the contract to manage the fighters at a fire-sale price for some quick money, Simard argues. "When Don King offered him $100,000 for the contract on the Hiltons, he accepted. But he said it's okay for me but you have to go and...discuss it with Frank Shoofey, the lawyer. Because Frank Shoofey was their manager... was the businessman of this affair. Frank Shoofey never accepted that deal."

The reason he never accepted the deal, according to Simard, was that Shoofey had heard that the fighters' father, Dave Hilton, Sr., had been tricked into signing with Frank Cotroni. Shoofey's obstinacy made him an impediment to the selling of the fighters' contract, annoying some very dangerous and well-connected people who weren't used to having their wishes denied; "Frank Shoofey was very disturbing for...them. Because he was helping the Hilton brothers."

Dave Hilton, Sr., later praised the deal with Don King productions which offered three of his sons, Dave, Jr., Matthew, and Alex, high profiles and high incomes. In boxing, as in other areas of Frank Cotroni's business life, the pull of the United States was overwhelming. "He'll get us big fights," Dave, Sr., said. "No one's better than

King. He has made all kinds of champions in the past, and he can make us champions...if we produce."

But the optimistic words were erased by a series of personal tragedies that shadowed the Hiltons for a decade. Alex Hilton fought his way to the Canadian middleweight title while still a teenager, but, by age twenty-one, he was an alcoholic and faced a three-month jail term for seven weapons and alcohol offences. In 1985, Dave, Jr., widely considered the most talented of the brothers, was in a motorcycle accident that shattered his leg, finger and, apparently, also his career. The cruellest blow came a year later when the baby of the family, Stewart, was driving with a girl, who was also seventeen. The car went out of control and crashed, killing both of them. Stewart and Matthew Hilton had been especially close; they had shared a room for years, and Stewart's death seemed to redouble Matthew's determination to win a world title.

Réal Simard says he always considered Matthew something special. When Simard and Cotroni paid frequent visits to George Cherry's Champion Boxing Club to watch the brothers train, "He [Dave Hilton, Jr.] wants to be a bigshot... He idolizes him [Frank Cotroni] the way I idolized Frank Cotroni when I was a kid. But Matthew, I have to admit, he's the only one that didn't pay any attention to us. Never, ever, ever accepted money from Frank Cotroni. Was never talking to him. We were always staying there in the gymnasium with girls. David, Jr., was always stopping his training and coming to us, talking to the girls, trying to impress them...

"Matthew was the only one who don't want to know nothing about Frank Cotroni, and I was always proud of that. Because, in my mind, I always said, 'This kid is smart. He doesn't pay attention to anybody.' You know what he was doing? He was punching on his punching bag. He didn't pay no attention to us. We were a piece of shit to him, you know? And he was right. You know what he was doing? Washing dishes in a restaurant instead of accepting Frank Cotroni's money... He [Frank Cotroni] destroyed those kids. You know why? Because they don't know, first they didn't know that discotheques exist, clubs exist. They didn't know that fast cars exist. They never had so much money. So, Frank, with his money, with girls around him, with the power that he's got, bring them to discotheques, to clubs, present them to girls, to everybody.

"So they lost control of their lives. For them, it was all new. You know an eighteen-year-old kid; on top with a big car, money filling his pockets, they were not interested any more in boxing. So, he killed those kids. Not purposely, but because he didn't know how to be with boxers. And George Cherry told me that one day. He said, 'Frank is no good for the Hilton brothers. He destroyed them because of the way he is with them.' Boxers have to be hungry... Why should people receive some punches in the face if it's not for money?"

By 1984, Cotroni could see something was going wrong with the Hiltons. That year *Journal de Montréal* sports columnist Jacques Beauchamp received a phone call from the mobster: "It was after the first Davey Hilton–Mario Cusson fight. 'Jacques, I have never bothered you before. But I know what you have done for old people, the handicapped and young people with personal problems. So, today, I am asking you if you can help the young Hiltons and their father. They have problems. I don't want them to go in the wrong direction. They are young and they can make errors. I think a sermon would do them an enormous amount of good.'"

Beauchamp obliged, but the problem continued. Simard argues that Cotroni didn't just kill them with clumsy attempts at kindness: "You know...[why] Dave Hilton, Jr., stopped boxing? Because the last time he boxed, he made $118,000 and he ended up with $50,000. Where do you think the rest go? In Frank Cotroni's pocket. I know that as a fact... If the Hilton brothers are finished, it's because of Frank Cotroni. He killed them. He destroyed them."

By 1988, people were asking if Matthew was in danger of being destroyed, too. He was locked into an exclusive contract with Don King, a former numbers runner who had found fame and fortune in promoting boxers after he served a prison term for manslaughter. A spokesman for King called Matthew Hilton "headstrong, stupid and uncontrollable" shortly before Matthew's first defeat in the ring. American Robert (Bam Bam) Hines, a four-to-one underdog, survived two early knockdowns to win a unanimous decision. His opponent didn't look like the Matthew Hilton that Réal Simard had respected, but rather a rusty, out-of-shape impersonator. Hilton had been the victor of his previous 30 fights as a pro and in 106 amateur bouts. When it was all over and he was no longer a champion, the press noted that the pride and last hope of the Fighting Hiltons seemed to be quietly sobbing.

Just two weeks after Matthew lost his world title, his older brother Alex was back in the headlines. A Montreal judge called him a "vicious and heartless person," said he had a split personality and sentenced him to five years in prison. Alex, just twenty-four, was already in jail when he received the second sentence, for ordering three sexual assaults on a Bordeaux Jail inmate and rupturing the spleen of a fellow prisoner who tried to halt the attack. In passing judgement, Quebec Court Justice Pierre Brassard said he was baffled at how Alex Hilton could respect the warnings of a referee in a ring but ignore his own conscience.

Dave Hilton, Sr.'s voice goes soft when he is asked if his family now suffers because of their friendship with the Cotronis. He talks quickly and loosely, as if hoping that the flow of his words will carry him to the answer. "I don't think it does us any good... Everybody knows Frank. I'm not the only one in sports. He's helped a lot of amateur boxers. And amateur teams to go away [on trips]. He's given a lot of donations for that... He never wanted publicity about it. He did it with his heart."

Stories that Frank Cotroni controlled boxing and his sons were, in Hilton's words, lies: "I wouldn't stand for it, for one thing. I wouldn't let nobody tell my sons what to do. He was like an uncle to them. He'd take them to a restaurant or something and that would be it. Most of the time, I was there. We went to so many restaurants. And he would barbeque. He was just an ordinary guy... Whatever the kids wanted. If they wanted to go to McDonald's and have a hamburger, he'd go out to McDonald's and have a hamburger with them."

Dave Hilton, Sr., refused to say this friend who helped him when he needed money for milk and rent was a villain. "I have no regrets at all whatsoever. He's still my friend."

Chapter Twenty-two

Uncle Sam's Revenge

"Frank Cotroni's probably finished."
— a Montreal police officer

Police in southern Florida watched nervously as members of the Dubois and Cotroni gangs drank together and shook hands on new business deals. The Dubois and Cotroni groups had a murderous rivalry in Quebec, but strange alliances grew in the "Petit Montreal" section of Hollywood, Florida. The sunny climes and potential for huge profits attracted a huge influx of French Canadians to southern Florida in the 1970s; many of them were fleeing the political turmoil and uncertain investment climate that had followed the election of the separatist Parti Québécois in 1976. Hotels in Hollywood, Florida, flew the Canadian flag and featured French menus and entertainment. Unlike New York City, southern Florida was considered a "free zone," open for anyone with nerve, ambition and a lack of morals. For the Cotroni group, it offered another avenue of expansion after the breakdown of their traditional Montreal-New York axis. South Florida's crime roots ran deep. It had been Al Capone's wintering nook six decades before. Now it was a key transit point in the enormously lucrative drug trade from South America.

The expectation that casino gambling would soon be legalized in Florida offered the promise of further profits for the Montreal gangsters, with their long-standing experience in gambling. The Canadians also found it easier to get guns in Florida than they did back home, and distance and language differences made it tough for Florida authorities to compare notes with their Quebec counterparts.

In the early 1980s, the Canadians raised underworld eyebrows by grabbing territory inside Hollywood, Florida, buying businesses including hotels, restaurants and body shops for stolen cars. A dozen pizzerias were firebombed between 1982 and 1984 as Canadian racketeers fought for a slice of the fast-food business. Perhaps anticipating trouble, the owners of one new pizzeria named their enterprise Kaboom Pizza. New York mobsters tried to counteract the infusion of Montrealers by moving in men of their own. The Gambino family sent a hundred men to the Miami area.

Portly Willie Obront, the Cotroni family's money-launderer, entered this volatile cauldron in 1980, but his freedom did not last long. Following an investigation dubbed the "Canadian Connection," he was arrested along with thirty-nine others on July 21, 1983. A kilogram of cocaine with a street value of about $387,000 was seized outside his home. His convictions on twelve drug-related charges brought him a twenty-year sentence. The Cotronis had lost another of their old stalwarts.

Operation Canadian Connection paled in comparison with Operation Avalanche. In March 1987, Obront was named with Vic Cotroni's son Nick in an indictment following a probe by the American Drug Enforcement Administration, the FBI and the Royal Canadian Mounted Police into a drug ring that brought millions of phony Quaaludes into the United States. The scope of the ring was enormous and, as well as Obront and Nick Cotroni, twenty Canadians, twenty-seven Americans and two Colombians were charged. The ring accounted for an estimated 70 per cent of the illegal Quaalude trade in the United States. The counterfeit pills had been shipped south from Quebec to Florida in trucks carrying loads of peatmoss and lumber. From Florida, they were shipped across the United States. Potential profits were staggering, as the 13.5 million tranquillizers the ring moved could be made for less than a nickel a piece, then sold on the street for six or seven dollars each. Obront's gang also shipped what authorities estimated was between 35 and 40 kilos of cocaine into Canada between 1981 and 1986.

Things were crumbling at home as well for the Cotronis. A police undercover operation provided a massive window into Frank Cotroni's businesses. Then, hitman Réal Simard turned on his former boss in return for a chance for parole after ten years in prison. Simard gives some of the credit for his turnabout to the spiritual writing of actress Shirley MacLaine. He says he was greatly moved by her book *Out on a Limb* which states, "Whatever action one takes will ultimately return to that person—good and bad—maybe not in this life embodiment, but sometime in the future. And no one is exempt."

Even more bad news for Frank Cotroni came from Connecticut where he was indicted in a heroin-smuggling conspiracy along with fellow Montrealers Giovanni (Johnny) Marra, Joseph (Joe Crow) Delvecchio and Oreste (Ernie Boy) Abbamonte and their Connecticut associate, Anthony (Gaetano, Toke, Guy Sr.) DiGorolamo. Cotroni had shared space in Mafia Row at Lewisburg Penitentiary with Delvecchio and Abbamonte, a particularly unnerving-looking criminal whose head resembled a bleached skull capped by a cheap wig. The Americans had offered Cotroni new connections into U.S. drug markets, but he was instead faced with the threat of a twenty-five-year term. There were eleven years remaining on his cocaine-smuggling charge. If he was sentenced to even a fraction of this, his family's empire would be all but dead.

Frank Cotroni's gut must have tightened considerably when Delvecchio and Abbamonte pleaded guilty and got five-year sentences for interstate travel in aid of racketeering and aiding and abetting. Their associate, Michael Corcione of New York, was sentenced to four years in prison after admitting his guilt.

In answer to the potentially disastrous American indictment, Cotroni's lawyer, Sydney Leithman, wrapped his client in Canada's new Charter of Rights and Freedoms and a plethora of other potential shields in an effort to keep him from being shipped to Connecticut. Leithman argued that only transcripts of telephone conversations between Montreal and the eastern seaboard had been produced, and not the original tapes, contrary to the rules of "best evidence." Those transcripts included suspicious allusions to "diapers," which police assumed was a code word for heroin. But prosecutors would later learn that the references were to the real thing. Cotroni was a devoted family man who considered some diapers available in the U.S. far superior to what was on sale in Quebec. Cotroni's right-hand man Claude Faber was a new father, and Cotroni was using his connections to import diapers for Faber's baby.

It seemed the Cotronis could not answer their doorbells without facing police officers and drug charges. The list of their troubles was dizzying, reminiscent of the family's woes with liquor inspectors a half-century before: Frank Cotroni's daughter Rosita Bruno and her husband, Nicola, were charged with cocaine-trafficking;

Frank Cotroni's son Francesco was convicted of possession when found with 1.5 grams of hashish at a downtown nightclub; Cotroni's son Michael was arrested at his home on Beaubien East and charged with possession of 25 grams of cocaine and seven grams of hashish for the purpose of trafficking. Worst of all, Cotroni's son Francesco was convicted along with Frank Cotroni and Claude Faber for slaying Giuseppe Montegano at Francesco's private club. Like fathers everywhere, Cotroni could not help but worry about his children. As he returned to jail for the Montegano murder, he left a message for a former Montreal police officer, asking him to keep an eye on his children so they wouldn't get into trouble.

Meanwhile, Quebec prisoners were learning there were worse things in life than sharing a cell-block with Frank Cotroni. One Christmas at Bordeaux Jail, he provided cellmates with fifty pairs of slippers, a dozen transistor radios and other stocking stuffers. He also sent Christmas food baskets to families in his old neighbourhood. While he was behind bars in Acapulco in the early 1970s, he fought successfully to upgrade the food and provide inmates with entertainment. A fellow prisoner who had contracted gangrene in his leg after a scuffle with a police officer had his medical bills handled by Cotroni. And when prisoners held their own version of the Olympics behind bars, it was Frank Cotroni who passed out the medals.

Now Frank Cotroni was behind bars again for Giuseppe Montegano's execution-style killing, and his bad fortune brought an improvement in living conditions for his prison-mates at maximum security Archambault prison. Cotroni treated 350 of them to a concert, which he arranged to be presented behind bars free of charge. "I'm not the kind of person to do free shows," said female singer Michele Richard. "But it was a great pleasure for me to accept this personal invitation from Mr. Cotroni who has been following my career for a long time. It wasn't like a normal show because all the lights in the hall were on. I could see their faces and the range of emotions they expressed. At the end of the show they all lined up to give me a kiss. They're all real gentlemen."

Frank Cotroni also granted a rare interview from jail, in which he announced he was preparing a recipe book. He said he was a scrupulously honest man in the kitchen. He admitted that only two-thirds of the recipes in his planned oeuvre would be his own creations; the rest would be from famous cooks, "because I don't like lies and I haven't created enough recipes for a whole book."

His fellow inmates may have been impressed, but police were

not. "Frank Cotroni's probably finished," said a Montreal police officer in December 1988. Right now, [Nick] Rizzuto has the power." But Nick Rizzuto and his son Vito were not in any position to gloat over the apparent ascendancy of their Sicilian wing of Montreal organized crime over the Calabrians. Nick Rizzuto was arrested in the family compound he maintained in Caracas in February 1988 when Venezuelan police said they found 800 grams of cocaine hidden in a special belt used to smuggle drugs through airports. Meanwhile, Italian police hoped to get their hands on him to charge him with Mafia associations. Things were tense for others in Rizzuto's circle, especially around the posh compounds of Gouin Boulevard in north Montreal. Threatening them — and all other Canadian mobsters — was a new weapon that was potentially more effective than the wiretap. It was Bill C-61 which gave authorities sweeping new powers to trace and seize proceeds of enterprise crime. And the bill was buttressed by companion legislation that allowed police of the United States and Britain to continue investigations on foreign soil. Bill C-61 made it an offence to channel criminal money into legitimate businesses and allowed the Crown to take assets of firms found to be fronts for crime. But while the bill's potential seemed great, its immediate impact was negligible, as authorities waited for proper test cases.

Meanwhile, police continued to complain that Canada lacked a witness-protection program comparable to that of the United States, one that would allow authorities to offer relocation, new identities and stipends for gangsters willing to turn on their old bosses. What was available was more modest and less uniform than the American model, and without a new program the Ciro Nieris and Réal Simards would continue to be few and far between.

As the 1990s began, the cast of characters on the streets continued to change dramatically, and there was increasingly vicious competition in the drug trade from Iranian gangs, Chinese, Colombians, Jamaicans and other ambitious newcomers, as well as numerous home-grown criminal groups, including biker gangs. The Cotroni's old benefactor Joe Bonanno, the only surviving member of the American Mafia Commission, was more of a museum piece than a major force in the underworld.

There were plenty of theories about the future of the Cotronis, but they all rang a bit hollow, since they could be ripped apart with the speed a bullet leaves the barrel of a gun.

PART FOUR

Convergence

"We need an approach that is as flexible, as integrated and as collaborative as the groups we are targetting if we wish to be successful."
— RCMP Commissioner Giuliano Zaccardelli

Chapter Twenty-Three

Growing Old

"I want to watch my children and grandchildren grow up."
— Frank Cotroni talks with
reporter from prison

rank Cotroni was in a reflective mood in September 1991
when he was approached by *Journal de Montréal* reporter
Yves Chartrand inside Laval's minimum-security Montée St-
François Institution. Cotroni was serving an eight-year term for the
contract killing of Giuseppe Montegano and fighting extradition to
the United States, where he was wanted on heroin-trafficking charges.
Chartrand was writing a general story about conditions at the prison.
But when he saw the mobster playing softball in the prison yard, he
seized the opportunity for an interview.

At sixty, Cotroni was far from nimble, but he was enjoying himself nevertheless. He was now a softball commissioner of sorts, the
organizer of the game between a visiting group of dentists and the
prisoners, including at least one other killer. The prisoners clearly
liked Cotroni and called him "Frank," but they also respected him
enough to keep a certain distance. The guards seemed to like him,
too.

"That's an organized man," a guard told Chartrand with what
might have been admiration.

Cotroni was amiable when asked if he had some words for the
reporter. "Do you have some liberty in this jail?" Chartrand asked.

"Come with me," Cotroni replied and then led Chartrand towards a building. Cotroni pulled out some keys, unlocked a door, walked a little farther and unlocked another door. As they approached a small room Chartrand could smell tomatoes. Cotroni led Chartrand into the room, where spaghetti sauce was simmering on a small stove. Between chomps on an expensive cigar, Cotroni announced that he was retiring from a life of crime to enjoy his six children and eight grandchildren.

"I want to watch my children and grandchildren grow up. It's in prison that one really comes to realize how precious a thing freedom is and that it's worth fighting for. During my stay here, I've tried to do my best to spread a little happiness." It was the early 1990s and Cotroni certainly had plenty to reflect on.

There's no record of how Cotroni reacted to news of the fate of Sydney Leithman, his former lawyer who had poured drinks for him at a press conference two decades earlier. On May 13, 1991, Leithman was alone in his black Saab convertible at 6:48 in the morning. Just a minute away from his home in Mount Royal, Leithman had been heading along his usual route to the office to present his final arguments in a trial in which he was defending Colombian drug-traffickers. The case had been going horribly for him and his underworld clients. Suddenly, a car in front of the Saab pulled up at a stoplight at the corner of Rockland Road and Monmouth Avenue. A young man walked towards Leithman from beside a telephone booth, pulling out a .45 automatic pistol as he did. The gunman fired slowly, accurately, and professionally, until he leaned right into the automobile. Another driver watched in horror, but the gunman ignored him as he fired methodically at the lawyer. When he stopped shooting, he threw a bag of smoked meat on to the body. Perhaps it was an anti-Semitic statement. Or perhaps the gunman had simply miscalculated how much time he had to snack before Leithman arrived in his Saab. The murder must have served as a grim reminder to Frank Cotroni that globalized organized crime was a high-stakes venture with precious little room for error or miscalculation. Although Frank Cotroni had certainly lost his share of court battles, he had never shot his lawyer afterwards.

It must have been bittersweet for Frank Cotroni, too, when he was briefly allowed out of custody in the company of a guard on July 6, 1991 to attend the marriage of his son Francesco to Mylena DiMaulo, the daughter of his long-time friend Joe DiMaulo. Perhaps that explained why Cotroni was so expansive about the importance of family when Chartrand approached him that September afternoon. However, a Montreal Urban Community police detective who had spent a couple of decades trying to unravel Cotroni's crime career was unmoved by the warm talk of family and happiness: "If you believe Cotroni's a changed man, you probably believe in Santa Claus and flying saucers."

The 1990s opened harshly, too, for Nick Rizzuto's son. Vito Rizzuto faced charges of conspiracy to import 16 tonnes of hashish into Canada. By November 1990, however, those charges had disappeared in a puff of smoke when it was revealed that the RCMP had wiretapped discussions between Vito Rizzuto's lawyer and other defence lawyers involved in the case.

Vito Rizzuto, who was usually mum with outsiders, cheerfully quipped to reporters, "One word can mean so much, especially when that word is 'acquittal.'"

Chapter Twenty-Four

Global Enterprise

*"The Mafia is not a curse from God. It's
a human phenomenon. And like all
human phenomena, it was born
and it can die."*
— Italian judge Giovanni Falcone

Some people called Guiseppe (Joe) Lo Presti "Poor Joe." But the nickname wasn't totally apt. The Montreal man with the sad, soft eyes twitched just a little when he spoke, and his flat voice, slight build and quiet manner didn't make him stand out in a crowded room. But one got the impression that Lo Presti wasn't seeking attention anyway. A closer look at Poor Joe, however, showed he wasn't so poor after all. He drove a late-model, cherry-red Porsche and he lived in a custom-built, neo-Tudor home on Montreal's toney Antoine Berthelet Street, an out-of-the-way cul-de-sac where his only close neighbours were Nick Rizzuto, Nick's son Vito and Nick's brother-in-law Paolo Renda. Lo Presti moved in a circle that motored about in Porsches, Mercedes, Jaguars and even the odd Bentley and Ferrari. But for some reason people close to him — including a businessman with close Liberal Party connections — still called him Poor Joe.

Bloody infighting and increased police pressure in Sicily in the sixties had sent a new wave of heroin-traffickers and money-launderers launderers out across the globe. Although they operated with the blessing of the old North American Mafia families, men such as Lo Presti and Cesare Bonventre emerged as laws unto themselves.

These newly-arrived Sicilians forced Canadian and American authorities to tear up and rework their charts of mob families. Lo Presti's fit in the underworld landscape was unclear. It was doubtless significant that he had been born in Cattolica Eraclea in the province of Agrigento, Sicily, a tiny village that was home to many of Canada's leading mafiosi. The FBI considered him a member of the New York City-based Bonanno family. However, he was also close to the Gambino family of John (The Dapper Don) Gotti. And his contacts stretched back to an associate of Lucien Rivard, the infamous Montreal heroin-trafficker of the 1960s.

Clearly though, Joe Lo Presti was a somebody in the underworld. Just a decade after arriving in Canada in 1969, he was rubbing shoulders with Sicilians close to Nick Rizzuto who had been involved in the murder of Paolo Violi. There were certainly those who thought Lo Presti himself had played a significant role in Violi's demise. Lo Presti's New York acquaintances included Cesare (Tall Guy) Bonventre, a newly-arrived Sicilian bodyguard for the Bonanno boss Carmine Galante. Bonventre later participated in Galante's July 12, 1979 murder. Lo Presti was also among those at the $64,000 wedding reception for Giuseppe (Pino) Bono at the Hotel Pierre in New York City on November 16, 1982. At the wedding, police noted members of the Ciaculli Mafia family of Palermo mingling with members of New York's Bonanno and Gambino families and with a leader of a Neapolitan Camorra organized-crime group.

Lo Presti's name surfaced in the breathtakingly complicated Pizza Connection case when he was charged with importing 30 kilos of heroin for the Gambino family of New York City. The drug busts created enormous problems within the Gambino family because Paul (Big Paul, The Pope) Castellano had decreed that there would be no drug-trafficking as long as he was boss. Castellano realized what countless legitimate lawmakers had known since the dawn of society — it's easier to make laws than to enforce them. (Eddie Lino and John Carneglia, who were also picked up on heroin charges with Lo Presti, were among a group that decided to change bosses rather than change behaviour. Lino and Carneglia were the triggermen when Gambino family members gunned down Castellano outside a New York City steakhouse. This opened the door for John Gotti.)

In the Pizza Connection case, an FBI bug caught Poor Joe making major heroin deals in 1982 with John Gotti's brother Gene and Gambino family soldier, Angelo (Quack Quack) Ruggiero. The jury heard a tape of a May 16, 1982 conversation in which Lo Presti reassured Ruggiero he had spoken to a member of the Cuntrera-Caruana family who had recently moved from Montreal to Caracus.

"He said he was 100 per cent certain our load is coming," Poor Joe Lo Presti said in the taped conversation. "It is in Canada, say a week and a half, before it's here."

There were delays and allegations of jury-tampering. But on February 7, 1990, after a three-week trial, a jury acquitted Lo Presti, Eddie Lino and former Montrealer Gerlando Sciascia of the Bonanno family. The acquittal came after a technical expert admitted it was possible that modern equipment could have been used to alter the tapes in ways that could not be detected. With that display of surprisingly good fortune for someone nicknamed "Poor Joe," Lo Presti slipped quietly back to his mansion on Antoine Berthelet Street.

A couple of years later, on April 28, 1992, there was a meeting of Montreal Calabrians at the home of a former frontman for a Cotroni family nightspot. The host was obviously respected in the underworld of Frank Cotroni, with the power to stop or start big things. The next day, as police wondered about the Calabrian meeting, Joe Lo Presti headed off to a meeting of his own. It was not clear who he planned to meet as he cruised away from Antoine Berthelet Street in his Porsche. It didn't seem like a big thing either, because Lo Presti was always motoring off to see someone at the racquetball courts, donut shops, discos, construction offices, bakeries and sports bars.

No one had to spell out the need for caution to Lo Presti. Since the day he'd been caught on tape talkng to Quack Quack Ruggiero, his old associates Lino and Bonventre had been murdered. The Bonventre slaying was particularly unsettling. He had been found in two pieces in two separate oil drums — a symbol perhaps of his double-cross of his old boss, Carmine Galante. Or perhaps "Tall Guy" was simply too big for one drum. Lo Presti, however, must have trusted whomever he met at a Decarie Boulevard restaurant that day in April, because he left in that person's vehicle.

It was already dark, around 10:30 p.m. at night on April 29, 1992, when the Canadian National rail worker saw a large plastic package lying by the side of the tracks at Fifty-Fourth Avenue and Henri Bourassa Boulevard East in northeast Montreal. As he got closer, he noticed blood. Soon homicide investigators were everywhere. The lifeless body had obviously been dumped by a pro. All identification was gone, but $4,000 was left on the body, a touch that was either arrogant or respectful, but clearly a sign that the hit was not the work of a street punk. When police located Lo Presti's car at the restaurant, a pager inside the Porsche was beeping. The caller was Lo Presti's twenty-three-year-old son, Enzo. He was called upon to identify his father's body at the Parthenais Street morgue.

Mourners looked edgy at the Beaubien Street funeral home where Lo Presti's body lay. There was a good chance that the men responsible for the murder were among them. A top Montreal Sicilian mafiosi and a number of important but low-key mafiosi from New York and Toronto came for the funeral, but there were notably few Calabrians from the old Violi-Cotroni group

Joe Lo Presti's death was like his life — certainly significant, but only a few people understood why, and they weren't sharing their secrets. It was perhaps a compliment to Lo Presti's subtle mind and wide-ranging influence that there were several possible assassins. Was Gotti territory being challenged? Was it Gotti infighting? Or had Lo Presti's long-time Calabrian rivals from the Cotroni group avenged old scores such as Paoli Violi's death a decade-and-a-half before?

What about the Calabrian gathering on the eve of the murder? Was the host a peacemaker? Or an agitator? And where did Frank Cotroni fit in? He was due to be released on parole that summer after serving time for heroin-trafficking and killing a suspected informer. Was Cotroni re-entering his milieu with a bang? Or was he just as confused as everyone else?

There were also questions about two Lo Presti associates who had been murdered earlier in 1992. Normand Hébert had been in the midst of a 300-kilo hashish deal when he pulled his Porsche into a Harvey's restaurant parking lot in North Montreal on January 4 and was gunned down. Then, on February 23, Santo Coverini was shot dead at a rendezvous in downtown Montreal's Little Burgundy district. Were these shootings related? Or were they just reminders of the violence that is inseparable from the drug trade?

Top Sicilian mobsters from Toronto huddled after the funeral, but no tit-for-tat slayings followed. Did this mean they authorized the hit? Or that they were in a fog about whom to attack? There was even a theory that the killer was a woman, which would have explained why the canny mafiosi were caught off-guard.

Quick answers — or even slow ones — were not really expected as some murders are next-to-impossible to solve, both for mobsters and the police. Poor Joe's influence was as real as the smoke from a gun, and just as hard to grasp.

In Italy, crusading judge Giovanni Falcone had devoted his adult life to trying to understand the actions of men like Joe Lo Presti. He knew this put him more at risk than his quarries and that his own murder might well be the inevitable result of his efforts. Only the time and method had yet to be determined. Falcone and his wife, Francesca, had as many as sixty bodyguards — an elite group with cool nerves, quick reflexes, and no spouses or children to slow them down. Sometimes they watched over Falcone's home by air as well as by land. Everyday activities such as jogging or walking alone to a corner store for a newspaper would have been suicidal for the judge. When he did go out for coffee, Falcone would order 10 cups and drink just one, reasoning that this would cut the chances of being poisoned. Once he tried to go to the movies. But security first had to clear the theatre, check everyone's papers, and then take over the front three rows of seats for the judge and his guards. "I don't go to the cinema anymore," he later said. "It's too much trouble for all the other people."

He had a villa by the sea but he found it difficult to relax there after his guards discovered a bag containing 20 kilograms of explosives and a timer on a sunbathing platform just 10 metres offshore. His Palermo neighbours feared they would get caught in a crossfire, and some pressured him to move away from their street. Other Italians took bets on when his death would come. Through it all, Falcone maintained a quiet sense of humour; but his hair was prematurely grey, he chain-smoked, and he admitted to being lonely.

Falcone often travelled to Canada, both for business and for relaxation. Besides Montreal, he spent time in Ottawa, where the RCMP are headquartered, and the Toronto area, where the Sicilian Mafia had made heavy investments in real estate, food stores, factories and restaurants. At times, he would speak to the RCMP about the Cotronis, Nick Rizzuto and the Cuntrera-Caruana clan. But his real focus wasn't the day-to-day, backyard squabbles or machinations of any one group. Falcone stressed that police must look at the big picture: how corruption and the Mafia were inextricably linked and how mafiosi were not Robin Hoods — that their victims included innocent women and children, as well as judges, police and journalists. Perhaps there had once been honour among thieves, but those days were long gone.

To demystify the Sicilian Mafia, Falcone explained the organization's pyramidal power structure. He wanted Canadian police to understand that there were vast differences in trust and decision-making between initiated members and close associates, who might be non-Sicilian. An associate might appear powerful, but he could never command the same respect as a true member. Such nuances were vital for police outside Italy to understand. The Sicilian Mafia could move to different countries, but its mentality and structures remained rigid and Sicilian.

Falcone insisted that police must learn to cooperate on a global level, because major crime groups were already working internationally. He noted that Mafia members were acting as financiers and money-launderers for emerging Colombian cocaine cartels and Asian heroin-trafficking groups. In the end, whoever controlled the money held the most power and was the hardest to catch. All others were little more than hewers of wood and drawers of water.

Ironically, Falcone found peace as well as information in Canada, the same country that offered refuge for many of his Mafia foes and much of their money. The judge loved to drive across the Prairies, and then wheel into the mountains of spectacular Banff National Park, with only his wife, Francesca, and a lone bodyguard from the RCMP sharing space in his car. It wasn't just the natural majesty of the scenery or the exhilaration of breathing the clean mountain air that made these trips so attractive. The popular resort area also offered the illusion, however fleeting, that he was free of the enemies who wanted to see him die a brutal, unnatural death.

There was reason for optimism for Giovanni Falcone in the spring of 1992. He was being touted as the next man to take charge of a new anti-Mafia agency later in the year, and he had already been named Italy's first national anti-Mafia prosecutor. But it was common knowledge that he and his wife often returned to Palermo on weekends — and there was only one highway from Punta Raisi airport to Palermo's downtown. Enemies like Salvatore (Toto, The

Beast) Riina had plenty of time to plot an ambush.

Realizing the threat against him would never die and suspecting there was a mole in the security service, Falcone often travelled in unmarked executive jets on unannounced flights.

That was the case on Saturday, May 23, 1992 when he and his wife drove from the airport towards Palermo's downtown. No one had paid much attention when a work crew tore open a stretch of the highway earlier that week and then repaved it. Also unnoticed that Saturday afternoon was a man perched somewhere on the rocky white cliffs overlooking the highway. With a press of a button, a ton of dynamite hidden under the highway ripped open an entire 500-yard section of pavement, leaving a gaping 40-foot-deep crater. Despite the incredible force of the blast, Falcone was not killed outright but died shortly after he reached the hospital. Francesca clung to life for five hours.

Falcone's associate, Judge Paolo Borsellino, had the honour and the curse of being considered his heir apparent. He lasted less than two months. On July 20, 1992, Borsellino was murdered while visiting his mother in Palermo. And on July 29, 1992, the head of Catania's anti-extortion team, Giovanni Lizzio, was slain.

It's a truism in the underworld that someone is ripe for murder if they are both isolated and dangerous, and that's how Italian law enforcement officials must have felt that horrible summer. The Mafia was too international now for Italy to win the fight alone.

Judge Liliana Ferraro, Italy's director of penal affairs for the minister of justice, appealed in March 1993 to the *Toronto Star* for Canada to tighten up its extradition laws, which she described as more cumbersome than those of Britain or the U.S.

"It is impossible," she warned, "to win this war without cooperation from other countries.

Chapter Twenty-Five

Broken Promise

*"Why don't they turn the whole
country into churches?"*
— Frank Cotroni associate Joe DiMaulo
ridicules the notion of non-smoking casinos

Joe DiMaulo was in a cheerful mood in July 1993 when approached by a reporter at his café in the Metropolitain Est-Viau Sud area of the St. Leonard district, kitty-corner to his nightclub. The reporter wanted to know what DiMaulo thought of new, government-run casinos that were planned for Ontario and Quebec. DiMaulo laughed and said that the best way to keep casinos clean would be to let the Mafia run them.

"That would be the best thing," DiMaulo said with a broad smile. "There would be no prostitutes, no pickpockets."

DiMaulo appeared more amused than angry about the surprise round of questioning, which took place under the gaze of a robust young man with a sweeping moustache, black T-shirt and a pager, who looked like a slightly spruced-up biker. DiMaulo chortled at the thought of the mob being put in charge of keeping crime out of casinos. Others might have shuddered. DiMaulo had been cited in a 1977 Quebec Police Commission report on organized crime as a key lieutenant of Frank Cotroni. Three months before the impromptu interview, Cotroni had been released from prison on parole after serving time for heroin-trafficking and five contract murders.

DiMaulo, a former nightclub doorman and massage parlour operator, had himself been acquitted of a triple-homicide in the early 1970s while his brother Vincenzo (Jimmy) was less fortunate, serving time in the late 1960s and 1970 for murder. Jimmy also had interests in the gambling machine industry. The month before the interview, in June 1993, Montreal police organized-crime squad head Richard McGinnis spoke out about what he saw as the dangers of mobsters in the video poker business. McGinnis claimed video poker machines were already the second highest money-maker for the Montreal mob — behind only the drug trade. Apparently heeding his warning, the Quebec government decided to keep private operators out of video machines in incoming casinos.

That day when he was approached by the reporter, DiMaulo looked cool and casual in a silk Hawaiian shirt. He barked out a one-word expletive to dismiss reports he had approached the Quebec government about getting involved in the casinos.

"It's strictly propaganda," DiMaulo continued, looking the very essence of control and good spirits. Then he ridiculed the idea that Ontario planned non-smoking casinos. "Why don't they turn the whole country into churches?" DiMaulo laughed.

That summer of 1993 there were explosions at two video-poker machine businesses owned partly by Frank Cotroni's forty-three-year-old son Nick. Perhaps they were messages to his father. Perhaps Joe DiMaulo was laughing. But others were obviously not amused.

The chic, ground-floor currency exchange at the busy corner of Peel Street and de Maisonneuve Boulevard in downtown Montreal might not have had the fancy calendars of some of its banking competitors, but it was enormously popular nonetheless. Among the many people who frequented the *Centre International Monetaire de Montréal* were Joe DiMaulo's brother Vincenzo (Jimmy) and Vito Rizzuto's associate, lawyer Joseph Lagana, who often showed up at the foreign-exchange counter with weighty sacks of small bills. The exchange was located at a convenient location, offered comfortable rates and, more importantly, appeared to be discreet to a fault. So perhaps it shouldn't have been surprising that the currency exchange's management had a problem other businesses could only dream of — far more business than it could ever hope to handle.

Soon after it was set up in 1990, the money exchange became a magnet for some twenty-five organized-crime groups. The business's owners were in a fluster. Their problem was the *Centre Interna-*

tional Monetaire de Montréal wasn't really trying to make money. The exchange's secret owner was the RCMP, and undercover officers there were running a police sting operation alternately called "Operation 90-26C" and "Operation Contract." What the Mounties found, however, was that the exchange attracted far more criminals than they could ever hope to handle. Among the regulars were Hells Angels, Sicilian mobsters, Colombian cartels, the West End Gang and the old Cotroni group.

Normally, this would be cause for rejoicing among the police. However, between 1990 and 1994, the Mounties' lack of resources meant the force could only investigate two of the twenty-five crime groups that used its services to launder money. The Mounties didn't even have the resources and manpower to identify all the crime groups doing business there. That meant the police ended up facilitating efforts by Colombian drug-traffickers and Canadian mobs to import close to 5,000 kilograms of cocaine into Central Canada. The coke's street value was about $2 billion. By the time the RCMP pulled the plug on the sting in 1994, the exchange had laundered $135 million of illicit money.

One of the exchange's frequent customers was Sabatino (Sam) Nicolucci who made at least 168 transactions over a two-year period and appeared on more than 400 RCMP wiretapped conversations. Nicolucci was seen as an important member of the Montreal Sicilian Mafia, and he was close to the lawyer Lagana. He was also scheming with David Rouleau, leader of the Hells Angels Sherbrooke chapter, to bring cocaine to Angels in England and to help Chinese gangs import heroin into New York State.

Nicolucci's activities were all the more interesting because he was doing them while out on parole after serving prison time for another drug scheme. In the end, it was criminals and not police who put a halt to Nicolucci's multi-tiered activities. He was kidnapped from a Jean-Talon Street strip club after falling behind in payments to his cocaine suppliers from Cali, Colombia. First, he was held north of Montreal while police frantically tried to locate exactly where he was, using a triangulation technique to trace his cell phone which was still active. Before police could locate him, Nicolucci was taken to Miami and then to the Cali region of Colombia. There was some speculation that he had been executed. But the Cali cartel wanted money more than blood. He was allowed to try to work off his debt while under Colombian house arrest, and Canadian police listening in on wiretaps picked up his voice calling north to a Montreal woman. At this point, his future was, to say the least, precarious. Canadian authorities wanted him on some 233 money-laundering and drug-trafficking charges, including helping the Hells Angels plot to ship 500 kilograms of cocaine into Britain. And the Cali cartel made it known in the underworld that Nicolucci wouldn't be seen again in Montreal until they received some $1.7 million they said they were owed. The police and underworld merged when Nicolucci's associates went to the bogus RCMP money exchange to draft ransom cheques. It was at this point that the police pulled the plug on the sting operation.

Agents of the U.S. Drug Enforcement Agency eventually liberated Nicolucci ninja-style from his Colombian captors — only to turn him over to American authorities in Bogota who, in turn, extradited him to Quebec in May 1996. There, Nicolucci was sentenced to nineteen years in prison in December 1997 for his role in attempting to import more than 400 kilos of cocaine and launder some $30 million.

Corporal Jocelyn Chagnon of the RCMP had participated in the arrests from the sting, which explained why he was approached by his landlord in July 1995. The landlord wanted to know if there was any way that Jimmy DiMaulo of the Frank Cotroni group might be sentenced to less time in prison than the fifteen years demanded by the Crown. If this could be arranged, the landlord continued, he had a friend who was prepared to give Chagnon a cool $100,000.

Chagnon informed his RCMP superiors of the offer, and then helped set up another sting. This time, hidden microphones and a video camera were placed in Chagnon's apartment, and he met there with his landlord on August 7, 1995. The cautious landlord mouthed the money offer but did not come right out and say the words.

That was enough for the Mounties to move anyway. And when the arrests for attempting to bribe the officer were made, Jimmy DiMaulo's brother Joe was among those caught in the Mountie net. However, there wasn't evidence for a case against him, and so, on August 18, 1995, he was set free. This time he looked grizzled rather than jaunty, but he still tried to joke to the press anyway, saying, "Two days in jail, in a 10-foot by 40-foot cell...it wasn't pleasant. But I love to follow the law."

There's no record of any of the DiMaulos laughing when, in March 1997, Jimmy pleaded guilty to the original charges and was sentenced to twelve years for drug conspiracy and eight years each on two money-laundering counts, all to be served concurrently. For his role in the botched bribery, the Mountie's landlord was given an eighteen-month conditional sentence — meaning he did not have to go behind bars.

The massive money exchange sting did not result in any cases against Vito Rizzuto, but it did disrupt his golf game. In 1995, at age fifty-one, Vito Rizzuto claimed he played golf a hundred times a year at exclusive clubs in the Montreal area. He said he enjoyed participating in tournaments for the benefit of Italian associations. When not on the links, Rizzuto was often spotted at a north-end social club on Jarry Street East that was also frequented by his father, Nick, who had returned to Montreal after being released from a Venezuelan prison where he'd been serving five years for cocaine-trafficking.

After the *Centre International Monetaire de Montréal* sting operation, however, Vito Rizzuto's golf foursome was broken up when authorities convicted his childhood friend and schoolmate Valentino Morielli of conspiring to bring cocaine into Canada via Miami and the Cayman Islands. Another potential golf partner for Vito, the lawyer Joseph Lagana, ended up behind bars as perhaps the Mounties' biggest catch. Lagana was sentenced to thirteen years in jail. (He would be released, though, after just two years under a non-violent offender program.)

While others were stumbling into the Mountie sting, Frank Cotroni was released on parole on April 17, 1993. It was soon clear that he had made many contacts while in custody, and now he was spending much time on the streets of Montreal and Toronto with Iranian and Iraqi immigrants, including Mahmood (Moe) Adolaymi, a former Iraqi soldier who ran an import business in downtown Toronto. Moe met Cotroni through Moroccan-born Shahrias Lalehzar of Montreal, who said the Cotroni clan planned to begin importing heroin from Europe and they could use Moe's help. This was in May 1993, just weeks after Cotroni's release, and Lalehzar was telling Moe that he had been working for Frank Cotroni for a year. Obviously, being locked up hadn't stopped Cotroni from minding his business.

In fact, Cotroni had actually expanded his contacts while in custody, much like a professor broadens his horizons during a sabbatical. He had become a better criminal. Now he was working with Mideast criminals who had done prison time with him.

"They worked very well together," Moe later recalled. "It's 'You scratch my back, I'll scratch yours.' Otherwise, it's war."

By September 1993, Moe was meeting face-to-face with Frank Cotroni and his son Francesco, family lieutenants Antonio (Tony) Volpato and Giovanni (Johnny) Marra, Lalehzar and others at Montreal restaurants controlled by the Cotronis.

Early on in their association, one of the crime family members made it clear that they weren't to be trifled with. "If you fuck with me," he warned Moe, "I'll find you. I'll find you now or in the future. Don't think we won't find you. We're a worldwide organization."

Cotroni also made a few trips to Toronto where he met with two old cronies on St. Clair Avenue West in the city's Little Italy district. One had been a bootlegger and was now a meatpacker and banquet hall owner. The other was a pleasant old baker. They were both considered cell leaders of the Calabrian *'ndrangheta* Mafia strain.

On December 16, 1993, Moe met Frank and Francesco Cotroni, Tony Volpato, and Lalehzar and others at a Montreal restaurant. Moe seemed a little offended. Why didn't Frank Senior call him when he was in Toronto? Cotroni replied that he did not want to put "heat" on Moe, as he felt he was constantly being watched by police. Things were going ahead, but they were moving extremely slowly and cautiously.

Then, on February 22, 1994, Lalehzar told Moe about a "seizure in the East" and that it had affected their "friends." That was about the time 5,385 kilos of cocaine were seized by the RCMP in Nova Scotia. Because of this, said Lalehzar, Frank and Tony had lost a lot of money. Now they would have no choice but to come to Moe. Shortly afterwards, Cotroni's old Toronto friend, ex-boxer Eddie Melo, said he would be going to Moe's export-import business, the Hudson Brownell Company, to check it out.

On July 22, 1994, there was a meeting at a swish non-mob Toronto restaurant that's popular with the Hollywood North movie crowd. This time there was Volpato, Melo, a Toronto lawyer, and Moe. The lawyer, who was close to Eddie Melo, always seemed to be around when the Montrealers came to town. Moe was again questioned about his business. Outside the restaurant, Volpato took Moe aside and said he would be going to Venezuela in a few weeks to "open a few doors."

By now, the mobsters had a Toronto warehouse, but still no drugs to put inside it. Moe was told to be patient. "Just wait. We'll tell you. Just wait till we tell you," he later recalled them saying.

On December 7, 1994, Lalehzar mentioned that Tony Volpato wanted to talk to Moe alone, without Frank Cotroni, because they might be able to do something with the Montreal Sicilians. While Cotroni was still important, when it came to the Italian mob, he clearly wasn't the only game in town.

On January 26, 1995, Frank Cotroni's conditional parole was revoked after he was seen with Volpato, among others. The fact that Frank Cotroni was back in custody didn't end the dealings. He dispatched a family member to travel to Colombia to meet two heads of the Cali cocaine cartel. Moe was told now that, after the tortuous wait, there would be a 200- to 500-kilogram shipment of cocaine in a cargo of shrimp from Ecuador. The second shipment of 2,000 kilograms was to follow almost immediately afterwards. Then there'd be further shipments of up to 10,000 kilograms, with some of the cocaine to be redirected to the Colombian organization in New York.

One of two containers of cocaine was to come in a shipment of tiles from Panama, while another shipment would be sent in "ecological coffee" from Peru. Just as the shipments were about to start, Cotroni was to be released on parole yet again. On the eve of his September 26, 1995 release from custody, Frank Cotroni must have been in a festive mood. The drugs were finally coming. His freedom was imminent. Life was good. And about thirty fellow inmates at the minimum-security Montée St-François Institution in Laval were giving him a touching little send-off with roast beef and pork chops that had been smuggled into prison. It was perhaps a bad omen for Cotroni that the farewell party was nixed when guards confiscated the uneaten contraband. He could only hope that authorities outside the jail weren't so vigilant.

Cotroni was released. And this time, his freedom lasted a little over half a year. On April 17, 1996, Cotroni was back in custody, charged with conspiracy to import 180 kilograms of cocaine into Canada. The cautious, slow-moving old mobster learned that "Moe" was, in fact, a paid RCMP double-agent, part of yet another police sting operation.

On April 4, 1997, Frank Cotroni was in court to face the new drug charges. By this time, his right-hand man, Giovanni (Johnny) Marra, had already been sentenced to fourteen years in prison. Things looked grim for Cotroni. Marra's case showed Cotroni had direct contact with the Cali cartel and influence throughout the eastern seaboard region of the United States. Cotroni wasn't in a fighting mood. He quickly pleaded guilty. From plea to sentencing, his court proceedings took just twenty-five minutes. Now, at age sixty-six, he heard himself sentenced to seven years in prison, and he would have to serve at least half of that before he had any chance of parole. His namesake son, Francesco Jr., got eight years.

Police love to talk about the "mistress factor" regarding wire-tapped conversations. That's when officers gain leverage after inter-cepting mobsters bragging about their extramarital sexual adven-tures. If a mobster is married to a woman from a significant crime family, this can be deeply disturbing on several levels, and so a quick guilty plea is often prudent. The alternative — hearing a rude tape played in open court in front of a spouse and in-laws as part of character evidence — is chilling, even for hardened underworld members.

This, however, wasn't the case with Frank Cotroni when he made his quick guilty plea. And it wasn't that he had seen the light or the error of his ways. Frank Cotroni simply took a cool look at the disclosure material and knew his best option was to concede defeat and cut his losses. He must have known that his notorious name would work against him with a jury. He must also have thought that it would be nice to get out of the rough jail where he was being held and back into the minimum security institution where he had been allowed to drive himself about in a golf cart. He needed two opera-tions to relieve pressure on his legs, and he could have that done in prison. He risked twice the time in prison — like the Morra sen-tence — if he fought and lost, and so the guilty plea made good business sense.

"I guess he did a risk assessment and thought the sentence rec-ommendation was reasonable," federal prosecutor Richard Starck said later.

Chapter Twenty-Six

Death of Johnny Pops

*"You never worry about your enemies.
It's your friends who bury you."*
— Ron Sandelli, former head of
Metro Toronto police intelligence unit

Ken Murdock was a streetfighter and small-time hood — not the type of person who worried about consequences. But Murdock was nervous. It was Saturday afternoon, May 31, 1997, as he walked up to the door of the Galaxy Vending office on Hamilton's dead-end Railway Street in the city's old Italian district.

For as long as anyone in Hamilton could remember, Railway Street was the centre of the personal fiefdom of Frank Cotroni's old associate, Johnny (Pops) Papalia. Back in 1924, the year Papalia was born in Hamilton, there were two murders on the tiny inner-city street as bootleggers fought for control of the illegal alcohol business. One of the top bootleggers back then was Papalia's father, Antonio, who worked for Rocco Perri, the Canadian lieutenant for Chicago's Al Capone. Years later, Perri disappeared and his wife, Bessie, was murdered. Suspicious fingers pointed toward Railway Street and Antonio Papalia. Now, Johnny Pops lived in a penthouse apartment a five-minute walk away, returning daily by foot or by Cadillac to one-block Railway Street where almost all the shabby homes were owned by family members and friends, and where eyes and ears were supposed to be sympathetic to him.

Ken Murdock had set out to see Johnny Pops twice over the past couple of weeks.

The first time was on Railway Street. But Murdock felt there were too many people around so he left quietly. The next time Murdock went to Papalia's penthouse on nearby Market Street, but he went to the wrong door. By the time Murdock realized his mistake, Papalia was greeting another visitor. Both times, Murdock had been packing a loaded gun, and both times he had lost his nerve and shuffled away before asking to meet the old mobster.

This time, Murdock finally summoned up the courage to open up the front door of Galaxy Vending. There, directly in front of him, was Johnny Pops. Murdock hadn't seen Papalia face-to-face before, but he recognized him instantly nonetheless. Everybody in Murdock's world knew what Johnny Pops looked like. His photo was often published in newspapers and books and flashed across the television screen, so that his hooked nose and scarred cheeks seemed as much a part of gritty Hamilton as its steel mills and omnipresent donut shops.

"I'm Ken Murdock," he said. "Could I have a minute of your time...outside?"

Inside the office that Saturday afternoon was another old man, and he and Papalia both took a hard look at the thirty-five-year-old. Johnny Pops had perfected the art of the cold hard stare, and, in a flash, he could make his eyes seem utterly devoid of emotion and humanity. That Saturday afternoon, however, Johnny Pops decided to give Murdock a few minutes of his time, stepping outside and leading Murdock around to the parking lot. Then he ordered Murdock to get to the point.

Murdock made up a story that Pasquale (Pat) Musitano, the son of deceased Mafiosi Dominic Musitano, owed him $10,000. Murdock was really just feeling Papalia out until he got the nerve to act on his real reason for the visit.

"I guess you'd say, [I was] working up the nerve to do whatever it is I've got to do," Murdock later said. What he felt he had to do was both simple and terrifying: murder the old gangster.

Murdock told Johnny Pops he wanted to know how he should go about collecting the $10,000. Papalia replied that he wanted to know why Murdock was asking him this.

"Well, apparently you're the godfather to him," Murdock replied.

Johnny Pops appeared to be chewing over these comments. But

218

Murdock was too nervous to keep quiet. Now, Murdock was talking about how his stepfather had done time with Johnny Pops in Collins Bay Penitentiary.

Papalia took out a pack of cigarettes and offered Murdock one. Then, about 20 minutes after the conversation had begun, Johnny Pops ended things abruptly, saying, "Do whatever you want. I'm not getting involved."

Papalia turned on his heels to walk away. That was when Murdock pulled out his .38 revolver and fired one shot to the back of Johnny Pop's head. Ella Lautenbach, who'd moved to Railway Street a week before, heard the gunshot and then a woman screaming, "Keep your kids in the house! Someone was just shot!"

Just days earlier, Lautenbach had seen Johnny Pops giving popsicles to neighbourhood children. Now she could see Johnny Pops — her landlord — lying on the pavement bleeding, and she ran towards him. She held him, checking his fading pulse in the tortuous minutes before an ambulance arrived.

Murdock sped away in a green pickup truck to an auto body shop, where he had left his getaway vehicle, a Chrysler Intrepid. Then he headed towards his home on Knox Avenue in industrial east Hamilton. As he drove, he put the revolver into a paper bag and tossed it in the bed of a pickup truck parked at one of the city's many Tim Horton's donut shops.

Around 2:30 p.m. — only an hour after the shooting — Murdock was paged by Hamilton-Wentworth police Detective Vic Rees. The message arrived just as Papalia was drawing his final breaths in hospital. Murdock called the police officer back, playing it cool. Rees wanted to know if Murdock had heard what had happened that day on Railway Street.

"No. I don't know nothin' about it," Murdock lied.

Police investigators knew enough to make theories but no arrests. Investigators noted it wasn't a clean hit. Johnny Pops was shot in the back of the head, so the killer didn't have to look him in the eyes. It was also a single bullet, so death wasn't instant or even certain. "It was a gutless one," concluded a veteran cop who had known Johnny Pops for decades.

Murdock didn't feel like being alone. So he turned his car west and headed to the Gathering Spot restaurant on James Street North, about a ten-minute walk from Papalia's office. Diners knew the Gathering Spot for its tasty thin-crust pizza. Mobsters thought of it as a place to meet with Pat Musitano, whose father, Dominic, had died a couple years earlier of a heart attack.

Murdock had been the triggerman for old Dominic Musitano in the drive-by machine-gun slaying of Salvatore Alaimo, a janitor at the Stelco steel plant. Murdock had nothing against Alaimo, but the elder Musitano had ordered the hit, and so Alaimo was gunned down as he worked in the garage of his home. Later, Murdock learned that Alaimo had done nothing wrong but had had the misfortune of being related to someone who angered the elder Musitano.

Now, Murdock was pulling a trigger for old Dominic's sons. Murdock considered Pat and his brother, Angelo, friends. And he liked to think they were showing their trust and respect when they once presented him with an expensive gold ring bearing his initials. As Murdock understood it, the hit on Johnny Pops was about money. Pat owed money to the old gangster and, Murdock later said, "There was pressure. And he went from that to, you know, that he didn't feel too comfortable owing John money is what it boiled down to. I don't feel he had the money to pay John back and, from the tone of the voice from him asking me to do basically John, that he was scared."

There were others who thought that Pat Musitano had more far-reaching reasons. He was considered friendly with Montreal Sicilians who had recently arrived in Ontario, and they considered Johnny Pops a relic from the old American La Cosa Nostra and a bothersome obstacle to their expansion. Naturally, the Musitanos would not feel the need to share this connection with a street-level criminal like Murdock.

That Saturday afternoon of the Papalia murder, Murdock later recalled, "I seen Pat outside, and that's when, while we were hugging each other, I told him, 'It's done.' He more or less said 'Thank you' and told me the place was crawling with cops and to 'Get out of there.'"

Murdock expected money as well as thanks, but now wasn't the time to ask for it. He was supposed to get $10,000 and 15 ounces of cocaine for the killing but said he would have done it for nothing because it was "for the family." Ultimately, he got about $2,000 for the hit. He also got the cocaine. Now, Murdock's habit jumped from one gram to about 10 grams a week.

"It numbs my mind," Murdock later said. "It does make you paranoid, but mostly it numbs my mind."

While Murdock was waiting to collect, there was plenty of speculation going on about who pulled the trigger on Johnny Pops. Papalia and his old associate Enio Mora had apparently invested money in real estate for the new group of Sicilian mobsters from Montreal who moved into Toronto in the 1990s, setting up a ritzy restaurant on Avenue Road and a splashy west-end nightclub. Millions of dollars went missing, and Johnny Pops had a new set of enemies along with the legions of old ones. Mora was murdered the previous fall, lending weight to the angry Sicilians' theory. Perhaps Johnny Pops was simply slain by a crazy person who wanted to kill someone famous. That, said some people, would explain the sloppiness of the killing. There were also sometimes rocky business dealings between Papalia and cigarette smugglers and biker gangs. Inside Papalia's own group there was grumbling as some Niagara region mobsters chafed at the feeling that he'd never step aside. Johnny Pops seemed ready to go on forever, unless someone did something about it. His relations with outlaw bikers were also a question. Johnny Pops was old school while the Hells Angels and Montreal Sicilians were new wave, and those who didn't embrace the change risked being swallowed up by it. There was general agreement among those familiar with the mob, however, that whoever killed Johnny Pops must have been someone he didn't fear, since he didn't turn his back on many people.

"You never worry about your enemies," said Ron Sandelli, former head of Metro Toronto intelligence, who worked for years on cases involving Papalia. "It's your friends that bury you."

There was a second shock for Papalia's family the week of his death. The Roman Catholic Church announced it was denying Johnny Pops a church burial because of his underworld lifestyle. The refusal was the first in memory in Canada, and Father Gerard Bergie, a spokesperson for the Hamilton diocese, admitted it was "extraordinary." Papalia's old Montreal mentor from the 1950s, Carmine Galante, had been denied mass with his funeral service back in New York in 1979, and a couple of decades before that, mass had been refused in New York for Albert (the Executioner) Anastasia. Domenic Pugliese, a close friend of the Papalias, said the family believed the Hamilton diocese had no authority to make such a decision. "Jesus was crucified with two thieves on the cross," he said. "Is the bishop above Jesus?"

From the Church's point of view, it was tough to give Johnny Pops the benefit of the doubt. Clearly, someone thought he was still dangerous at the end of his life or he wouldn't have been shot. And since he was shot in the back of his head, he didn't see his death coming that afternoon. While Jesus forgave those who repented their sins, Johnny Pops' killer didn't give him a final chance to make his peace with God.

"We have no indication [Papalia] repented the criminal activities he was involved in," Bergie said.

The final snub for Johnny Pops came from his old cronies. The turnout of 350 mourners was relatively sparse for the funeral service on Barton Street East, just a ten-minute walk from Railway Street, where Johnny Pops was born, raised, and murdered. Adding insult to fatal injury, Pat Musitano held court outside the funeral home, providing an easy photo opportunity to press and police photographers gathered on the other side of the street. "I didn't think this [funeral turnout] was very respectful," a veteran police officer specializing in organized crime said. "When you think of the people of his generation...they weren't there to be seen." Inside the funeral home, a female relative tearfully denounced his killer as a "coward" and a priest said prayers for Papalia's soul and his family's comfort.

In his day, Johnny Pops had been considered big enough in the underworld that U.S. Senator and Attorney General Bobby Kennedy mentioned him during his organized crime probe of the early 1960s. And in the late 1980s, a police intelligence report ranked him as Ontario's top mobster. The day of his funeral, however, watchers noted that his final send-off paled compared to those of his contemporaries. Just one vehicle carrying floral arrangements was needed to escort his casket to the Bayview Crematorium in Burlington. Vic Cotroni's funeral procession required 23 cars sporting spectacular floral arrangements — as well as a brass band. Even Papalia's little-known associate, Enio Mora of Toronto, had rated five vehicles carrying flowers after his bullet-riddled body was found in the trunk of his gold Cadillac the previous September.

"For his [Papalia's] connections, I would have thought...there'd be better flower arrangements," a police officer said, sounding oddly like a commentator at the Rose Bowl Parade.

It wasn't long before shockwaves from the Johnny Pops murder were felt from Buffalo, N.Y., about an hour's drive from where he was slain. The Musitano brothers learned about a meeting in Buffalo attended by Johnny Pops' Niagara Falls lieutenant, Carmen Barillaro. What the Musitanos heard about that meeting was both insulting and threatening. "Word came back to Pat more or less that he was next," Murdock later said. "The only details I got was the meeting took place and supposedly through the leader over there, the right-hand man trickled information back and Carmen was stated as saying at the table, at the meeting, 'I'll take care of that fat piece of shit myself.'"

That's why Murdock and his friend Angelo Musitano drove down to the Falls on July 23, 1997, on the eve of Barillaro's fifty-third birthday. With Angelo Musitano waiting in a car outside, Murdock knocked on the front door of Barillaro's upscale home. When Barillaro came to the door, Murdock asked him if the red Corvette in the driveway was for sale. Barillaro wasn't one to humour idiots or strangers and Murdock appeared to be both, so Barillaro told him to shove off. The niceties were suddenly over and Murdock pushed his way past the heavily-muscled mobster.

"Barillaro seemed to understand what was about to occur," Murdock later said.

Murdock pulled out a 9-millimetre pistol. Barillaro ran to another room but then suddenly turned back and rushed Murdock. The hitman squeezed off two shots, killing the Papalia lieutenant.

Late in 1998, Murdock was arrested for extortion. At first, awaiting trial on that charge, Murdock was stoic in jail. But his mood turned angry when police played him a tape that suggested his life was in danger from the very gangsters he'd tried so hard to impress. He felt he had no options left except to turn on his old associates. And so, on October 22, 1998, Murdock signed an agreement to cooperate with police. He pleaded guilty to three counts of second-degree murder in the slayings of the janitor Salvatore Alaimo, Papalia and Barillaro and was given life in prison with no chance of parole for thirteen years.

When Murdock took the witness stand on June 16, 1999 to testify at the preliminary hearing of his former friends, the Musitano brothers looked at him from the prisoners' dock with expressions of utter disdain and disgust. Pat and Angelo were each charged with one count of first-degree murder and Angelo was also charged with the murder of Barillo.

"I've known Ang since he was yay-high," Murdock testified in cross-examination by defence lawyer Dean Paquette. "You know, like this is the hardest thing for me to do right here. It's tearing me apart inside because I do love these guys, in a sense."

Then Murdock turned towards Pat and Angelo Musitano and asked, "Do you understand? Even though you don't believe it. I know you're hurt. I'm...hurt."

Pat, who was thirty-two, shrugged and rolled his eyes while twenty-two-year-old Angelo shot a look at his mother, sister, brother and the coterie of Musitano supporters. The brothers might be disgusted but they knew they were caught. They pleaded guilty to conspiracy to murder Barillaro and were sentenced to ten years in jail.

Four months after the murder of Johnny Pops, Frank Cotroni received yet another reminder of mortality. On Saturday August 30, 1997, an elderly group returned to the old Little Italy neighbourhood around Notre Dame della Difesa Church for the funeral of Antonietta (née Seminaro) Cotroni, who died at age seventy-three. Antonietta was the widow of Frank's brother Pep, and she had died after a long illness. Most of her post-Pep life had been lived in the Town of Mount Royal. She also ran a wig business out of a shop on Ste. Catherine Street East. Plus she managed a family-owned real estate company and administered a number of properties she owned. Pep had been in and out of prison before dying of natural causes in September 1979, and so it had fallen to Antonietta to raise her family almost single-handedly. One of the last matriarchs of the Cotroni clan, she was remembered fondly for her love of cooking big Italian meals for her daughters and grandchildren.

By the time of Antonietta's death, the only surviving Cotroni brother, Frank, and his namesake son Francesco, then thirty-six, were both in prison for cocaine-trafficking, and so they couldn't hear the eighteen elderly Italian musicians in blue uniforms playing Chopin's mournful funeral march as her coffin was carried out into the grey hearse. There were some nine matching grey limousines with huge funeral bouquets, a couple of which were shaped to read "Mamma" and "Ma Tante." It was like a scene from another time.

By now, the old neighbourhood where the Cotronis had built their power base had a strong South American flavour, and the families of old Italians like Antonietta Cotroni returned only to get married or buried.

Chapter Twenty-Seven

Dirty Laundry

"Everything is false."
— Former pig farmer and international
money-launderer Alfonso Caruana

It was a blunt, rude, tactless question — just what you might expect from a lawyer working for Revenue Canada. Lawyer Chantal Comtois asked Alfonso Caruana during an income tax hearing in Montreal in March 1997 if he was the Mafia's godfather.

"If only it were true," Caruana replied.

Comtois was undaunted, and continued, "Is it true that you owned 160 square kilometres of land in Venezuela near the Colombian border?"

"Everything is false," replied the fifty-one-year-old man who now lived in the community of Woodbridge north of Toronto. Caruana had been compelled to appear in the courtroom in an attempt to fend off Revenue Canada's demand for $29.8 million in unpaid taxes and penalties. That was a hefty financial burden, especially if one was inclined to believe Caruana's claim that he made just $400 a week washing and waxing vehicles at a car wash he owned.

During his income-tax hearing, Caruana was hard-pressed to explain why people seemed to keep bringing him money, or how that money found its way eventually to Switzerland.

"You went back and forth — Venezuela, Montreal, Switzerland?" Justice Derek Guthrie asked.

"No, I had it brought to me," Caruana replied.

"By whom?" the judge asked.

"By travellers," Caruana replied, declining to elaborate.

Superior Court Justice Derek Guthrie noted that some $21 million passed through Caruana's bank account in 1981 — one of several years when he didn't file an income tax return. Caruana acted puzzled by the amount and said he was unable to offer an explanation. After the mystery mega-sums had passed through his account, Caruana had declared bankruptcy.

For many years, Caruana had been able to escape this unwanted attention. His father learned the ways of Mafia stealth in Agrigento, Sicily, under Don Giuseppe Settecasi, the same man who was sent to Montreal to mediate the Paolo Violi–Nick Rizzuto feud back in the seventies. Caruana's family originally came to Canada around 1967, when he was a teenager. He arrived in the Montreal courtroom in 1997 via a circuitous route: from the dusty village of Siculiana in southern Sicily to Montreal, then on to South America and Britain where he lived in a Sicilian enclave nicknamed the "Stockbroker Belt" in the south-eastern town of Woking. (Woking's claim to fame is as the site where the Martians landed in H.G. Wells' novel *The War of the Worlds*.) Caruana left Europe shortly before a wave of money-laundering and drug-trafficking arrests hit his business associates. During their travels, the Caruana and Cuntrera families of Siculiana intermarried, creating in the words of academic researcher Tom Blickman, "a curious mix of Sicilian old-fashioned patriarchal clannishness (which protects them from infiltration) and modern global enterprise in illegal commodities."

Tax problems were irritating, but not the worst of Caruana's woes. The rival Corleonesi Mafia clan of Sicily wanted to kill him because they thought he had become too rich and too arrogant. And Italian authorities had been after him for twenty-two years to lock him up after he was convicted *in absentia* of drug-trafficking and Mafia association.

His problems with Revenue Canada dated back to the mid-1980s. At that point, he moved to Venezuela, where he said he worked as a pig farmer. Meanwhile, up in Canada, Revenue Canada seized some $800,000 of his assets. When the 1997 hearing was over, the news wasn't so bad for Caruana. Judge Guthrie ordered him to pay only $90,000 of the tax bill over the next three years.

"I don't believe a word he said . . . ," Guthrie concluded. "I don't believe the bankrupt [Caruana] and his wife, whose testimonies were full of holes, hesitations and incomplete explanations, but I must render my judgement based on proof, not suspicions."

But within a year, on July 15, 1998, the former pig farmer with the poor memory was subjected to even harsher scrutiny. Alfonso Caruana was arrested with thirteen others on charges of conspiracy to import cocaine, conspiracy to traffic in cocaine and importing cocaine in a series of pre-dawn raids by some two hundred officers in Toronto, Montreal, the U.S. and Mexico.

Police said that when he wasn't washing cars or raising pigs Caruana moonlighted as the head of a multibillion-dollar Mafia group, one of the most powerful in the world, that specialized in drug-trafficking and money-laundering. His group had bases throughout the world, including Miami, New York, Mexico City, Toronto, Montreal, Houston, Italy, Spain, the Netherlands, Venezuela, Aruba, England, France, Germany, Spain, Thailand and India. The sophisticated organization moved drug profits from accounts in Toronto and Montreal to Miami, Houston, Mexico City, through numbered accounts in Lugano, Switzerland, and from there to Colombia.

The Cuntrera-Caruana clan was called "the Mafia's Rothschilds" by journalist Giuseppe D'Avanzo in the Italian newspaper *la Repubblica*. Canadian police called their effort to bag them, Project *Omertà,* which meant conspiracy of silence in Italian, a name wholly appropriate for the tight-lipped Caruanna.

Arrested along with Caruana for conspiracy to import cocaine were his brothers Gerlando of St. Leonard, Quebec and Pasquale of Maple, Ontario. It was a coup, both by police and by underworld standards, when the Canadian police scooped them up. Until that point, despite his notoriety in police circles, Alfonso Caruana enjoyed relative privacy in his $400,000 home on Goldpark Court in Woodbridge. He and his family had no record of violence and were financiers and facilitators, not gunmen. In a milieu where leaders had nicknames like "The Executioner" and "The Beast," Caruana was known as "The Ghost."

Caruana held his head high when arrested, even when the police cruiser in which he was travelling was surrounded by news photographers. It was a dignified and sharp contrast to a flabby co-accused, who looked bewildered as he was helped from a police cruiser and led into the police station wearing shorts, a plaid shirt and slippers while an officer carried a tray of his medications.

Arrested by Italian police that spring of '98 was Caruana's

brother-in-law, Pasquale Cuntrera, who was picked up in Spain. He was in his seventies and confined to a wheelchair, but that didn't stop him from somehow escaping custody in May while awaiting sentencing in a drug-trafficking case. The escape caused a national scandal in Italy.

Pasquale and his brothers Paolo and Gaspare had lived in Venezuela before being expelled for "security reasons." They'd managed to accumulate widespread real estate investments in Montreal and indirect investments in the Toronto area. Police heard of their operations from Frank Cotroni's old associate, informer Tommaso Buscetta. In Buscetta's time in Montreal, Alfonso Caruana had flipped pizzas in a modest pizzeria in Montreal and his wife had operated the cash register.

By the time of their arrest, they were accused of laundering some $70 million in Mafia heroin profits between 1980 and 1984. The multibillion-dollar operation was hit by police operating on a shoestring budget.

Because it's extremely difficult to infiltrate or pry informers from a traditional Mafia group, police had to go the expensive route of using electronic bugs. It takes a lot of money to pay for wiretaps. Much of the cost is in labour— transcribing phone calls, surveying suspected smugglers. And because smugglers don't work office hours, a lot of overtime is involved. The two-year police operation cost $2 million, and funds dried up at one point until the Criminal Intelligence Service of Ontario kicked in a "substantial" amount of money to keep things going. Police knew of other alleged organized crime figures living comfortably in Woodbridge and other parts of Canada, but didn't have the resources to also combat them.

When Alfonso Caruana was sentenced to eighteen years in prison, police could say that they had lopped off the head of a state-of-the-art, multibillion-dollar, transnational crime enterprise. They could not, however, say that they had killed his organization. They also couldn't say that there weren't countless other still-alive groups with different faces but similar intentions. Authorities estimated that some $17 billion was laundered in Canada each year making Canada, in the words of RCMP Chief Superintendent Ben Soave, head of the Toronto Integrated Intelligence Unit, "a haven for organized crime."

Soave's words were borne out in the sentences served by the money-launderers. Antonio LaRosa of Montreal was sentenced to four years for his role in conspiring to import some 1,500 kilograms of cocaine into Canada. He qualified for an accelerated parole review because he was classed as a first-time, non-violent offender, and got his parole within eight months.

Alfonso's nephew, Giuseppe Caruana, was paroled eight months into his four-year-sentence because he didn't have a criminal history and his crimes were considered nonviolent. "There has been no evidence to suggest that you are planning to commit a violent offence," the National Parole Board concluded.

And Alfonso Caruana was somehow eligible for parole because of time already served when he pleaded guilty in February 2000, despite his conviction and sentencing *in absentia* by an Italian court to a twenty-two-year-term.

This time, though, the board exercised some discretion and did not let him walk out of the courtroom a free man the day of his conviction. Parole was denied. Caruana would stay in jail.

Chapter Twenty-Eight

Hitting Home

*"I made a deal with the Italians. That's
the price now."*
— A Hells Angel fixes the price of
cocaine with the mob.

If his last name had not been "Cotroni," then what happened to Frank's son Paul on August 23, 1998, would not have made the national news. That night, Paul Cotroni had just returned home to his modest split-level house on Pigalle Street in Repentigny, just east of Montreal. As he stepped out of his blue Corvette, two men opened fire. By the time his wife ran outside to find him lying on the driveway, he was bleeding from three bullet wounds to his head and neck, and the gunmen were gone. Paul was still alive the next morning when police found two handguns in a vacant lot nearby a Jehovah's Witness meeting hall. By this point, the two dried puddles of blood on Paul's driveway were attracting curious neighbourhood kids. Their parents told reporters what neighbours usually say about underworld figures who live nearby — they were quiet but friendly. Finally, after a thirty-six-hour battle to stay alive, Paul Cotroni died in the neurological unit of the Sacre-Coeur Hospital.

Naturally, the murder of Frank Cotroni's son was noticed by police.But officers didn't consider Paul a major player in the underworld. He had been known to mingle in Hells Angels circles, and he had associations with their affiliated clubs, the Rockers and the Death Riders. He had been charged with drug possession in 1990 and 1992, but both cases were dropped before trial. In 1991, he pleaded guilty to possession of stolen goods and was fined after police found a motorboat and a trailer in his garage. He wasn't an innocent, but he was hardly a godfather.

There were rumours, however, that he was selling diluted cocaine to bikers and that he felt safe doing so because of his family name. Then, as the stories went, the bikers did their own risk assessment and decided that Paul's father, Frank — who was in custody yet again — was no longer a major threat. "They [Frank's crime family] didn't have the clout in place," a veteran police officer said. The shooting of Paul Cotroni sent a chilling message to the old Italian underworld. No one could remember the last time the son of a crime boss had been executed. Suddenly the bosses, and their families, were all a little more vulnerable.

Paul's younger brother, thirty-seven-year-old Francesco, was tough enough to avenge Paul's murder — he'd been found guilty of the 1981 fatal shooting of a drug dealer. But Francesco wasn't on the streets to back up his brother. He was in prison serving an eight-year-term for conspiring to import 180 kilograms of cocaine.

There was a small bit of good news within the Cotroni family, though. On May 19, 1999, Frank's daughter Rosina was spared time behind bars and given an eighteen-month suspended sentence after pleading guilty to conspiracy and cocaine-trafficking charges. She was ordered to do community service and be under curfew for the duration of her sentence.

By the new millennium, it was hard to remember the days when Paolo Violi criticized Frank Cotroni for being too soft on outlaw bikers, saying that he would have "gone into the club [where the bikers hung out], clients or no clients, lined everybody up against the wall and rat-a-tat-tat." Now, Violi was long-dead and the bikers were far stronger than anyone had ever imagined. And Hells Angels' leader Maurice (Mom) Boucher, with his close-cut grey hair, steelrimmed glasses and muscular frame, was as familiar to Quebecers as most entertainers or politicians.

Back in 1973, when Violi was making his tough comments about outlaw bikers, Boucher was making his first appearance on court records with a conviction for theft of $200. That court appearance came four years before the Hells Angels even existed in Canada.

Boucher was before the courts again in 1976 and subsequently spent forty months behind bars for an armed robbery. He rebounded nicely to an estate with horse stables on Montreal's south shore. His employment was alternatively listed as a used-car salesman, real estate manager, cook and construction worker.

Boucher belonged to the SS motorcycle gang until it disbanded in 1984, and he gained full membership in the Hells Angels on May 1, 1987. By the early 1990s he was head of the Montreal chapter, and in 1995 he took over the notorious Nomads chapter after serving four months in jail for carrying an unregistered pistol. The Nomads' mission was to spearhead the Angels expansion into Ontario and to lead the war against the Rock Machine in Quebec. Bikers felt he did both jobs very well. "Mr. Boucher was considered like a god," informer Serge Boutin remarked at Boucher's trial.

In July 2000, there was a meeting at a south-shore Montreal restaurant between Hells Angel Normand Robitaille of the Nomads chapter and a group of junior bikers, including a man who appeared in police files as Agent No. 3683. On the streets, Agent No. 3683 was known as Danny Kane, a member of the Hells Angels puppet club, the Rockers. Kane was Robitaille's driver and bodyguard. Kane was known on the streets as a potentially violent man, having beaten a murder charge in Halifax.

What wasn't widely known was that Kane was also gay, something that would have ostracized him within the biker community. If the bikers had also known that day that Kane was wearing a police wire, he most certainly would have been dead.

The topic in that south-shore restaurant meeting was cocaine, and Robitaille told a group of Rockers, "The price of a kilo is now $50,000. I made a deal with the Italians. That's the price now." That meant that the price of cocaine had just jumped by $10,000. The Mafia were supplying the Nomads chapter with cocaine, and the Nomads were supplying all the other Quebec chapters with cocaine and hashish (except for the Sherbrooke chapter, which was autonomous). The bikers were setting the resale prices, and heaven help anyone who undercut them. In the legitimate business world, price-fixing is illegal. In the underworld, price-fixing is the preferred way of doing business.

The Hells Angels also collaborated with the Italian mob and some Irish-heritage dockworkers at the Port of Montreal. The Italians would import drugs by ship and the dockworkers would take a third of the cargo as a fee for letting it through. Then the remaining cargo would be picked up by people associated with the bikers. They would drive it around Quebec long enough to set up their own counter-surveillance to check for police. It was believed that police could only afford to follow them for a couple of weeks because of the prohibitive costs of around-the-clock surveillance that often took some thirty officers, divided between surveillance, search and interception teams.

So the bikers would wait things out for a month or two until police budgets were exhausted. Then they moved the drugs on to the streets.

The bikers made a massive miscalculation in September 2000, however, when gunmen connected to the Hells Angels tried to kill *Journal de Montréal* reporter Michel Auger. Auger had pointed out that the Bandidos were ahead of the Angels in expanding into Ontario, and that the Angels-Rock Machine war meant that scores of people with no connection to the biker gangs had been killed.

"I was shot because I told the truth," Auger said later.

He survived the murder attempt, even though he was hit six times in the back after a gunman emptied his silencer-equipped pistol into him.

Auger is a particularly well-liked and well-respected journalist both inside and outside Quebec, and the public reaction to the murder attempt was swift and powerful. Journalists marched in Ottawa and Montreal in a show of solidarity.

Hard-hitting questions about the need for tougher anti-gang laws — similar to what would later be used for terrorists — were posed in the Quebec legislature and in the House of Commons in Ottawa where even Prime Minister Jean Chrétien was grilled.

Meanwhile, Auger learned that the bikers also had plans to kill TV personality Jocelyne Cazin of TVA; Serge Menard, the Quebec minister of public security; Jacques Duchesneau, the former chief of the Montreal Urban Community police; as well as some judges.

It was nothing less than an organized attempt to terrorize the population and undermine law enforcement officials and democracy. Canadians could no longer pretend that attacks like the one that killed crusading Judge Giovanni Falcone of Italy were foreign to their shores.

The people who plotted to kill Auger, Cazin, Menard, Duchesneau and others were home-grown criminals, more deadly than anything that sneaked in through the country's immigration system.

After the Auger shooting, the Hells Angels were increasingly seen as domestic terrorists, and not just as rough-hewn mavericks. Faced with the massive public reaction against Auger's attempted murder, the bikers decided to shelve their plans to kill Cazin, Menard, Duchesneau and others.

Chapter Twenty-Nine

Down for the Count

*"I haven't seen anyone associated with
the Mafia in three or four years.
They're all in jail."*
— Boxer Eddie Melo in 1999

There was a time when Eddie Melo seemed to want nothing more out of life than a tough image. He was a neighbourhood legend on the streets and in the gyms of Toronto's west-end Ossington Avenue area, and when he wasn't fighting he was going out of his way to look tough. "I was always fighting," Melo later said. "If I had a black eye, I didn't put on dark glasses to hide it. If I got a little scratch and came home bleeding, my mother would go crazy. But the way I figured it, you can't give pain to somebody else and not expect to get a little bruised yourself."

"On Ossington, nobody screwed with him," said David Brown, who used to spar with him at Sully's Gym. "As a kid he used to walk with two Dobermans."

Melo, a construction worker's son and the eldest of five children, quit school in grade nine and moved to Verdun where his tough personality and a forged birth certificate allowed him to turn pro as a fighter at seventeen. There, his hell-bent, "no-prisoners" boxing style earned him the nickname "Hurricane" and he quickly caught the eye of Frank Cotroni. Melo didn't just swing a lot; he also hit hard and was, in the words of former Canadian heavyweight champion George Chuvalo "a world-class puncher."

By his mid-twenties, however, Melo was a spent force in the ring, and he retired with a record of 32 wins (27 by knockout), nine losses, and two draws. When he left the ring, he had plenty going for him. He was married to a former Miss Montreal Alouette, drove a new Lincoln Continental, had $20,000 in jewellery, a new house in the Toronto suburbs, a newborn baby and a job as an organizer with the Hotel and Restaurant Employees Union. He also had a furious temper, some brain damage from taking blows to the head, and a tight friendship with Cotroni whom he called "my number one fan." In the Toronto area, Melo ran Cotroni-related businesses that supplied strippers for bars and rented video machines. During this time, Melo grated on the nerves of Hamilton mobster Johnny (Pops) Papalia who, according to a police source, told Frank Cotroni, "Put a leash on Melo or I'll kill him."

Johnny Pops wasn't the only one who felt that way about Melo. In 1989, a group of young mobsters decided it was time for Melo to die. Melo had slapped one of them around in a College Street pool hall in Toronto's Little Italy. They were mad. A hitman was given a .357 magnum to kill Melo, and a smaller .22 for Melo 's less-threatening associate, Frank Natale Roda. The murder plot was foiled by police, but it took a toll nonetheless. Perhaps the stress of almost being slain is what finally ended Melo's first marriage. He and his wife, Sine, separated, reconciled, and then split for good in April 1989. Shortly afterwards, she moved to the West Coast with their two young daughters.

Police knew that if they wanted to find trouble, they could always follow Eddie. Surveillance officers noted him meeting at a trendy Yorkville eatery with a B.C. Hells Angel who was active in loan-sharking. And a 1993 police report from the southern Italian province of Calabria listed him as a member of the Toronto Siderno Mafia group, even though Melo was born in Portugal and maintained tight ties with Cotroni.

In August 1994, a police wiretap caught him on the phone with Cotroni's associate, Tony Volpato. It was easy to draw ominous conclusions when Melo told Volpato, "I went there when they had the meeting. I had a couple of guys. We took care of things. You know what I mean. . .went down and took care of things, so there is no problem. . . . So what I'm doing I think, is the right thing here for us . . . and fuck the other guy."

The wiretaps also picked up Volpato telling Melo, "I already told the other guy, my *compadri,* whatever my *compadri* decides the family here goes with him. . . . He called me back. He says, 'Tony, I gotta see you.' . . . I said, 'Look, you wanna come, come.'"

Melo wasn't caught in the sting by Iraqi immigrant Mahmood (Moe) Adolaymi, but the RCMP operation meant that by the mid-1990s Cotroni and his right-hand man Volpato were in prison for drug-trafficking. Suddenly, Melo was isolated.

Now, as he approached middle age, Melo decided to go back to a place where he had always felt in control and alive — the boxing ring. He planned to re-establish his name with bouts across Europe and South America, and then earn the shot at a world title he had dreamed about since his teens. His manager was Harold Arviv, a Bay Street businessman whose checkered past included time in prison for blowing up his own Bloor Street disco for insurance money.

However, before Melo could get things restarted in the ring, he found himself in a far more serious fight. Canadian police discovered that he had never taken out citizenship, and they sought to deport him to Portugal on grounds of criminality, even though Canada had been his home for three decades.

"My parents brought me here for a better life," he protested. "I did everything in Canada. Had two daughters and now a baby. And I have to add I got in a lot of trouble here, too."

The immigration fight would affect his father's health, family members said. It also caused enormous strains for family members who protested that Melo would lose valuable family support and on-going psychiatric counselling for anger management.

Melo admitted to immigration officials that his friends included ex-boxer Joe Dinardo. Known in police jargon as "a leg and arm man," Dinardo had some thirty criminal convictions stretching back to 1958 for matters ranging from arson, robbery, passing counterfeit money to illegal possession of guns.

When questioned by authorities, Melo didn't have an unkind word for Cotroni or his underworld associates, saying they never turned their backs on him, and were still his friends. He admitted that Tony Volpato was in fact the godfather to one of his daughters. Melo added that he was the godfather to the daughter of Arviv, "the disco bomber" and would-be boxing manager.

Melo was asked in an immigration hearing if he would avoid the likes of Cotroni, Volpato and Arviv, should he be allowed to stay in Canada. He was clearly on the ropes: "Well, sir, it's really kind of hard for me to avoid them because it's not just a friend relationship. It's more like, you know, twenty years you get to know somebody.

Whatever they've done through the courts, I mean, I'm not one to pass judgement or to make them pay to society. All I know is that they've been okay with me. They've never asked me to do any criminal activity or get into trouble. They've only been supportive in whatever it was that I had to do. So I . . . you know, I really can't judge them that way except the way they were judging me."

As he fought to stay in Toronto, Melo remained a celebrity of sorts. He posed for photos at the 1998 Toronto Film Festival with his new live-in partner Rhonda Sullivan who, the press gushed, was a Pamela Anderson look-alike. He liked to say he was working legitimately now, promoting shares in a B.C. mining company. He told immigration officials that he was receiving regular psychiatric counselling and also two types of medication — a chemical straight-jacket — to control the anger that had worked so well for him in the ring.

As he approached his forties, Melo made some amends for his violent past, buying new pews for St. Helen's Church in Toronto's Portugese district. It was where Eduardo Jr., his son with Rhonda, had been baptized. Eduardo Jr. and Rhonda seemed to have a calming effect on him, as did his advancing years. Now he enjoyed downloading free songs from Napster on the Internet as he held Rhonda in his arms. He loved taking the family to the Golden Griddle every Saturday morning so preschooler Eduardo Jr. could get his beloved waffle fries. He didn't seem to really mind, after years of sculpting his body for fighting, that he was now developing a soft belly and a junk-food habit that included smoked meat and pizza almost every night in bed. He got a laugh out of answering his mother's personal telephone with "Hello, you've reached the morgue." Now that he wasn't so tough, perhaps his life was finally getting on track.

However, with Melo's past it was tough for him to age gracefully because there always seemed to be someone who wanted to make a name by putting a fist in his face or, even worse, a bullet in his body.

"I wish I could be treated as a normal person," he once complained. "I always seem to be in a mess, with someone challenging or provoking something. I'm afraid to go out. I hate to fight. It goes on everywhere I go."

The struggle to keep from being deported dragged on for years. He complained to the Immigration and Refugee Board that police harassment almost drove him out of the vending-machine business.

Police noted that close associates were still active in that business and wondered if they were merely fronts for Melo. He declared his income as exactly $24,000; yet, somehow he was able to maintain $2,000 monthly condo expenses for his home on Lake Shore Boulevard West, another $1,500 monthly for his first wife, an undisclosed amount for a condo on upscale Queens Quay and payments on his sport utility vehicle and sleek Jaguar.

The first week of April 2001, Rhonda was suffering a bout of depression, and Eddie stayed home from his new job as a stock promoter at a Bay Street brokerage firm to help her cope. A day after he turned forty — on Friday, April 6, 2001 — Rhonda was feeling well enough to go to lunch with Eddie and a lawyer friend at the Movenpick restaurant on downtown York Street. Later, after stopping for a coffee, Eddie and Rhonda headed west to pick up four-year-old Eduardo Jr. at his daycare, which was run by Catholic nuns.

"I remember we were stopped at [the downtown intersection of] Richmond and University [Streets]," Rhonda later recalled. "I held his hand and told him how much I loved him, and how I forgave him for everything bad he'd ever done to me. Ever. Because he'd been so supportive. And I'd never said that, you know? It was so weird."

They returned to their condo overlooking Lake Ontario at about five p.m. Within fifteen minutes, Eddie told Rhonda he was taking her Jeep Cherokee to a nearby coffee bar at a tiny plaza just off the Queen Elizabeth Way highway. It was called the Amici Sport Café — "*amici*" is Italian for "friends"— where, in Rhonda's words, he "used to go to drink cappuccino and hang out." He wasn't going to be long because they had tickets to see tenor Andrea Bocelli that evening at the Air Canada Centre. Shortly before 7 p.m. Rhonda says she got a telephone call from her mother who asked some unusual questions about her vehicle. It was strange, and Rhonda recalled that her sister called moments later: "She said 'Ra' . . . that's what they call me . . . she said, 'Ra, where's Eddie?' And I said 'Oh, he went out to Amici.'

"And she's like, 'Is he driving your Jeep?' I said, 'Yeah, why?' She didn't say anything. I asked her again and she said because we heard there was a double homicide. . . She said just give me your plate number. And I gave it to her and she said, 'Oh, Ra.' It was probably fifteen minutes after it happened."

Sullivan said she later learned from family that her cousin had

241

been at the same mall when the gunfire erupted. "My cousin Pam, who I never see, she was at the plaza, at the liquor store. She heard shots and when she came out of the liquor store, she said to the police officer, 'Oh my God, that looks like my cousin's Jeep.'

"And they're like, 'Who's your cousin?' And she said, 'Her name is Rhonda, she's married to Eddie Melo.' So then she called my mother and then my mother called me. That's what is so weird, the way I found out," Sullivan later recalled to *Toronto Star* reporter Jack Lakey. "It was probably fifteen minutes after it happened.

"He was my whole life. We had our ups and downs, but I will never find another love like him. Ever."

There were a lot of questions. Eddie Melo had left Amici that Friday night at 6:25 p.m. with his friend Joao (Johnny) Pavao, a salvage-truck driver from the Toronto suburb of Mississauga. Pavao and Melo were long-time friends. Police weren't sure if this was an arranged meeting or if the two happened on each other that evening. Whatever the case, a gunman walked up to the Jeep and fired several shots into it, and then hijacked a red 1990 Honda Civic. The startled Honda driver had been ordered out of the car at gunpoint, and the killer fled the scene. These were clearly execution-style shootings. Why did the killer do the hit in front of so many witnesses? Was it a brazen message of strength? Or was it done out of sheer panic? Why didn't he have his own escape vehicle ready?

There was some speculation that Frank Cotroni might get a day-pass from prison to attend Melo's funeral. By this point, Frank was sixty-nine, morbidly obese and had difficulty walking. "Frank adored this kid," a Montreal source close to Cotroni said.

"I would think that he [Cotroni] would [attend] because of everything that Eddie did for him over the years," said Ron Sandelli, former head of Toronto police intelligence.

Cotroni treated Melo "better than his sons," another veteran police investigator said. "Eddie was the guy who was hustling and moving."

During the funeral arrangements, people familiar with Melo offered several motives for his killing, including a falling-out with an old friend who collaborated with him on stock market scams and the work of Hells Angels bikers who were expanding into Toronto. Other theories that were floated included rival mobsters who had tried and failed to kill him years before. There was also talk about a jewellery heist in which some $100,000 worth of goods was taken.

During the visitation to the funeral home, some people close to Melo offered up another possible motive — an affair he'd had with the wife of a Toronto-area police officer. There was whispering about other affairs, and other angry husbands. Because Melo and Pavao were in a Jeep Cherokee, a make of vehicle that was often stolen by car-theft rings, police considered but more or less rejected the idea that the shootings could have been a carjacking gone horribly wrong.

"We don't know what the motive was," Inspector Tom Slinger, head of the homicide unit for Peel Regional Police, said shortly after the killings, "but I wouldn't put car-jacking at the top of the list,"

Was Melo expected at Amici? He had only a short time between taking Eduardo Jr. home from daycare and going out to the Andrea Bocelli concert. Why was he in such a rush to get there?

"Was he followed there?" asked Detective Steve Gormley of Peel Regional Police. "Did he [the killer] bump into him there?"

Melo was always under threat of some sort, but police said there was nothing above the normal level of hostility in the weeks before his death. Melo was more into stock market fraud than street violence towards the end because such crimes were high-return and low-risk ventures. Could the killer have been from that white-collar world? Usually in a homicide, investigating police start with the family and friends and work outwards. And Melo's friends certainly gave them plenty to work with. "There's a lot of history between a lot of people," Gormley understated.

Meanwhile, a source close to Melo said chances were the former boxer knew his killer and had gone to Amici to meet him. "I would bet this was someone he [Melo] knew and knew well, otherwise he wouldn't have gotten that close to him," said the associate, who asked not to be identified. The source thought Pavao was probably killed because he also knew the shooter. The source said Melo knew he had "a lot of enemies" and conducted himself accordingly by being on the alert.

"He wasn't paranoid, but he was very alert. When he went into a restaurant or a bar, he always sat in a place where he could see what was going on," the long-time associate said.

In his final years, Melo didn't talk much about his days working for Frank Cotroni. But he did have a picture of himself and The Big Guy in a prominent place in his condominium home, the source said. Police also found a mass card for the funeral of Frank's murdered son Paul in Melo's condo.

"Cotroni hasn't been part of his life for a long time," Melo's old associate said.

Ironically, Melo might still be alive if he had not won his fight with Canadian authorities against deportation to Portugal. Melo had argued that he didn't know anybody over there — but then nobody there wanted him dead.

Harold Arviv was out of the country on a vacation that had been planned before the killing. The two hadn't been close in the final months of Melo's life, and Arviv didn't return for the funeral. Well-known former Toronto boxers George Chuvalo and Nicky Furlano were asked to serve as pallbearers, but Chuvalo said he couldn't because of an out-of-town, anti-drug speaking engagement. Three of Chuvalo's sons had died from drug addictions, so such speaking commitments were sacrosanct to the aging boxer. As the funeral was being planned, Chuvalo said he could close his eyes and vividly see Melo as a nine-year-old playing in the gym with his sons.

"My sons, who died, were around his age," Chuvalo said softly in an interview. "I always see him as a kid when I think of him…It was, I guess, an innocent time. He would have been a world-class contender — big-time — if he was allowed to mature. His life should have been different. …By the time he was twenty-five, he was burned. A kid at twenty-five shouldn't be burned and he was… To me, I see him as a kid — a kid who could have made it."

The funeral was at St. Helen's Church on Dundas Street West, where Eduardo Jr. had been baptized four years earlier and where Chuvalo once served as an altar boy.

Only the best was said about Melo at a service that was both heavy-hearted and light-spirited. Some four-hundred people, including former boxers Nicky Furlano, Clyde Gray and Spider Jones, gathered under the church's soaring arches. But noteworthy mobsters were conspicuously absent, especially Frank Cotroni. And there were no Hells Angels to be seen, even though Melo had had a close friendship with some of them for more than a decade. There were, however, about half a dozen undercover police officers scanning the crowd for underworld faces.

At one point, Reverend Fernando Couto looked directly at Melo's three children, nineteen-year-old Jessica, fourteen-year-old Elise, and four-year-old Eduardo Jr., and said, "He loved you, he tried to be a good father, you can always treasure that in your heart. Remember the good he did, because the rest we don't know."

Outside the church, television camera operators jostled for a better view and Melo's younger brother Joey shouted angrily, "You're here and you want a piece of my brother." He then turned to mourners gathered on the steps of the church and thanked them for their presence, drawing a cheer in response.

Melo's widow, Rhonda, appreciated the media presence, however. As the casket was carried by pallbearers to a polished hearse, tearful family members traded hugs. Sullivan climbed into the royal-blue Jaguar and blew kisses to reporters across the street. "Thank you so much for coming," she said before she drove herself to the cemetery.

Melo's gleaming black casket was layered with birds of paradise, his favourite flower, and draped with an old Portuguese flag, one he had worn decades ago into the ring, emblazoned with the words: "Hurricane, Number 1."

At his gravesite at Mount Pleasant Cemetery, his best friend Joey "Popeye" Bolarino, who grew up with Melo, reminisced about training with him. "Our favourite day was Friday so we could watch Baby Blue movies on TV," he said to laughter and applause.

"Boxing is corrupt," Bolarino continued. "All Eddie wanted was to be loved and accepted."

Daughter Jessica, an elegant young woman with a striking resemblance to her father, talked about his gentle side. She told how he once offered to wash the blackened, shoeless feet of a homeless man in downtown Vancouver, and she said he had cheered the loudest of all the fathers at his daughter Elise's recent dance competition.

"Everything that's been said about him, it's all sensationalized," she said. "He was a good man and a good father."

Then, surrounded by dozens of Melo's relatives, friends and acquaintances, Rhonda and Joey cracked open a coppery $6,000 bottle of Louis XIII cognac, shared a glass and washed the burial ground.

It was an elaborate gesture for a man who had recently claimed an annual income of $24,000.

"Only the best for Eddie," Rhonda said.

The cognac was followed by champagne. One of Melo's favourite songs, "The Prayer," a duet by Sarah Brightman and Andrea Bocelli, was playing loudly in repeat mode on the stereo of the Jaguar with its door open.

Over and over, the assembled mourners could hear the words:

Let this be our prayer,
When we lose our way,
Lead us to the place,
Guide us with your grace,
To a place where we'll be safe.

A year after Eddie's murder, Rhonda Sullivan tearfully said she spent her days waiting for the phone call when police would "tell me they've caught the person who robbed my five-year-old son of his beautiful father. Little boys need their dad. Eduardo goes to soccer games and sees all the other dads are there and his papa isn't there."

By then, police said they had interviewed more than five hundred people and many of them several times. However, they were still left with no answers to the questions: Who killed Eddie Melo and Johnny Pavao, and why? They weren't even sure if Melo was the intended target. Could the killer have been after Pavao, and Melo was just in the wrong place at the wrong time?

"We explored every conceivable connection as they came up," said homicide investigator Detective Steve Gormley of Peel Regional Police.

"The more complex a person's life is, the more complex an investigation is going to be," added Detective Tom Slinger. "The possibilities I wouldn't say are endless. I would say they are numerous."

They were numerous, in part, because the two men had been executed.

"When you double the victims, you double the investigation," Slinger said. The investigation was a crash course on the Toronto-area's rapidly changing organized-crime scene, as literally dozens of criminals from varied groups had to be considered as suspects. "It's hard to mention a name that you can think of that doesn't come up," Slinger said.

Criminals like Melo aren't in the habit of sharing business secrets with their spouses, and so Sullivan couldn't be too much help to investigators. Meanwhile, Sullivan said the year following the murder had been a struggle for her and the namesake son.

"There isn't a day goes by that he doesn't ask about his papa," she said. "At night, when he says his prayer, he says that his papa is in his heart and in his mind and that he thinks of him every day. Then he blows a kiss to the sky, to his papa, who he knows is in heaven."

Eduardo Jr. also grew troubled whenever his mother had to go somewhere without him, always asking, "Are you sure you're coming back, Mommy?"

It must also have hit the imprisoned Frank Cotroni hard. First he lost his son Paul, and now Melo, who was like a son. In both cases, the old boss was helpless to protect them.

When police finally arrested Melo's killer on July 15, 2003, they found he was a man who had never even met the ex-boxer or his friend Pavao until the evening of their murders. Thirty-three-year-old Charles Gagné said he was just doing a job for a couple of old west-Toronto neighbourhood acquaintance of Melo's, including small-time mobster Delio Manuel Pereira, 50.

Gagné brought violent credentials to his work — he'd once used an AK-47 assault rifle to rob a supermarket. At the time of the Melo–Pavao slayings, Gagné was on a temporary absence pass from the Portsmouth Community Correctional Centre in Kingston where federal officials had assessed him as a low-risk parolee.

Police never revealed a motive for the murders. But Melo's younger brother Joey proudly blamed simmering jealousy.

"Eddie walked into a lot of places and people respected him," Joey Melo said. "These guys could never face him one-on-one, even if my brother had only had one arm and one leg."

Joey Melo said his brother knew the men accused of plotting his brother's murder, but never got close to them.

"They were never really friends," Joey Melo said. "They were associates. That's it."

The week Melo was being buried in Toronto, Davey Hilton, Jr., the most talented member of Canada's most infamous boxing family, the "Fighting Hiltons," was in court in Montreal. He faced the worst of that family's many charges — sexual assault accusations for repeated attacks on his own two underaged daughters. It was a numbing, revolting court case. At one point, Davey Jr. called on New Yorkers Jackie Coonan and Sean Cumminskey to speak as character witnesses. They told of how they had been guests of Davey, Jr., at a heavyweight boxing bout in Las Vegas in January 1999. The court also heard that they were frequent houseguests of Hilton in Quebec, partying with him about two weeks a month over a six-month period. Throughout that time, the court heard, the men saw Hilton do nothing untoward with his two young daughters. So far, so good for Hilton.

However, the prosecutor then said he was curious about Coonan's uncle, Jimmy Coonan, the imprisoned leader of the brutal Westies gang that ruled New York City's Hell's Kitchen neighbourhood in the seventies and eighties. Cumminskey's father was the late Eddie "The Butcher" Cumminskey and one of the elder Coonan's favourite hitmen. He had learned the butchery trade in prison and used it when free to chop murdered victims into unrecognizable bits before tossing them in the East River. Not so good for Hilton.

The judge ruled that family relationships weren't relevant to the case against Hilton, but not before the court heard how eager young Hilton was to meet the two men, and how he was enthralled by organized crime. During a break in testimony, Hilton commented that people shouldn't read too much into this, and that people should not burden children with the sins of their fathers.

Davey Jr. had plenty of sins of his own to answer for, anyway. And many would argue that among those sins was the wasting of so much talent.

Davey Hilton, Jr., was blessed with speed, grace, a granite chin and his father's knockout punch. He was supposed to fight for the Continental Americas welterweight title back in 1985 against junior welterweight champion Aaron Pryor. (Pryor would move up in weight to meet him.) The next step for the Hilton brother would be a 1986 world title shot. That chance was lost when Davey Jr. broke a leg and a finger in a motorcycle accident while preparing for the Pryor bout. By the time his bones healed, he had bloated up forty pounds. Five years later, Davey Jr. and his brother Matthew (who had won and lost a world title of his own) were arrested for a particularly stupid crime — an armed robbery on a donut shop that netted just $160.

But the fighter's promise in the ring was so great that it could survive his stupidity outside of it.

Veteran Montreal fight trainer Russ Anber said, "He was as good a prodigy as ever came around. Without a doubt, pound for pound, he was probably the best our country has ever produced."

Finally, in December 2000, fourteen years after he was to get his first shot at a world title, Hilton climbed into the ring with South

African Dingaan "The Rose of Soweto" Thobela. At stake was the World Boxing Council's Super Middleweight world championship. Davey Jr. had moved up a weight class for the fight. Thobela was taller and heavier, but it was Hilton who won by split decision.

"It wasn't even his weight class and to win a world title at thirty-seven . . . that's phenomenal," Anber said. "That shows you the talent he has."

Just four months later, however, Hilton was in the headlines again, convicted of nine charges of sexual assault against his daughters, now young women. The World Boxing Council stripped him of his title — he obviously could not defend it, since he faced the next seven years in prison. The Hilton saga, once one of hope and promise, was now immeasurably tainted. It was another story of opportunity lost in the world of Frank Cotroni.

Frank Cotroni didn't even show up for his parole hearing on July 25, 2001. It wasn't that Cotroni, now seventy, didn't value his freedom. It was more that he didn't like losing or wasting his time. He couldn't have been surprised when he was denied both day and full parole because he was deemed to be uninterested in rehabilitation and because, in the past, he had used unescorted day-passes to visit Mafia hangouts.

"Your case-management group considers that you demonstrate little motivation to change your criminal behaviour and your attitude," a parole board report understated. The report noted that in 1998, during brief, unescorted leaves from prison, he had visited places "that police authorities consider to be frequented by members of Italian organized crime." The report concluded that: "Even at the age of seventy, and even taking into consideration your family and the state of your health, your criminal attitudes are still the same."

It wasn't pleasant news, but it was hardly surprising either. Cotroni would qualify a couple of months later anyway for "statutory release" after serving two-thirds of his seven-year sentence. The parole board would have no discretion then, and his statutory release meant there would be few conditions beyond residing within a specific area and providing a monthly statement of his finances. Canadian criminals serve an average of just 32 per cent of their federal sentences before receiving day parole, and only 39.8 per cent of their time before getting full parole, and Cotroni had been a frequent beneficiary of this tolerance.

On December 3, 2001, Cotroni was released from minimum-security custody at Montée St-François Institution in Laval. The only real restrictions were those imposed on him by health, but they couldn't be taken lightly.

He had severe problems walking. In prison, he'd been wheeled about on a golf cart. Frank Cotroni was now entering his eighth decade.

Chapter Thirty

Gone Bananas

"He literally just faded away."
— Joe Bonanno's personal physician

Old-school mafiosi such as Vic Cotroni had never been too comfortable around outlaw bikers. What kind of a man wears a patch on his back announcing that he's a bad guy? Where's the finesse, the tact? There was something unreliable, hotheaded and unnecessarily violent at play here. Why invite trouble? Cotroni's world was based on influence and infiltration. But the bikers used the crudest of means to control their turf. They were upfront and easy to see, almost asking for trouble.

For their part, the outlaw bikers had traditionally been respectful of the mobsters' seniority in the underworld. In Vic Cotroni's glory days, the way things generally played out was that the mob got the drugs and the outlaw bikers distributed them. And when mobsters needed someone to do a dirty job like debt collection or murder, they could do worse than to call upon an outlaw biker.

Back then, the bikers weren't much of an organized force. It wasn't until 1977 that the world's largest outlaw biker gang, the Hells Angels, even entered Canada. It began with the Popeyes of Montreal being given their Angels colours by the Oakland, California-based parent organization. By 1985, another seven Hells Angels chapters had opened up between Vancouver and Halifax. But there was still nothing in Ontario where a dozen independent gangs blocked the Angels' entry.

By late 2001 when Frank Cotroni was released once more on parole, there had been seismic shifts in the underworld. After six years of vicious turf war against other biker gangs, the Quebec Hells Angels had virtually eliminated all rivals. The Rock Machine, originally a collection of drug dealers who opposed the Angels, now had to merge with the Texas-based Bandidos gang just to stay alive. The forces of convergence, much talked about in mainstream, multinational, information-driven businesses, were also rapidly reshaping the underworld. And the Bandidos communications were now carried via the Internet with its immediacy and total lack of international borders. (Alas for the Bandidos, the Canadian expansion would not be a great success. On April 8, 2006, the bodies of five full patch Bandido members and three prospects were discovered inside cars abandoned in a wooded field near Shedden, Ontario. They'd been shot dead. It would be the worst mass murder in Ontario history. The accused in the killings included other Bandidos. And the murders all but put an end to the Bandidos as an organized crime force in Canada.)

While Cotroni was still in jail, the Angels had expanded en masse into Ontario, instantly converting some 170 members of old biker gangs into Angels. At the start of December 2000, there were just two Hells Angels in the entire province. But by the end of the month, Ontario was home to the largest concentration of the gang in the world, with some half-dozen chapters within an hour's drive of Toronto's CN Tower. As a grand gesture, it was atop the tower where the Angels made their formal offer of membership to bikers of the old Toronto gangs. With the addition of the Toronto bikers, there were now about the same number of Hells Angels in the Toronto-area alone as in the entire province of Quebec. And the expansion pushed on. Within a year, Ontario had some 200 full patch Hells Angels and another 200 associates. Until the Angels arrived, there had been no puppet clubs of junior members in Ontario. Now these clubs were popping up throughout the province with young members eager to do rough jobs in return for the chance to one day become an Angel.

On February 26, 2001, the *National Post* ran a page-one story by Adrian Humphreys under the headline "Mafia Begins Unity Drive: Canadian Leaders Face Common Threat from Hells Angels." It told of a meeting at the end of January 2001 in north Toronto where there was an apparent attempt to forge an alliance among quarrelsome Mafia clans from Ontario, Quebec, British Columbia and possibly New York State. The goal was to present a united mob front to the Hells Angels and Bandidos.

According to the story, Montreal Sicilian mobsters had been coming to Toronto every couple of weeks, apparently trying to pull together Mafia families from the Golden Horseshoe area of southern Ontario and the northern United States. The mafiosi had a difficult decision to make — should they get tough with the bikers, or work with them? In the end, they decided just to wait.

There was an irony to the situation. The Montreal mob was in part responsible for the bikers' strength and for the violent turf war. It was the mob that had given the downtown Montreal drug market to the Hells Angels in the first place. And once the Angels swallowed up that market, they became hungry for more. The Angels began muscling in on the operations of other Québécois criminal groups — who responded by banding together to form the rival Rock Machine.

A generation earlier, the formidable Siderno Calabrian *'ndrangheta* group of Toronto had employed Satan's Choice biker Cecil Kirby as an enforcer and hitman. Back then, bikers such as Kirby were disposable muscle to do messy jobs for mafiosi who didn't want blood or dirt on their hands. Now, the Satan's Choice members had patched over *en masse* into the Hells Angels, and the Siderno group was treating the bikers with a new respect. At the same time, the bikers showed little fear of young mobsters.

After the fallout from the September 13, 2000 shooting of journalist Michel Auger, there was a much-publicized move by the Hells Angels and Rock Machine to show that the war between them was over. Mom Boucher of the Angels and Fred Faucher of the Rock Machine met on September 26 in the Quebec City courthouse to start negotiations.

On October 8, a peace agreement was announced and documented with photos in the the Quebec crime tabloid *Allô Police*. Many people who were familiar with the underworld suspected that this peace accord was a sham orchestrated by the Montreal Sicilian underworld.

"He [a Sicilian underworld leader] probably had something to do with it," retired Quebec police biker expert Guy Ouellette said. "He probably had some sensitive information that the government would pass a new law."

But in March 2001, before anything could erupt between the Mafia and Hells Angels, the top leaders of the Quebec Hells Angels were arrested in a massive police operation.

By mid-2004, the final chapter in one of the Canadian underworld's most bloody confrontations was closed when Walter (Nurget) Stadnick, 51, and his friend Donald (Pup) Stockford, 42, of Hamilton and Ancaster were convicted of conspiracy to murder, gangsterism and drug trafficking.

The Crown admitted during the trial that it had no direct evidence linking Stadnick with the murders but argued that his senior position within the Nomads biker gang essentially made him guilty by association. The convictions were seen as the end of the Quebec Nomad chapter. This was the chapter that had led the drug wars. Now all its members — except David (Wolf) Carroll who was a fugitive reportedly hiding out in Latin America — were either in jail or dead. However, by this point, the Angels were established as a coast-to-coast-to-coast operation in Canada, and policing critics charged they were benefiting from the 1997 federal dismantling of a separate police department for the ports. There were now some 500 Hells Angels in Canada (more than forty of whom worked in the Port of Vancouver), compared with 700 in the U.S. (which has ten times the population) and a total of 2,500 to 3,000 worldwide.

Nick Rizzuto's son Vito must have been a little nervous at this time, despite his wealth and apparent good health. In July 2001, two men were charged with conspiracy to murder him and Francesco Arcadi as well as with conspiracy to kidnap acquaintance Frank Martorana. In one of the accused's home, police found a Kalashnikov-style automatic rifle, two 9-millimetre pistols, one .357 magnum revolver, two bulletproof vests and several ammunition clips and walkie-talkies. In February 2002, there was a bomb discovered near a social club that Vito Rizzuto frequented. Word was that these attacks were based on a personal grievance, rather than some underworld motive.

A couple of months later, Vito Rizzuto was pulled over by Montreal police and charged with impaired driving and refusing a blood test. He had been at the wheel of a Jeep Grand Cherokee registered to OMG Media Inc., a company with a long-term contract to supply recycling bins to the City of Toronto. An OMG official said he knew nothing about Rizzuto, and the executive who loaned Rizzuto the Jeep resigned after the story broke in the press. While authorities were not able to put him behind bars, Rizzuto was said to be embarrassed by the incident.

Rizzuto liked to sip coffee quietly in the modest Cosenza Social Club located in a north Montreal strip mall. But that came to an end in January 2004 after the FBI, U.S. Justice Department and the New York Police Department fingered him as one of the hitmen in the unsolved 1981 "three captains" slayings that had taken place in a Brooklyn, N.Y. social club.

Vito was scooped up in a crackdown of the New York-based Bonanno crime family along with such colourfully-named American "goodfellas" as Patty Muscles, Mickey Boots, Mickey Bats and Baldo as authorities leveled charges of everything from fixing baccarat games to murder. Relying in large part on information from the mobster-turned-informer known as "Good Looking Sal," American authorities alleged that, on May 5, 1981, Rizzuto hid in a closet of the Brooklyn social club to ambush three underbosses— mobsters who were thought to be staging a takeover of the powerful Bonanno family's empire.

Also in on the plot, according to American authorities, was Rizzuto's Montreal neighbour, Gerlando Sciascia. The prosecution story was that Sciascia ran his hands through his hair as a signal to start shooting. When it was over, Alphonse (Sonny Red) Indelicato, Philip (Philly Lucky) Gicaonne and Dominick (Big Trin) Trinchera lay dead or dying. (Readers who have difficulty visualizing the hit can rent the 1997 film *Donnie Brasco* starring Johnny Depp to see the killing recreated on celluloid.) A day later, Rizzuto and Sciascia were photographed by police surveillance officers leaving a room at the Capri Motor Lodge in the Bronx and walking towards a black sedan. With them was Joseph Massino who soon became the new godfather of the Bonanno family.

In Canada, Rizzuto's Toronto-area manager, Spanish national Juan Ramon Fernandez (aka Joe Bravo), was found guilty in Newmarket, Ontario in June 2004 of a half-dozen gangland charges, including conspiring to murder a 460-pound rival cocaine trafficker. Looking fit and well-groomed in a perfectly tailored black business suit and silver handcuffs and leg-irons, Fernandez admitted guilt to charges of plotting a murder, conspiring to import cocaine with Montreal's Rizzuto crime group and a Woodbridge Hells Angels biker, using a forged passport, possessing a counterfeit credit card and defrauding a bank. He didn't flinch when he got a twelve-year-sentence. But he became visibly upset to hear much of his jewelry would be confiscated as proceeds of crime.

As the bikers and mafiosi jockeyed for power and survival, an old man in his tenth decade made international headlines by *not* being murdered. Joseph Bonanno, the notorious gangster (who detested his nickname "Joe Bananas") died quietly of natural causes at age ninety-seven. Bonanno's lifespan was remarkable for any man, but astounding considering his milieu and the fact that his contemporaries had included Al Capone, Lucky Luciano and Meyer Lansky. He had lived more than double the lifespan of his underling Paolo Violi whose birth in 1931 came just months before Bonanno helped found the U.S. Mafia Commission to mediate disputes among crime families. Eddie Melo hadn't even been born back in 1955, when Vic Cotroni and Louis Greco were appointed joint heads of the Canadian arm of the Bonanno family, nor in 1957 when Bonanno attended the Palermo meetings to reorganize the world's heroin traffic. The old man had outlived them all. In the end, said Bonanno's personal physician Dr. David Ben-Asher, Vic Cotroni's old benefactor and boss "literally just faded away."

Throughout his life, Bonanno had denied engaging in such "unmanly" activities as narcotics-trafficking or prostitution, though authorities argued otherwise. As Bonanno told it, he was a "venture capitalist" who invested in businesses with owners who sought out his connections. Stories of his death suggested the old man had found a measure of peace — a stark contrast to the turbulence that swirled around the only still-living member of Canada's most enduring crime family, Frank Cotroni.

By the time Frank Cotroni was freed again on parole, it was December 3, 2001, and he had lived almost thirty years of his life behind bars. Even at his peak, Frank couldn't pretend to be the branch plant manager his elder brother Vic had been. And Frank was now far from his peak. "He has a name, but not the first name," quipped someone familiar with his milieu who was still leery enough of that name to ask that his comments not be attributed. Frank Cotroni had to be content simply to survive amidst the competition from the Sicilians and emergent biker gangs. Many of his old crew had departed, either by death, prison or defection to the Sicilians.

"He's slowed down quite a bit," a veteran police officer said at the time. "The organization's in tatters…if you want to call it an organization."

Frank Cotroni knew enough about the underworld that he could have had enormous impact as a police informer. But everyone who knew him said that would never happen.

"Not him, he's too long down the road," said a police officer at the time who knew him well. His devotion to the old ways led him back to prison on June 3, 2002 after he was picked up for a parole violation. He had been seen meeting with a man in a Montreal restaurant who then went on to talk with some old Cotroni associates. That was enough for police to pick up Cotroni yet again.

Frank Cotroni's comment to *Journal de Montréal* reporter Yves Chartrand back in 1991 about wanting to quit crime so that he could watch his children and grandchildren grow up now seemed hopelessly faraway — both a distant memory and a sour joke.

Frank's long-awaited cookbook finally came out in early 2004, and its preface included the understated observation that his life had not always been "a long, tranquil river." The 128-page *oeuvre* included a full-page photo of his first communion and a photo of him in later years in prison (which he called "college") stirring tomato sauce for fellow prisoners—or "*mes compagnons d'infortune.*"

"Of course, he's a gangster," said Anne Béland, a spokesperson for his publisher *éditions du Trécarre* Inc. "But he likes to cook. Even in prison he cooked. He wants to be remembered for other things than crime."

A few months later, Frank moved into his daughter Rosina's nondescript east-end Montreal duplex.

It was there, on August 17, 2004, that the last of the underworld Cotroni brothers died in his bed of brain cancer. He was seventy-two-years old. As he took his last breaths, he was surrounded by family members, much as his brother Vic had been when he'd died two decades earlier. The end was painless. Frank slipped from the world while heavily sedated with morphine.

News of his passing brought a sudden boom in business to Little Italy flower shops, with calls for elaborate arrangements of hearts and crosses made from white chrysanthemums, red roses gerbera, casablancas, star gazers, fujis, gladiola and solidago. (However, the death also meant that the florists had lost a steady and generous customer, as Frank Cotroni had often sent flowers to families of the departed, even when he was behind bars.)

It was overcast for his send-off at *Notre Dame della Difesa* Church on Rue Dante in the north end of Montreal with the sky, in the words of journalist Miro Cirnetig, the "colour of gun-metal grey."

Mourners gathered under the fresco of dictator Benito Mussolini on his stallion surrounded by Catholic saints, just as they had done at the funerals for Frank's older brother Vic and for Paolo Violi a generation before.

As expected, the ceremony attracted underworld rounders, gawkers and sidewalk philosophers, as well as grieving loved ones. And they all seemed to be aware that something historic was happening before them. This was the last great funeral for the Cotroni Mafia family. Observers counted sixteen limousines bearing 192 elaborate floral displays—about five times the amount for the average Little Italy funeral (although seven vehicles short of the number for Vic Cotroni's funeral in 1984).

"You're born, you die," an old man said, pausing from his morning game of the traditional Italian card game *briscola* to philosophize with the press. "The hard part is to live well in the middle."

By now, the Cotroni crime family was more a curiosity than a feared force. Montreal *Gazette* columnist Mike Boone noted that the mobster/cookbook-author's death came just four days after the passing of famed chef Julia Child. "Barely enough time," he wrote, "to marinate a pot roast or dispose of an informant."

A three-man band featuring accordion, guitar and mandolin played on the church steps as a funeral director placed four wooden cages filled with seventy-two white doves on tables set up in front of a waiting hearse. A singer launched into *"Calabria Mia,"* a nostalgic tribute to the southern Italian province of Cotroni's parents. (Although Cotroni had never actually visited Calabria, he loved to sing the song at weddings. And so it seemed fitting.)

Gesturing towards the caged doves, the funeral director explained, "One dove for each year of Frank's life. Nice, huh?"

"It's never easy to lose someone we love," she continued. "We hope that in the next life Frank finds peace."

As the casket was loaded onto the hearse, the caged birds were set free, and many flew straight to a nearby building where undercover police were believed to be stationed...watching.

Chapter Thirty-One

Life After Death

"I seen Vito shoot. I don't know who he hit."
—Salvatore (Good Looking Sal) Vitale

The old boys of Collège Jean-de-Brébeuf in Montreal are a *Who's Who* of Quebec's francophone elite, and their ranks include former Canadian Prime Minister Pierre Trudeau and former Quebec Premier Robert Bourassa. The collège was once run by Jesuits. It offers a secure, even staid, environment for the province's future leaders. Among those keeping watch over the collège's hallowed stone and brick walls and the privileged teens inside in October 2004 was a middle-aged security guard named Charles Bouchard. He quietly did his rounds, locked up windows and was best known for a quick smile and friendly manner.

Collège officials weren't prone to rash decisions. Before hiring Bouchard as a night watchman, they first verified that he had no criminal record and then questioned his previous employers, which included a school for handicapped children and another for autistic children. No problems were found in his background, and Bouchard was offered a job.

So, naturally, it came as a shock for collège administrators to learn that the polite guard who had worked for them for nine months was in fact Réal Simard — the same Réal Simard who had murdered five people for Frank Cotroni in the 1980s while he helped Cotroni expand his drug and nude dancer businesses into Ontario.

After he'd turned on Cotroni, Simard was put on the fast-track for release from prison and was granted full parole in 1994. He first worked under an assumed name as an aide to a Parti Québécois

MNA and then served as campaign manager for a Bloc Québécois candidate. Those jobs were lost after police tipped his political employers off to his underworld past. The supposedly-unemployed former hitman then began collecting welfare but failed to report that he was also working three days a week with the Red Cross.

Eventually caught and charged with welfare fraud, Simard found his parole revoked. Rather than face the prospect of a return to prison, he bolted and stole the name "Charles Bouchard" from a gravestone in Notre-Dame-des-Neiges cemetery in Montreal. (The real Charles Bouchard died when he was just a month old in the 1950s.) In January 2000, Simard adopted the name as his own, using it to obtain a birth certificate and social insurance number.

By the time of his arrest in October 2004, Simard had been on the run from police for five years. Before arriving at the collège, his flight from justice and the mob had taken him to Latin America where he'd worked as a lay minister, marrying a woman there and fathering a child. But despite its dangers, the pull of his old home remained strong and he moved back to Quebec with his new family. Craving adrenalin, he was soon taunting the parole board with e-mails, saying they would never be able to track him down. He also mocked them by publishing a book and appearing in a television interview.

In February 2005, four months after his arrest, Simard burst into tears as he told a National Parole Board hearing in Drummondville that he should be set free yet again.

The waterworks began when he was asked by a parole commissioner why he'd turned against Frank Cotroni two decades before.

"There was this combat between good and evil going on," Simard said, barely getting the words out before the sobbing began.

Not convinced that "good" was winning Simard's internal battle, the parole board denied his new bid for freedom.

Sixty-seven-year-old Vincenzo (Jimmy) Di Maulo had more reasons than Simard for being optimistic in October 2004. Arrested in 1994 in one of the largest money-laundering sting operations in Canadian policing history, Di Maulo was hopeful he might finally be getting out early, rather than having to serve his full 12-year prison stretch. In his money-laundering days, Di Maulo had washed some $10-million in drug money over a four-year period. Now, Di Maulo stood to be rewarded by the National Parole Board for acknowledging his past ties to the underworld, as well as for his good works behind bars, including helping out in a suicide-prevention program.

However, in order to get his freedom, Di Maulo had to promise he wouldn't associate, in the words of the parole board, with known criminals "related to the drug milieu and/or organized crime, including your brother Joe Di Maulo, who is known as an influential member of the Montreal Mafia."

That was acceptable to Di Maulo who vowed he wanted to spend his time with his granddaughter, not mobsters.

"She seems to be at the centre of your motivations for integrating into society and severing all links (with organized crime)," the parole board report concluded. The board granted him parole.

Ambition, it turned out — not hatred or jealousy — drove Charles Gagné to kill former pro boxer Eddie (the Hurricane) Melo.

And it was a matter of convenience, Gagné told a trial on September 25, 2005, that drove him to end the life of Melo's friend Joao (Johnny) Pavao. Pavao was simply in the wrong place at the wrong time, sitting beside Melo in his Jeep Cherokee in a west Toronto plaza, when Gagne showed up to shoot Melo.

Gagné, 32, was promised $75,000 for the Melo hit, although he was eventually only paid $50,000. However, as good as it was, money wasn't the most important thing about the job for Gagné. He needed to show he could kill in the big leagues.

"When you want to play with the big boys, you got to do what you got to do," Gagné testified at the trial of Manuel (Mike) DaSilva, Melo's longtime West Toronto neighbour, who was accused of arranging the hit. "I had never killed anybody before, but I knew what had to be done to move up in the criminal ranks."

Gagné told the court he had dreams for himself and his family. He wanted more from life than breaking legs or intimidating people.

"I had done all that before," said Gagné, who had been in and out of prison since he was 18 and also admitted to committing at least 20 bank robberies for which he was never arrested.

Speaking in a cold, clinical voice, Gagné said he walked up to Melo's SUV, raised his .38 snub-nosed revolver and shot Pavao in the head. "Then Mr. Melo tried to press the gas," Gagné said, "and I started shooting him. I shot him twice… I shot Melo twice in the head, left side. I saw the blood. It was the first time that I ever killed anybody...the adrenalin was pumping."

The killing excited him, but Gagné still considered himself a family man. He was almost bragging as he told court that he refused to kill Melo in front of his family at little Eduardo's day care.

"There was no way I was going to kill him in front of his wife and kid."

DaSilva denied involvement. And in the end, the jury chose to believe him over Gagné. It found DaSilva not guilty on both counts of first-degree murder. (Another Toronto man, Delio Pereira, 53, was earlier sentenced in the case to four-and-a-half years in prison, after pleading guilty in January 2005 to conspiracy to commit murder.) Melo's widow Rhonda sat in the courtroom with her son Eduardo as DaSilva was pronounced not guilty. She was wearing a gold necklace with "Eddie" on it, and later said to Bob Mitchell of the *Toronto Star* that she hadn't yet told little Eduardo that his father had been murdered.

"Eduardo thinks his father was killed in a car crash," she said. "How do you tell him two bullets were put into his father's head?"

The headline in the March 2, 2006 Montreal *Gazette* was cheeky and eye-catching. It read: "Like father, like Godfather." Under it was a story on drunk driving charges facing Nicolo (Nick) Rizzuto, 82, and referring to the still-pending earlier charges involving his son Vito, 60.

The Rizzutos were the butt of nervous jokes and curious public speculation now. The latest scrape with the law for the elder Rizzuto — who served five years in a Venezuelan prison for cocaine possession in the late 1980s and early 1990s — came after his arrest on New Year's Eve 2005 when his Mercedes collided with a fire truck.

At the time Nick Rizzuto was crashing into the fire engine, his son Vito was still in jail fighting an extradition order to the U.S. where he was charged with racketeering involving the 1981 "three captains slayings" in Brooklyn.

There were also legal woes in Italy. Vito Rizzuto faced charges of using laundered money in a $6-billion-dollar tender for a contract to build a 3.6-kilometer suspension bridge across the Strait of Massino linking Sicily with mainland Italy for the first time. The proposed bridge was to be three times the length of San Francisco's Golden Gate Bridge, which would make it the world's longest suspension bridge. Even before the Mafia allegations, the project was controversial because of its cost, potential environmental impact and safety concerns — the proposed construction site was in an earthquake zone.

Clearly, his drunk driving charges – or those of his father – were not the top thing on his mind in March 2006. It couldn't have been comforting for Vito Rizzuto, as he sat in jail on the American racketeering charges, to read fresh reports in the *Montreal Gazette* about the 1981 murders in Brooklyn of Bonanno family members Alphonse (Sonny Red) Indelicato, Dominick (Big Trin) Trinchera and Philip (Phil Lucky) Giaccone.

Rizzuto had long denied the allegation he had been involved in the triple-murder. He claimed he was nothing more than an ordinary businessman with interests in a construction company. However, the *Gazette* noted that Salvatore (Good Looking Sal) Vitale, the Bonanno underboss-turned-informant, testified in the 2004 trial of former Bonanno captain Joseph (Big Joey) Massino that Vito Rizzuto not only was involved, he was one of the killers.

At the trial, the prosecutor had asked Vitale, "Was someone designated as the lead shooter?"

"Vito and Emmanuel," Vitale replied.

Vitale noted that mobster Dominick Napolitano suggested the hit-team should include his underling, Donnie Brasco, so that Brasco could achieve Mafia member status. He didn't realize that Brasco was really undercover FBI agent Joe Pistone. Massino rejected the suggestion of getting Brasco to help out with the murders because, he said, he wanted Canadians instead.

"Was there any discussion where the shooters...why some of the shooters were from Canada?" asked prosecutor Greg Andres.

"Because of a security issue," Vitale replied. "It would never leak out. And after the murders, they would go back to Montreal."

Vitale was asked who ultimately made up the hit-team.

"Vito Rizzuto, a man named Emmanuel, an old-timer, and myself," Vitale said.

"Do you know where Vito Rizzuto was from?" Andres asked.

"Montreal, Canada."

"How about Emmanuel?"

"I believe from Montreal also."

(Emmanuel and "the old-timer" were never identified by the authorities.)

Vitale described in detail how the four gunmen hid in a closet of the Brooklyn social club before bursting out together when their associate Gerlando (George from Canada) Sciascia signaled them by running his hands through his silvery hair.

"I heard Vito say, 'Don't anybody move. This is a holdup.' And then shots were being fired," Vitale testified.

"I seen Vito shoot. I don't know who he hit," Vitale added.

Sciascia, who helped orchestrate the slaughter, had fallen out of favour with his old Mafia associates. He'd become another of their murder victims and was no longer a threat to anyone. But Massino was convicted on eleven racketeering counts, including ones that said he was involved in setting up the Indelicato, Trinchera and Giaccone hits. Soon after his conviction, Massino, who faced the threat of the death penalty, also turned informant. He was available and he had the motivation to testify against Rizzuto.

On March 16, 2006, the Supreme Court of Canada declined to hear Vito Rizzuto's appeal of the extradition order. Now Rizzuto sat in his cell knowing that, if extradicted and convicted, he faced the very real prospect of some 20 years in prison. And at his age, that amounted to a life sentence.

If he felt the need for a drink, well, it was understandable.

Endnotes

CHAPTER 1

This chapter draws from numerous sources, including news accounts of Vic Cotroni's funeral. One of the most valuable reference books for the entire book was Pino Arlacchi's *Mafia Business: The Mafia Ethic and the Spirit of Capitalism* (Oxford: Oxford University Press, 1986). The section on the virginity-shame aspect of Mafia tension is from page 7 of that book. Arlacchi also aided me through an interview in Rome. The anecdote about Vic Cotroni's reaction to the TV crew comes from journalist James Dubro of the CBC *Connections* series.

The description of Vic Cotroni's house comes from a two-hour visit I paid to it in July 1989 when it came on the market, and the description of how Vic Cotroni rated in the Canadian underworld and the composition of the underworld comes in large part from not-for-attribution interviews with police and police reports.

Palermo journalist Daniele Billitiere, a long-time Mafia observer, helped me make sense of it all, including tensions between Sicilian and Calabrian mobsters.

CHAPTER 2

Robert F. Harney's "Montreal's King of Italian Labour: A Case Study in Padronism," *Labour/Le Travailleur* 4, no. 4 (1979): 57–84, and "The Padrone and the Immigrant," *Canadian Review of American Studies* 5 no. 2 (Fall 1974): 101-17, were a great help in dealing with King Cordasco. Also useful was "The Royal Commission appointed to inquire into the Immigration of Italian Labourers to Montreal and the Alleged Fraudulent Practices of Employment Agencies," *Report of the Commissioner and Evidence,* Issued by the Department of Labour, Canada (J.N.O. Winchester, commissioner) (Ottawa: King's Printer, 1905).

The Blackhand letter to Cordasco was printed in *La Presse* on September 3, 1904. The Salvatore Tino file is in the RG 13 section at the National Archives, along with other previously sealed Blackhand files, which I had opened, including a 1913 conviction for Frank Rocco for unlawful conspiracy and a 1914 case in which Joseph Ranieri was convicted of sending threatening letters. The Tony Frank trial material is also from RG 13 at the National Archives in Ottawa.

The second commission is by Superior Court Judge Louis Codèrre, which was published verbatim in *Le Devoir* on March 14, 1925. Police commissions over the past century in Quebec are analysed in depth by Jean-Paul Brodeur in *La Délinquance de l'Ordre; récherches sur les commissions d'inquête, I*(Québec: Hurtubise, 1984).

Details specific to the Cotronis can be drawn from numerous court cases in the downtown Montreal courthouse, including Le Roi *vs.* Vincent Coutroni, April 16, 1928; Quebec Liquor Commission *vs.* Joseph Catoni, April 18, 1928; Quebec Liquor Commission *vs.* Nick Catroni, August 9, 1928; Quebec Liquor Commission vs. Jim Cotroni, September 11, 1928; Le Roi *vs.* Nick Catroni, August 10, 1928; Le Roi *vs.* Wm. Tanguay (alias Lucien Lacoste), April 16, 1928; Rex *vs.* Emila Millano Catroni, June 6, 1931; Le Roi Contre John Catoni (alias Catroni) and Fran Searpabegga, February 1, 1934; Regina *vs.* Jos Catroni and Paul Gauthier, September 10, 1937; Rex *vs.* Vincenzo Catroni, February 16, 1938; Regina *vs.* Giuseppe Cotroni, October 19, 1959.

Much of my information about Montreal at the time the Cotronis arrived comes from *The Italians of Montreal: From Sojourning to Settlement, 1900–1921* (Montréal: Les Éditions du Courant, 1980) by Bruno Ramirez and Michael Del Balso.

The estimates on the number of brothels in the old Cotroni neighbourhood come from page 169 of Jean-Pierre Charbonneau's definitive *The Canadian Connection* (Montreal: Optimum Publishing, 1976) and pages 147 and 174 of *Pax: lutte a finir avec la pègre* by Alain Stanké and Jean-Louis Morgan (Montreal: La Presse,

1972). Anyone writing about Montreal organized crime owes a huge debt to Charbonneau, who survived a murder attempt from a Cotroni associate while breaking stories for *Le Devoir.* Brothels, booze, jazz and the general mood of the jazz age in Montreal times is nicely captured in *Swinging in Paradise: The Story of Jazz in Montreal* (Montreal: Vehicule Press, 1988), by John Gilmore.

I also read a good deal of *Maclean's* magazine and *Saturday Night* from the time period, the September 11, 1909, September 25, 1909, May 2, 1912, and March 1, 1926, issues of *Saturday Night* and the March 1, 1926, issue of *Maclean's* being of particular interest. *Saturday Night* ran much copy on the "national menace" of smuggling in issues between November 22, 1924, and January 3, 1925, with more on June 13, June 27, and December 26, 1925.

Journalist Ralph Allen's *Ordeal By Fire: Canada 1910–1945,* Volume Five of the Canadian History Series, Thomas B. Costain, editor (Toronto: Doubleday Canada Ltd., 1961) offers insights into the custom 's scandal as well.

The Second World War detention records, in the RG 18 series at the National Archives in Ottawa, were first discovered by James Dubro and Robin F. Rowland for their *King of the Mob: Rocco Perri and the Women Who Ran His Rackets* (Toronto: Viking, 1987).

CHAPTER 3

I gathered some fresh material on Carmine Galante through the Freedom of Information Act in the United States.

Figures on heroin dollar-values are from pages 63 and 65 of *Organized Crime and Illicit Traffic in Narcotics;* report of the committee operations, United States Senate, made by its permanent subcommittee on investigations (Washington: U.S. Government Printing Office, 1965).

The woes of Salvatore Giglio, Frank Pretula and their confederates, as well as the rise of Vic Cotroni and Carmine Galante's activities in Montreal in the 1950s were chronicled by Charbonneau (op. cit.), as well as by Alan Phillips in a five-part series that ran in *Maclean's* magazine on August 24, September 21, October 5, and December 2, 1963; and March 7, 1964. The old *Star Weekly* had another important piece by Pax Plante and David MacDonald called "The Shame of My City: Crime in Montreal," in the supplement to newspapers, including the *Toronto Star* and the *Montreal Star,* on June 24, 1962, pp. 2–6; July 1, 1961, pp. 6–11; July 8, 1961, pp.

10–13; July 15, 1961, pp. 14–17; and July 22, 1961, pp. 15–17.

I also benefited from interviews with Mario Latraverse, former head of the Montreal Urban Police's anti-gang squad, and with other police organized-crime experts, on the basis that their names not appear in print. I also gained access to some police files on the time period.

CHAPTER 4

The conversation between Pep Cotroni and the FBI team is taken verbatim from trial transcripts.

Regarding Vic Cotroni's lack of convictions for drug-trafficking, it's worth noting that he was held in February 19 60 in Miami for conspiracy to violate narcotics laws. The charges were dropped for lack of evidence.

The 1957 meetings in Palermo were described in *Men of Honour: The Confessions of Tommaso Buscetta, the Man who Destroyed the Mafia*

(London: Collins, 1987) by Tim Shawcross and Martin Young. I gained atmosphere by staying at the site of some of the meetings, the Hotel des Palmes, while researching the book in Sicily.

CHAPTER 5

My visit to Vic Cotroni's Lavaltrie summer home helped again, as did police files and a chat with the newspaper editor who spent a night in jail with Frank Cotroni. Understandably, he request anonymity.

CHAPTER 6

Joe Bonanno's autobiography, *A Man of Honor: The Autobiography of Joseph Bonanno* (New York: Simon and Schuster, 1983), is self-serving, but provides a look at the mobster's poisonous relationship with his cousin, Stefano Magaddino of Buffalo, with his quote on Carlo Gambino coming from page 226 and his description of jail in Montreal from page 240. Federal Immigration department documents that I opened under the Access to Information Act gave a look into Bonanno's time in Montreal, as well as that of his son, Salvatore. It's interesting that these government files directly contradict Bonanno's claim in his book that he had no intentions of settling in Montreal.

Honor Thy Father by Gay Talese (New York: Dell, 1981) is a revealing book on life in the Mafia, centred on Salvatore Bonanno. Joe Bonanno's version of why he headed north comes, in part, from a *60 Minutes* interview by Mike Wallace on March 28, 1983. Sam (The Plumber) DeCavalcante unwittingly provided some of the quotes of this chapter, via Henry A. Zeiger's *Sam the Plumber* (New York: Signet, 1970) and quotes used on the Montreal adventure are from pages 43, 44 and 138.

The interview with Salvatore Bonanno on the importance of family was done by Martyn Burke of the CBC *Connections* investigative team and is taken from page 17 of transcripts from the June 12, 1977, airing. More interesting notes on the Saputo situation came from confidential police files and page 15 of the *Connections* transcripts for June 12, 1977. Files on the Saputo cheese operations were closed under the Access to Information Act, although I gained access to closed police files on Saputo cheese through another source. As well, author James Dubro's files were generously opened to me as well, including the transcript to a July 10, 1978, WCAX-TV Burlington, Vermont, broadcast on Saputo cheese. Jonathan Kwitny, author of *Vicious Circles: The Mafia in the Marketplace* (New York: W.W. Norton & Company, 1979), which deals with the cheese industry, also generously gave me access to portions of his files. Also, the Ontario Milk Marketing Board records files in Guelph, Ontario, included a defence by Giuseppe Saputo against Mafia allegations, which was interesting since he claimed that he was a Mafia victim, not an associate, and said that he left Sicily to get away from the Mafia. He said his business went from modest beginnings to becoming a huge success in part because of the boom in popularity for pizza.

As usual, not-for-attribution police sources were of help.

CHAPTER 7

My thanks to *Toronto Star* reporter Don Dutton for allowing me to make a copy of the "Orbit" wiretap transcripts, which record conversations in the Giacomo Luppino household.

Arlacchi's *Mafia Business* (op. cit.) was, again, extremely important here, with the "populist everyman" quote coming from page 117. Phillips again was useful and venerable *Toronto Star* crime reporter Jocko Thomas helped out through interviews, as did confidential police sources and reports. As proof that Paolo Violi wasn't a major crime player early in his career, police files state he didn't even meet Vic Cotroni until 1962.

Journalists Lee Lamothe and Rob Lamberti did a valuable series on Rocco Zito, which ran in the *Toronto Sun* May 19–22, 1988, and should be clipped by anyone interested in this underworld figure.

Government sources include "Royal Commission on Crime," by Justice Wilfrid D. Roach, March 18, 1963; "Report of the Ontario Police Commission on Organized Crime," by Judge Bruce Macdonald, January 31, 1964; "Crime, Justice and Society," Vol. 3, Crime in Quebec, organized crime, Commission of enquiry into the administration of justice on criminal and penal matters in Quebec, 1969 .

Dubro kindly helped me gain some understanding of Giacomo Luppino. The intricacies of the wedding of his daughter Grazia to Paolo Violi are from confidential police files, interviews and the June 12, 1977, transcripts from the *Connections* television series, which first noted that the wedding brought together crime interests as well as two people.

Off-the-record interviews with police sources gave me a sense of Violi 's position in the mob as well. The CBC *Connections* series pointed out Violi's pivotal position in the Canadian underworld and a diagram of this is in *Making Connections* by Wade Rowland (Toronto: Gage, 1979). The *Connections* series inspired a good many journalists, myself included.

Aside from the Brigante killing, Paolo Violi was also questioned for the 1969 Toronto murder of Filippo Vendemini, a Calabrian immigrant who did some work delivering illegal liquor for Violi and who ran a shoe store on Bloor Street West.

CHAPTER 8

Background sources on the FLQ include *The Assassination of Pierre Laporte* by Pierre Vallières, translated by Ralph Wells (Toronto: James Lorimer, 1977); *Pierre Vallières: The Revolutionary Process in Quebec,* by Nicholas M. Regush (Toronto: Fitzhenry & Whiteside, 1973); Louis Fournier's *FLQ: The Anatomy of an Underground Movement,* translated by Edward Baxter (Toronto: New Canada Publications, 1984). On page 54 of this work, a meeting between the Cotronis and Pierre Vallières is described, in which the mobsters attempt to learn just what the "Cotroni" reference in the FLQ manifesto means.

Talking it Out: The October Crisis from Inside by Francis Simard, translated by David Homel (Montreal: Guernica, 1982), provides the quote by Simard on the election that disillusioned him on pages 95 and 96; Laporte in shock is from page 49 and 51–52; and Simard's musings on why Laporte was their victim are on pages 21 and 22.

Harold Crooks 's *Dirty Business: The Inside Story of the New Garbage Agglomerates* (Toronto: James Lorimer, 1983) also has useful material of political connections of Montreal criminals. Much of the news broken at the time came from Robert McKenzie and Ronald Lebel of the *Toronto Star*, including July 7, 1973, on the South Shore election; police surveillance on the meeting between Laporte and mobsters on July 7 and 12, 1973; the planned forced "confession" of Laporte on August 4, 1973; Rose's reported confession March 16, 1973; and the Gagnon-D'Asti relationship from January 16, March 2 and May 16, 1974. *Canadian* magazine noted his great affection for his wife in a lengthy piece shortly after his murder.

The meat scandal is discussed in *L'introduction frauduleuse de viande impropre sur le marche de la consommation humaine et la fraude en rapport avec la viande chevaline; rapport interimaire de l'enquête sur le crime organisé* (Montreal: Centre de reproduction Ministère de la Justice, October 16, 1975) and the Laporte scandal in *Rapport d'enquête sur l'étude de liens possible entre Nicolas Di Iorio et Frank Dasti, membres du crime organisé, Pierre Laporte, ministre, René Gagnon, chef de cabinet, et Jean-Jacques Côté, organisateur politique* (Ste.-Foy, Que.: Commission de Police du Québec, 1974). It's worth noting, for people who think mobsters hurt only other mobsters, that this isn't the only time the Cotroni clan has put rotten meat into consumers' stomachs, as Vic Cotroni and Paolo Violi's Reggio Foods was shut down for selling unfit meat.

CHAPTER 9

Frank Cotroni's bizarre press conference was described in amusing detail by Wade Rowland in the February 18, 1971, Toronto *Telegram*. News photos taken helped with some of the physical details. The November 5, 1967, *Allô Police* provided details of his arrest. While this is a flashy tabloid, it has a wide readership and input from both the law enforcement and law-breaking fraternities and is considered an accurate record by a number of criminologists.

Again, I benefited from access to Dubro's personal files.

I interviewed A.J. Campbell on his recollections of the trial as well. There was an even sadder ending to what had been a fine career for lawyer Jean-Paul Ste. Marie. He was convicted in 1978 of misappropriating $112,654 entrusted to him by a client and disbarred for life by the Quebec Bar later that year. In 1979, he was sentenced to twenty-three months in jail for taking the money. After his disbarment, the once-zealous prosecutor worked as a taxi driver and administrator for a Montreal taxi drivers' association.

Again, not-for-attribution police sources and records were of help.

CHAPTER 10

Former Montreal undercover officer Bob Menard, as well as Mario Latraverse, the former head of the Montreal Urban Police anti-gang squad, and Normand Ostiguy, an anti-gang squad member, helped here, as well as not-for-attribution police sources. William Marsden of the Montreal *Gazette* has written intelligently of the Sicilian element in Montreal organized crime, with a particularly interesting offering on April 8, 1988. The Violi ties to the Getty kidnapping were first made public in Canada on March 28, 1979, by the *Connections* team, while Arlacchi has written with knowledge and insight on the changes in the nature of Mafia capitalism in *Mafia Business*.

I got the 1936 Tribunal of Agrigento concerning Mafia members through the Access to Information Act. It had apparently been passed from the Department of the Secretary of State to the Citizenship and Immigration branch of the federal government.

The detail that Desormiers was listening to "Les Portes de Pénitencier" at the moment of his death came from a finely written piece by Martha Gagnon in the October 15, 1982, *La Presse*.

Secret police files note that Paolo Violi once said that, if he had it all to do over again, he would have eliminated the Dubois brothers before they grew too strong.

Arlacchi's *Mafia Business* (op. cit.) suggests on page 152 that Paolo Violi was involved in drug-trafficking, although he had no Canadian convictions. The book says American police agents were told by a southern Calabrian mafioso that he could get them heroin from "his friend Paolo Violi, a well-known Italo-American mafioso resident in Toronto." It's curious the mafioso refers to Violi as being from his former home of Toronto, rather than his then-current home of Montreal.

CHAPTER 11

Sources on Giuseppe Catania and Tommaso Buscetta include Shaw-cross and Young (op. cit.) and police sources who didn't want to be identified. The fact that D'Asti's lawyer was provided by legal aid can't help but raise questions about the myth that all powerful mobsters are rich.

D'Asti's unsuccessful lobbying effort in Ottawa comes from secret police files.

CHAPTER 12

The financial machinations of this time of Willie Obront are catalogued in *Organized Crime and the World of Business: Quebec Police Commission Report of the Commission of Inquiry on Organized Crime and Recommendations,* released on August 2, 1977. Also useful in a general sense are *Crime, Justice and Society,* Vol. 3: Crime in Quebec, organized crime, Commission of Enquiry into the Administration of Justice on Criminal and Penal Matters in Quebec, (1969); *Report of the Commission of Inquiry on the Exercise of Union Freedom in the Construction Industry,* by Robert Cliche, chairman, along with Brian Mulroney and Guy Chevrette, released on May 2, 1975. The *Financial Post* examined Obront's association with businessman Gerald Pencier in its September 8 and 9, 1988, issue in a series written by Philip Mathias and edited by Tessa Wilmott.

The Bronfman Dynasty by Peter C. Newman (Toronto: McClelland and Stewart, 1978) deals with Mitchell Bronfman's involvement with Obront.

An unsung hero of the *Toronto Star*'s award-winning discovery of Gerda Munsinger is Jack Granek, a German-speaking editor who tirelessly worked the overseas phones to locate her, but received negligible glory for the discovery.

Closed police files show that, in the late 1960s, American crime expert Ralph Salerno had suggested that Canadian police target Vic Cotroni, Louis Greco, Willie Obront and Joe DiMaulo for further probes.Salerno recommended more use of wiretapping and the use of flowcharts to show the relationships between gangsters. His suggestions were apparently followed, with great success. Salerno had pointed out the danger of leaking material to the media, which could result in huge lawsuits, like the Vic Cotroni suit against *Maclean's* and a number of suits against *Life* magazine.

CHAPTER 13

No one outside the Mafia, and not very many people inside it, knew more about Paolo Violi than former undercover police officer Bob Menard, and again, he helped me here. Conversations quoted in this chapter are from his recollections. A not-for-attribution police source helped me with details of Violi's wedding. An October 25, 1980, Montreal *Gazette* piece by Eddie Collister on police officer Nick Guerra shows Menard wasn't the only brave officer fighting the Cotroni group.

I also enjoyed and benefited from Ann Charney's "The Life and Death of Paolo Violi" in *Weekend Magazine,* January 20, 1979.

The St. Leonard situation during the language debate of the late 1960s is dealt with in "The Italians of Quebec: Key Participants in Contemporary Linguistic and Political Debates," by Paul-Andre Linteau, in *Arrangiarsi: The Italian Immigration Experience in Canada,* edited by Roberto Perin and Franc Sturino (Montreal: Guernica, 1989). Excellent coverage of Paolo Violi's funeral was provided in the January 28, 1978, Montreal *Gazette* by Tim Burke. This article described how Violi "protected" an English-language advocate, as does Charney (op. cit.).

CHAPTER 14

Latraverse and other police sources were helpful here, as were the commission reports cited for Chapter 13 and certain confidential police reports. *Contrepreneurs* by Diane Francis (Toronto: Macmillan of Canada, 1988) goes into more detail for those interested in more on the Buffalo Gas and Oil scam.

It's worth noting that a rash of bombings and beatings plagued the Italian ice-cream industry in Montreal, after Paolo Violi's lock on the industry was broken. This is the subject of a January 12, 1985, Montreal *Gazette* article.

The overseas scam mentioned involved problems that an Italian contractor had with gangsters, which Violi said he could solve for 10 million lire (apr. $17 million), plus a cut of 10 per cent of all future railway contracts. A soldier was sent to Italy to work out the details and told to refer to the payment on the phone as "10 cases of tomatoes." Montreal police didn't learn the outcome of the operation but the soldier sent overseas was arrested for murdering the attorney general of the province of Cotenzo, as recorded in the Montreal *Gazette,* November 29, 1975.

CHAPTER 15

The list of Vic Cotroni's ailments was filed with court documents on the extortion trial, while the quote from Vincenzo Macri comes from page 146 of *Mafia Business* (op. cit.). Mario Latraverse, former antigang squad head in Montreal, was obviously very helpful in this chapter as well. John Papalia's pithy quotes come from the June 12, 1977, airing of *Connections* on CBC. I can attest to Papalia's ill humour, having been called a "parasite" by him when I approached him in his Hamilton office for an interview. Peter Moon of the *Globe and Mail* had an interview with the foul-mouthed gangster, which appeared in the *Globe* on November 28, 1986.

Charboneau (op. cit.) furnished the fact that Papalia had worked for Carmine Galante and Louis Greco.

CHAPTER 16

I benefited here from above-mentioned police sources as well as the March 27, 1979, *Connections* program, which featured an amusing Martyn Burke interview with Vincenzo Randisi. The Mafia associate quote on Paolo Violi in prison comes from page 12 of the transcripts first show of the second *Connections* organized-crime series which aired in March 1979. The Vic Cotroni-Paolo Violi exchange about the Menard operations comes from Menard, who heard it through a contact.

Ann Charney's *Weekend Magazine* piece (op. cit.) was fascinating, particularly her interview with Grazia Luppino.

The movements of Joe DiMaulo and Vic Cotroni after the Paolo Violi murder come from confidential police files, as did Vic Cotroni's reactions. The statement about danger increasing with longevity for criminals comes from *The Occupational Hazard of Doing Crime: Deterrence Theory Reconsidered,* by Gilbert Cordeau and Pierre Tremblay (Montreal: Centre International de Criminologie Comparée, Université de Montréal, October 1988).

The movements of Paolo Violi's killers are from secret police files, as are the theories for why he was killed. Not-for-attribution police sources and police files provided the theory that Vic Cotroni and Violi's brother-in-law Jimmy Luppino knew of the hit in advance.

The record turnout for Vic Cotroni's mother's funeral can be explained in large part as a show of respect for her offspring.

CHAPTER 17

The Freedom of Information Act was useful here, as were articles by Lucinda Franks *(New York Times,* February 20, 1977, "An Obscure Gangster Is Emerging as the Mafia Chieftain in New York"); William Federici and Paul Meskil *(Sunday News,* February 20, 1977, "Galante Climbing Mob Hill"); Paul Meskil *(New York* magazine, February 28, 1977, "Meet the New Godfather"); and Michael Daly *(Rolling Stone,* August 23, 1979, "Death of a Godfather: Anatomy of a Gangland Murder").

The previously mentioned Carmine Galante profile was invaluable here, along with the other Galante sources used in Chapter 4. Nicholas Pileggi's *Wise Guy: Life in a Mafia Family* (New York: Pocket Books, 1985) helped with the Lewisburg prison description. This book also helped Montreal police figure out why Frank Cotroni had a new set of chums when he was finally let out. He simply made friends in Lewisburg and stayed on close terms with them after his release. A *New York Times* magazine magazine profile published April 3, 1989, on John Gotti by Selwyn Raab noted that Galante was impressed by young Gotti in jail, but was told by others that Gotti "belongs to Dellacroce."

A fascinating and insightful counterpoint to the Galante magazine and newspaper pieces in 1977 is Thomas Plate's "The Making of a Godfather: Leaked Federal Intelligence Report Prompts Press Promotion of Galante as New Mafia Don," in the June 1977 edition of *More* magazine.

An interesting article in the May–June 1978 *Harvard Business Review* by Harry Levinson entitled "The Abrasive Personality" deals with legitimate business executives, but offers some insight into Galante's failure to hold power once he had attained it. It describes short-tempered, abrasive managers who are consumed with a need for perfection, and who need total control and discourage discussion. Such executives may be good at securing power but are poor at wielding it, although few suffer for their failings as dramatically as Galante.

Once again, Arlacchi's *Mafia Business* (op. cit.) helped with the business underpinnings of the frantic on-street activity; the part on Mafia codes being supplanted by money is from page 207.

The description of Galante sometimes looking professorial comes from Dubro, who pulled off a journalist coup by capturing the little mobster on film at a church.

CHAPTER 18

Not-for-attribution police interviews helped enormously here, as did secret police files. Charbonneau was again valuable. Louis Freeh of the South Manhattan U.S. Attorney's office helped me with the New York–Canadian connection. *New York Times* reporter Ralph Blumenthal helped me plan my trip to Sicily, and his *Last Days of the Sicilians: The FBI Assault on the Pizza Connection* (New York: Times Books, 1988) was useful.

I interviewed Réal Simard for more than three hours as well. Simard's autobiography *The Nephew: The Making of a Mafia Hitman* (Scarborough: Prentice-Hall Canada Inc., 1988) which he co-authored with Michel Vastel, is self-serving but nonetheless intriguing. Simard is also the focal point of "Broken Honour: The Making of a Mafia Hitman," Greg Foad, executive producer, which aired on CHCH-TV in Hamilton on May 25, 1989.

I also interviewed some of Simard's police handlers and reviewed police files on him.

CHAPTER 19

Anyone interested in the Sicilian mob in Montreal should read William Marsden's Montreal *Gazette* series, which appeared April 7–8, 1988.

Not-for-attribution police sources helped, as did Pino Arlacchi, whom I interviewed in Rome.

CHAPTER 20

Secret police files and not-for-attribution interviews aided me immensely here. Paul Volpe's relationship with Frank Cotroni and Cotroni's movements in Toronto are from a not-for-attribution police source in Toronto and secret police intelligence reports.

The economics of the table-dance business in southern Ontario in the early 1980s is from a confidential Toronto police source.

James Dubro 's *Mob Rule: Inside the Canadian Mafia* (Toronto: Macmillan, 1985) is a journalistic breakthrough in this genre and required reading for anyone interested in Volpe or the Canadian Mafia in general.

Mafia Assassin: The Inside Story of a Canadian Biker, Hitman and Police Informer, by Cecil Kirby and Thomas C. Renner (Toronto: Methuen, 1986), gives a look at the Toronto mob scene in the 1970s and early 1980s. The underworld theory that the Cotronis were the authors of Volpe's murder is from pages 235 and 236.

Much drama came out in mobster Richard Clément's trial in March 1988 in Toronto, in which he was charged with the Seaway Hotel attack. Journalist Darcy Henton followed up on the story, reporting on the front page of the *Sunday Star* on July 16, 1989 that Hétu was charged with four counts of sexual assault since being given a new identity after the trial under the provincial witness-protection program. Henton also reported Hétu's brag that he has killed four people.

The union section drew, from a story I wrote for the *Toronto Star* on June 18, 1989. That article took three months and involved more than twenty-five interviews. Further articles appeared in the *Star* on November 23, 1989, and December 31, 1989.

The hotel union wasn't the Cotroni's first association with organized labour, as reported in *Report of the Commission of Inquiry on the Exercise of Union Freedom in the Construction Industry,* by Robert Cliche (chairman), Brian Mulroney, Guy Chevrette. This report notes the Cotroni backing of "a private army of goons, without peer in the history of Quebec labor relations." Francesco Fuoco, one of the men convicted in the effort to tunnel into the Montreal City and District Savings Bank on Decarie Blvd., reappears here. The commission noted Fuoco wrote a construction company in 1973, offering "protection" and listing his qualifications in this manner: "I was a soldier in the Mafia in Montreal, I was what you call a smal *[sic]* soldier, my job was to falow *[sic]* orders, keep my mouth shout *[sic]* end *[sic]* do what I was told. In 1966 the boss of the mafia decided to organid *[sic]* the bigest *[sic]* Bank Roberie *[sic]* evr *[sic]* pul *[sic]* in Canada . ...dont *[sic]* be shy I can always use my old conection *[sic].*"

The relationship in Ontario between the Luppinos, Violis and Volpe is described in *Report of the Royal Commission on Certain Sectors of the Building Industry* (Toronto: Queen 's Printer for Ontario, 1974), Judge Harry Waisberg, commissioner.

CHAPTER 21

Secret police files helped again immensely. This section obviously also benefits from interviews with Dave Hilton, Sr.; Henri Spitzer; Simard; George Cherry; and my usual police sources. The quote from Pauline Desormiers is from *Allô Police,* March 25, 1984. Claude Jodoin's *Qui a Tué Frank Shoofey?* (Montreal: Les Éditions de L'Epoque, 1985) is clearly more a tribute to the author's friend

Shoofey than unbiased journalism, but it's interesting nonetheless.The quote by Dave Hilton, Sr., on signing with Don King is from the Montreal *Gazette,* February 4, 1985, while the Jacques Beauchamp quote is from *Journal de Montréal,* March 13, 1984.

It's worth noting that mob ties to boxers in Canada are nothing new, and that the gang was using pro boxers to tear up bars for extortion purposes in the mid-1950s.

CHAPTER 22

Again, Shawcross and Young (op. cit.) is useful.

I was aided by the 1983 Annual Report of the Governor's Council on Organized Crime; State of Florida. My *Toronto Star* colleagues Cal Millar and Don Dutton were unselfish in helping me out with the Florida section of the book, and I also benefited from their May 6, 1974, piece in the *Star.* Eddie Collister of the Montreal *Gazette* turned in an interesting article on October 19, 1983. Selwyn Raab wrote a January 2, 1984, piece on Canadian gangs in Florida for the *New York Times. The Canadians* by Andrew Malcolm (Toronto: Paperjacks, 1985) deals with Canadian mobsters in Florida on pages 358 and 359.

The detail on Frank Cotroni's prison generosity comes from Charbonneau's *Canadian Connection* (page 456) while the amusing quote about Cotroni's prison concert organizing appeared in the Toronto *Sun* on May 28, 1988. Simard and police sources helped with the section on Rizzuto's record woes. Francis (op. cit.) writes with emotion on Bill C-61, and I used the Access to Information Act for background reports by the Canadian Bar Association and the Canadian Bankers' Association on the bill.

William Marsden of the Montreal *Gazette* had a piece published in that newspaper on July 8, 1989, called "Police Are Slow to Put Bite on Drug Dealers' Assets," which shows the strength of Bill C-61 was not being used to its full potential. I also talked with police on their views of the act.

My understanding of the new influence of Iranians in the Montreal heroin-traffic was aided by "Busting the Heroin Pedlars" on CBC's *the fifth estate*, April 18, 1989, with reporter Sheila MacVicar and producer Brian McKenna and through an interview with Montreal police crime analyst Bob Perreault.

CHAPTER 23

Yves Chartrand of the *Journal de Montréal* shared with me his memories about Frank Cotroni in prison. The fact that Cotroni was allowed out of prison for his son Francesco 's wedding is from "Cotroni Must Wait Till '93 for Parole: Prison Officials Rebuff Hopes for Early Release," by Eddie Collister, Montreal *Gazette,* September 4, 1991.

On December 21, 1992, four days before Christmas, senior Mountie Claude Savoie put his service revolver to his head and pulled the trigger at the RCMP's Ottawa headquarters, amidst allegations that he took bribes totaling $200,000 from drug dealer Allan (the Weasel) Ross of Montreal's West End Gang.

Mounties investigating the death were troubled by Insp. Savoie's relationship with Ross, who was then serving a life sentence at Leavenworth Penitentiary in Kansas, and were preparing to question him that morning about whether he channeled sensitive police intelligence to Ross through mob lawyer Sidney Leithman.

The suicide came as Savoie faced questioning by the force's internal investigators, and as the CBC public-affairs program *the fifth estate* was preparing to broadcast a documentary Ross, which included mention of his relationship with Savoie. Savoie had told the news program this about his relationship with Ross: "He wasn't an informant, nor was I an informant for him. But I knew him. Put it that way. I met him."

CHAPTER 24

For more on this topic, see *Deadly Silence: Canadian Mafia Murders* by Peter Edwards and Antonio Nicaso (Toronto: Macmillan Canada, 1993).

Gerlando Sciascia outlived Joe Lo Presti, but was also murdered in New York City in March 1999.

CHAPTER 25

The Joe DiMaulo interview is from "Mafia's Casino Interests Run Deep" by Peter Edwards in the *Toronto Star,* July 6, 1993. "How the RCMP Helped 'Push' $2 billion Worth of Cocaine" by Andrew McIntosh is taken from the Ottawa *Citizen* on June 11, 1998.

I met several times with Mahmood (Moe) Adolaymi and interviewed federal prosecutor Richard Starck. The material about Frank

Cotroni and the behind-bars party that fell through is from "Le 'party' d'adieu de Frank Cotroni gache par ses geoliers" by Andre Cedilot in *La Presse* on April 28, 1995.

It's interesting that Cotroni was granted parole, despite having been convicted in the early 1990s also by American authorities of a plot to smuggle drugs into the U.S. That plot was hatched while he was already in custody in the 1980s.

I also benefited from Paul Cherry's story in the Montreal *Gazette* on August 18, 2001.

CHAPTER 26

Quotes of Ken Murdock's memories of the day he killed Johnny Papalia are from *Hamilton Spectator* reporter Barbara Brown and were published on February 5, 2000, in the *Toronto Star* and the *Hamilton Spectator.*

Papalia's life is the subject of Adrian Humphreys' *The Enforcer: Johnny Pops Papalia — A Life and Death in the Mafia* (Toronto: HarperCollins, 1999).

CHAPTER 27

The Cuntrera-Caruana story is the topic of *Bloodlines: Project Omertà and the Fall of the Mafia's Royal Family* by Lee Lamothe and Antonio Nicaso (Toronto: HarperCollins, 2001) and *The Rothschilds of the Mafia on Aruba* by Tom Blickman, *Transnational Organized Crime* 3, no. 2 (Summer 1997).

Money on the Run; Canada and How the World's Dirty Profits are Laundered by Mario Possamai (Toronto: Viking, 1992) deals with Alfonso Caruana to a point, but also with the process of money-laundering in Canada. The quote from the National Parole Board regarding Giuseppe Caruana is from *Bloodlines* (op. cit.), page 381.

Antonio LaRosa's quick parole is from *Con Game: The Truth about Canada's Prisons* by Michael Harris (Toronto: McClelland & Stewart, 2002).

The point that Alfonso Caruana was eligible for parole immediately after pleading guilty is from journalist Michel Auger.

CHAPTER 28

This chapter drew in part from George Kalogeraskis's article in the Montreal *Gazette* on April 11, 2001, and "Dead Man Talking" by Daniel Sanger in *Saturday Night* 117, no. 1 (April 2002).

The shooting of Michel Auger is dealt with in depth in his book *L'Attentat* (Montreal: Les Éditions Trait d'Union, 2001)

CHAPTER 29

I drew from Melo's Immigration and Refugee Board, Immigration Appeal Division, files (Board File: T94-07953), which contained comments from Melo, his friends, family and police.

I interviewed the Peel Regional Police officers investigating his murder: Inspector Tom Slinger, Detective-Sergeant Frank Roselli and Detective Steve Gormley and also retired Quebec biker intelligence officer, Guy Ouellette.

Details of Melo's funeral are from "$6,000 Last Call as Slain Ex-Fighter Buried — Louis XIII Cognac Poured on Casket of Eddie Melo," *Toronto Star,* April 17, 2001, by Andrew Chung and Peter Edwards.

George Chuvalo quotes are from "Melo Burned Out Too Soon: Chuvalo" by Peter Edwards, *Toronto Star,* April 11, 2001. Quotes from Rhonda Sullivan are from "Melo's Widow Relives Agony" in the *Toronto Star,* April 9, 2001, by Jack Lakey, and "Melo Shooting Unsolved a Year Later — Police Issue Appeal for Public's Help after 400 Interviews" by Bob Mitchell, *Toronto Star,* April 5, 2002.

George Kalogerakis of the Montreal *Gazette* wrote on February 12, 2001, in the *National Post* about Davey Hilton, Jr.'s, attempt to use relatives of the Westies gang of New York City as character references.

Bill Beacon wrote an excellent article in the *Toronto Star* that ran March 17, 2001, on the "Fighting Hiltons" and their troubles with the law and triumphs in the ring.

André Cédilot wrote "Frank Cotroni recouvre la liberté," which was published in *La Presse* on November 8, 2001, and noted that he had gotten about in custody in a golf cart.

Statistics about average time in federal prison before day parole and full parole are from Harris (op. cit.).

CHAPTER 29

On February 26, 2001, Adrian Humphreys wrote in the *National Post,* "Mafia Begins Unity Drive: Canadian Leaders Face Common Threat from Hells Angels."

I drew on several interviews with police sources for the conclusions about Frank Cotroni.

Under-aged victims of sex crimes are normally not identified, for obvious reasons. In this case, the sisters themselves success-fully fought to allow their identitiesto be made public. They wrote a book about their ordeal entitled, *Le Coeur au beurre noir*, which translates as "The Heart with a Black Eye."

CHAPTER 30

An investigation by the *Vancouver Sun* identified fifty-three sepa-rate criminal cases that were launched against full-patch members of the Angels since 1994, and found that only twenty – thirty-eight per cent — ended in prosecutors obtaining convictions. In thirty-three of the cases – sixty-two per cent — the prosecutions failed.

Select Bibliography

Albini, Joseph L. *The American Mafia: Genesis of a Legend.* New York: Appleton-Century-Crofts, 1971.

Allen, Ralph. *Ordeal By Fire; Canada 1910–1945.* Volume 5 of the Canadian History Series. Thomas B. Costain, editor. Toronto: Doubleday Canada Ltd., 19 61.

Arlacchi, Pino. *Mafia Business: The Mafia Ethic and the Spirit of Capitalism.* Oxford: Oxford University Press, 1986.
———. *Mafia Peasants and Great Estates: Society in Traditional Calabria.* Cambridge: Cambridge University Press, 1983.

Auger, Michel. *The Biker Who Shot Me: Recollections of a Crime Reporter.* Toronto: McClelland & Stewart, 2002. Trans. Jean-Paul Murray.

Barzini, Luigi. *The Italians: A Full-length Portrait Featuring Their Manners and Morals.* New York: Atheneum, 1986.

Block, Alan. *East Side–West Side: Organizing Crime in New York 1930–1950.* Cardiff: University College Cardiff Press, 1980.

Blok, Anton. *The Mafia of a Sicilian Village, 1860–1960: A Study of Violent Peasant Entrepreneurs.* London: William Clowes & Sons,1974.

Blumenthal, Ralph. *Last Days of the Sicilians: The FBI 's War Against the Mafia.* New York: Pocket Books, 1989.

Bonanno, Joseph, with Sergio Lalli. *A Man of Honor: The autobiography of Joseph Bonanno.* New York: Simon and Schuster, 1983.

Brodeur, Jean-Paul. *La Délinquence de L'Ordre; récherche sur les comcommissions d'inquête I.* Québec: Hurtubise, 1984.

Charbonneau, Jean-Pierre. *The Canadian Connection.* Montreal: Optimum Publishing Co. Ltd., 1976.

Dubro, James. *Mob Rule: Inside the Canadian Mafia.* Toronto:

Macmillan, 1985.

Dubro, James, and Robin F. Rowland. *King of the Mob: Rocco Perri and the Women Who Ran His Rackets.* Markham, Ont.: Viking Canada Ltd., 1987.

Edwards, Peter. *The Big Sting; The True Story of the Canadian Who Betrayed Colombia's Drug Barons.* Toronto: Key Porter Books, 1991.

Edwards, Peter and Michel Auger. *The Encyclopedia of Canadian Organized Crime; from Captain Kidd to Mom Boucher.* McClelland & Stewart. Toronto. 2004.

Edwards, Peter, and Antonio Nicaso. *Deadly Silence: Canadian Mafia Murders.* Toronto: Macmillan Canada, 1993.

Fournier, Louis. F.L.Q.: *The Anatomy of an Underground Movement.* Translated by Edward Baxter. Toronto: New Canada Publications, 1984.

Francis, Diane. *Contrepreneurs.* Toronto: Macmillan of Canada, 1988. Gilmore, John. *Swinging in Paradise: The Story of Jazz in Montreal.* Montreal: Vehicule Press, 1988.

Gray, James H. *Booze.* Toronto: Macmillan of Canada, 1972. Hobsbawm, E.J. *Primitive Rebels: Studies in Archaic Forms of Social Movement in the 19th and 20th Centuries.* Manchester: Manchester University Press, 1959.

Humphreys, Adrian. *The Enforcer: Johnny Pops Papalia — A Life and Death in the Mafia.* Toronto: HarperCollins, 1999.

Ianni, Francis A., and Elizabeth Reuss-lanni, editors. *The Crime Society: Organized Crime and Corruption in America.* New York: New American Library, 1976.

Jodoin, Claude. *Qui a Tué Frank Shoofey?* Montreal: Les Editions de L'Epoque, 1985.

Kirby, Cecil, and Thomas C. Renner. *Mafia Assassin: The Inside Story of a Canadian Biker, Hitman and Police Informer.* Toronto: Methuen, 1986.

Kwitny, Jonathon. *Vicious Circles: The Mafia in the Marketplace.* New York: W.W. Norton & Company, 1979.

Lewis, Norman. *The Honoured Society: The Sicilian Mafia Observed.* London: Eland Books, 1984.

McKenna, Brian, and Susan Purcell. *Drapeau.* Markham, Ont.: Penguin Books, 1981.

Moore, Robin. *The French Connection.* New York: Bantam, 1970.

Nelli, Humbert S. *The Business of Crime: Italians and Syndicate Crime in the United States.* Chicago: The University of Chicago

Press, 1976.

Newman, Peter C. *Bronfman Dynasty*. Toronto: McClelland and Stewart, 1978.

Nicaso, Antonio, and Lee Lamothe. *Bloodlines: Project Omertà and the Fall of the Mafia's Royal Family*. Toronto: HarperCollins, 2001.

Pileggi, Nicholas. *Wise Guy: Life in a Mafia Family*. New York: Pocket Books, 1985.

Pistone, Joseph D., with Richard Woodley. *Donnie Brasco: My Undercover Life in the Mafia*. New York: New American Library, 1987.

Plante, Pacifique Roy (Pax). *Montréal sous le règne de la Pègre*. Montréal: Éditions de L'Action Nationale, 1950.

Ramirez, Bruno, and Michael Del Balso. *The Italians of Montreal: From Sojourning to Settlement, 1900–1921*. Montreal: Les Editions du Courant, 1980.

Regush, Nicholas M. *Pierre Vallières: The Revolutionary Process in Quebec*. Toronto: Fitzhenry & Whiteside, 1973.

Rowland, Wade. *Making Connections: The Behind-the-Scenes Story*. Toronto: Gage, 1979.

Salerno, Ralph, and John S. Tompkins. *The Crime Confederation: Cosa Nostra and Allied Operations in Organized Crime*. Garden City, N.Y.: Doubleday & Company, 1969.

Shawcross, Tim, and Martin Young. *Men of Honour: The Confessions of Tommaso Buscetta, the Man who Destroyed the Mafia*. London: Collins, 1987.

Sher, Julian and William Marsden. *The Road To Hell: How Biker Gangs Conquered Canada*. Random House, Toronto. 2003.

Simard, Francis. *Taking it Out: The October Crisis from Inside*. Montreal: Guernica, 1982.

Simard, Réal, and Michel Vastel. *The Nephew: The Making of a Mafia Hitman*. Scarborough: Prentice-Hall Canada, 1988. (First published as *Le Neveu*. Montreal: Québec/Amerique, 1987.)

Talese, Gay. *Honor Thy Father*. New York: Dell, 1981.

Teresa, Vincent, with Thomas C. Renner. *My Life in the Mafia*. Garden City, N.Y.: Doubleday & Company, 1973.

Vallières, Pierre. *The Assassination of Pierre Laporte*. Translated by Ralph Wells. Toronto: James Lorimer & Company, 1977.

DOCUMENTS

The Royal Commission appointed to inquire into the immigration of Italian Labourers to Montreal and the Alleged Fraudulent Practices of Employment Agencies. *Report of the Commissioner and Evidence.* J.N.O. Winchester, commissioner. Ottawa: S.E. Dawson, Printer to the King's Most Excellent Majesty, 1905.

"Rapport sur l'administration de la ville de Montréal." L.J. Cannon, commissioner. Montreal: Published in December 18, 1909, *La Presse.*

"Rapport d'enquête sur la police de Montréal." Louis Codèrre, commissioner. Published in March 14, 1925, *Le Devoir.*

"Rapport d'enquête sur la moralité." François Caron, commissioner. Published in October 9, 1954, Montreal *Gazette,* and October 16, 1954, *Le Devoir.*

"Royal Commission on Crime." Justice Wilfrid D. Roach, commissioner. 19 63.

"Report of the Ontario Police Commission on Organized Crime." Judge Bruce Macdonald, commissioner. 1964.

"Organized Crime and Illicit Traffic in Narcotics: Report of the Committee on Government Operations, United States Senate, made by its permanent subcommittee on investigations together with additional combined views and individual views." Washington: U.S. Government Printing Office, 1965.

Report of the Commissioner, The Honorable Frederic Dorion, Chief Justice for the Province of Quebec, June 1965.

"Crime, Justice and Society." Vol. 3. Crime in Quebec, organized crime. Commission of enquiry into the administration of justice on criminal and penal matters in Quebec. Associate Chief Justice, Yves Prévost. Quebec: 1969.

"Rapport d'enquête sur l'étude de liens possible entre Nicolas Di Iorio et Frank D'Asti, membres du crime organisé, Pierre Laporte, ministre, René Gagnon, chef de cabinet, et Jean-Jacques Côté, organisateur politique." 1974.

"Report of the Royal Commission on Certain Sectors of the Building Industry." Judge Harry Waisberg, commissioner. Toronto: Queen 's Printer for Ontario. 1974.

"Report of the Commission of Inquiry on the Exercise of Union

Freedom in the Construction Industry." Robert Cliche, chairman. Brian Mulroney, Guy Chevrette. May 2, 1975.

"*L'introduction frauduleuse de viande impropre sur le marche de la consommation humaine et la fraude en rapport avec la viande chevaline; rapport interimaire de l'inquête sur le crime organisé.*" Montréal: Centre de reproduction Ministère de la Justice. 1975.

"*La Lutte au Crime Organisé au Québec.*" Commission de Police du Québec. 1976.

"Organized Crime and the World of Business." Quebec Police Commission Report of the Commission of Inquiry on Organized Crime and Recommendations. August 2, 1977.

"CECO; the fight against organized crime in Quebec. Quebec Police Commission report of the commission of inquiry on organized crime and recommendations." Éditeur officiel du Quebec. 1977.

"The Sicilian Connection; southwest Asian heroin en route to the United States." Senator Joseph R. Biden Jr. report to the Committee on Foreign Relations and Committee on the Judiciary, United States Senate. Washington: U.S. Government Printing Office, 1980.

"Organized Crime in America." Hearings before the Committee on theJudiciary. Ninety-Eighth Congress. First session on Organized Crime in America. May 20 and July 11, 1983. Serial No. J-98-2. Part 2.

"Governor's Council on Organized Crime; State of Florida 1983 annual report." Eugene T. Whitworth, chairman. 1983.

"Hotel Employees and Restaurant Employees International Union." Permanent Subcommittee on Investigations of the Committee on Governmental Affairs, United States Senate. Washington: U.S. Government Printing Office. 1984.

Eduardo Melo Immigration and Refugee Board file. Immigration Appeal Division (Board File: T94-0753).

ARTICLES/PAPERS

Auger, Michel. "Frank Cotroni and boxing." *Journal de Montréal.* March 11 and 13, April 14, 1984.

Auger, Michel, and Dan Burke. "Frank Cotroni and Boxing." *Sunday Express,* March 11, 1984.

Boone, Mike. "Reputed lovers of food," The Montreal *Gazette*, August 18, 2004.

Cernetig, Miro. "Mandolins and miniskirts: How to mourn a mafioso; Cotroni's sins forgotten at funeral Crime boss 'a giving guy,' admirers say," *The Toronto Star*, August 22, 2004. Page A1.

Charney, Ann. "The Life and Death of Paolo Violi." *Weekend Magazine,* January 20, 1979.

Cherry, Paul. "Hundreds mourn mob boss Cotroni: No eulogy at service for last of 3 brothers," The Montreal *Gazette*, August 22, 2004. Page A1.

Edwards, Peter. "'Le Gros' goes quietly; Montreal mob boss who ordered five deaths dies in bed Ontario police once called Cotroni 'our most serious threat'" The Toronto *Star*. Aug. 18, 2004. Page A3.

Edwards, Peter. "Metro's Powerful Hotel Union Boss Laughs at Link with Mafia Kingpin." *Sunday Star,* June 18, 1989.

Ha, Tu Thanh. "Montreal crime family's last member dies at 72," *The Globe and Mail*, August 18, 2004. Page A3.

Harney, Robert F. "Montreal's King of Italian Labour: A Case Study in Padronism." *Labour/Le Travailleur*4, no. 4 (1979): 57–84.

———. "The Padrone and the Immigrant." *Canadian Review of American Studies* 5, no. 2 (Fall 1974): 101–17.

Lamothe, Lee, and Rob Lamberti. Toronto *Sun*. Series on Toronto mobster Rocco Zito, May 19–22, 1988.

Lebel, Ron; and Robert McKenzie. *Toronto Star* coverage of October Crisis. March 1 6, July 7 and 12, August 4, 1973; January 1 6, March 2, May 1 6, 1974.

Linteau, Paul-Andre. "The Italians of Quebec: Key Participants in Contemporary Linguistic and Political Debates." In *Arrangiarsi: The Italian Immigration Experience in Canada,* edited by Robert Perin and Franc Sturino. Montreal: Guernica, 1989.

Marsden, William. "Police Gear Up to Seize Drug Mob's Assets,"